CHURCHES OF CHRIST IN OKLAHOMA

Also by W. David Baird

Peter Pitchlynn: Chief of the Choctaw (Norman, 1972; 1986)

The Osage People (Phoenix, 1972)

The Choctaw People (Phoenix, 1974)

The Chickasaw People (Phoenix, 1975)

(ed.) *The Dictionary of the Osage Language,* by Francis La Flesche
(Phoenix, 1975)

The Quapaw People (Phoenix, 1975)

Years of Discontent: Doctor Frank L. James in Arkansas, 1877–1878
(Memphis, 1977)

Medical Education in Arkansas, 1879–1978 (Memphis, 1979)

The Quapaw Indians: A History of the Downstream People (Norman, 1980)

(ed.) *A Creek Warrior for the Confederacy:
The Autobiography of Chief G. W. Grayson* (Norman, 1988)

The Quapaws (New York, 1989)

(with Danney Goble) *The Story of Oklahoma* (Norman, 1994; 2020)

(with Danney Goble) *Oklahoma: A History* (Norman, 2008)

Quest for Distinction: Pepperdine University in the Twentieth Century
(Malibu, 2016)

CHURCHES
OF CHRIST IN
OKLAHOMA

A History

W. DAVID BAIRD

UNIVERSITY OF OKLAHOMA PRESS : NORMAN

This book is published with the generous assistance of the
Wallace C. Thompson Endowment Fund, University of Oklahoma Foundation.

An earlier version of a section of chapter 2 was published as "R. W. Officer and the Indian Mission: The Foundational Years (1880–1886)," in *And the Word Became Flesh: Studies in History, Communication, and Scripture in Memory of Michael W. Casey,* ed. Thomas H. Olbricht and David Fleer (Eugene, Ore.: Pinwick Publications, 2009), 3–20. It is used here by permission.

Library of Congress Cataloging-in-Publication Data

Names: Baird, W. David, author.
Title: Churches of Christ in Oklahoma : a history / W. David Baird.
Description: First [edition]. | Norman : University of Oklahoma Press, 2020. | Includes bibliographical references and index. | Summary: "An examination of the key characteristics, individuals, and debates that shaped the Church of Christ in Oklahoma from 1853 to the end of the twentieth century"— Provided by publisher.
Identifiers: LCCN 2019022666 | ISBN 978-0-8061-6462-5 (paperback)
Subjects: LCSH: Churches of Christ—Oklahoma—History.
Classification: LCC BX7075.Z5 O353 2020 | DDC 286.6/766—dc23
LC record available at https://lccn.loc.gov/2019022666

To the memory of
Silas Webster and Mary Fyffe Baird
and their descendants

CONTENTS

ILLUSTRATIONS

PREFACE

This is a book about the history of Churches of Christ in Oklahoma. It begins with a brief account of the Stone-Campbell movement, a religious crusade that had its genesis along the American frontier early in the nineteenth century. The first representatives of the movement came to Oklahoma as missionaries, first to the Cherokees, then to the Chickasaws, and then to the Choctaws. Additional missionaries followed during the era of the Twin Territories, Indian and Oklahoma. Because of disagreements regarding faith and practice, the movement nationwide separated into Churches of Christ and Disciples of Christ, a division recognized by the U.S. Census Bureau in 1906. The narrative then focuses only on Churches of Christ in Oklahoma.

This telling includes a history of Cordell Christian College and pacifism, O. E. Enfield and Christian socialism, African American evangelism, and the WPA survey of religions in Oklahoma. This story also addresses the 1950s when, by percentage, Churches of Christ were recognized as the fastest-growing religious organization in the United States. Locally, the move of Oklahoma Christian College from Bartlesville to Oklahoma City and the establishment of an impressive number of new congregations demonstrated that growth. But growth did not exclude division, and Churches of Christ quarreled over everything from Sunday schools and the support of orphans' homes to the elements of worship, gender roles in the church, and the application of a new hermeneutic. And there was also no agreement as to why membership began to decline in the 1970s. This narrative of the history of Oklahoma Churches of Christ closes with the onset of the twenty-first century.

I have wanted to write this story ever since I was a doctoral student at the University of Oklahoma. Indeed, I even proposed it as a PhD dissertation topic to one of my mentors at the University. He did not give the proposition even modest consideration but said, "You are not ready for it." Fifty-five years later that may still be the case, but I going to make an attempt nonetheless.

It is appropriate that I confess up front to being a native Oklahoman and a lifelong member of Churches of Christ, actually a fifth-generation member. I spent almost thirty years as the Howard A. White professor of history and dean of Seaver College at Pepperdine University, which has a historic relationship with Churches of Christ. Rather than encourage bias, my hope is that my church membership, association with Pepperdine, and Oklahoma citizenship will enable me to better explain Oklahoma Churches of Christ to readers.

Researching this story has been a challenge. Churches of Christ are congregational in polity. They cherish their independence and their right to make decisions on matters of faith and practice. While other denominations have conventions, synods, and dioceses, whose deliberations and resolutions are chronicled, published, and circulated, Churches of Christ have only the minutes of the elders' meetings as the principal record of the congregation. Moreover, those minutes quickly become ephemera and are lost to the historian. My survey of Oklahoma congregations provided some additional insights, but the response rate to those instruments was less than 20 percent. Absent records from a majority or more of the congregations and lacking documents from some kind of convention, scholars are forced to depend upon religious periodicals that print communications from evangelists in the field to provide a sense of what was going on prior to and after Oklahoma statehood.

It would be difficult to complete a project like this without support of a host of people. Roy B. Young, long the minister of the Apache Church of Christ, shared with me his collection of historic material, which he had gathered over the years, intending to write his own history of the church in Oklahoma. Eric and Linda King of Edmond opened their home to me for many days in 2008. The same was true of my sister-in-law and brother-in-law, Jean and Mike Hornsby, of Tulsa, in 2008 and 2018. Patti Loughlin, a former student of mine at Pepperdine University, arranged housing for me at the University of Central Oklahoma, of which I am an alumnus and she is a professor of history, in 2018. I have benefited from the research assistance of Pepperdine University student Michelle Carriger and from lengthy conversations about the substance of this study with John Wilson, dean emeritus of Seaver College, Pepperdine University, and Jim Wilburn, dean emeritus of the School of Public Policy, Pepperdine University, who also shared treasures from his personal library. Lynn McMillon, editor of the *Christian Chronicle* and professor of Bible at Oklahoma Christian University, was a constant source of encouragement. I am grateful for all this assistance, but I am especially thankful to my good wife of fifty-seven years, Jane. One more time, she has given me the freedom and encouragement to complete a project, perhaps the last one.

CHURCHES OF CHRIST IN OKLAHOMA

1

CHARACTERISTICS OF THE STONE-CAMPBELL MOVEMENT

The Churches of Christ in Oklahoma are part of a religious tradition—the Stone-Campbell movement—that had its genesis on the American frontier in the early years of the nineteenth century. The movement began in response to the divisiveness of European sects and denominations, which "had splintered in Europe and splattered onto the American shores." Its primary objective was religious unity. Leaders reasoned that unanimity was possible if men and women of goodwill would throw away their man-made creeds and limit their faith and practices to those ordained by Christ, taught by the apostles, and recorded in scripture. The restoration of this "primitive gospel" along with the "New Testament church" would usher in the nondenominational unity for which Christ prayed.[1]

Barton W. Stone

One of the major influences on this "restoration" movement was Barton W. Stone (1772–1844). Born to Scotch-Irish parents in Port Tobacco, Maryland, in 1772, Stone received his education from local tutors, independent study, and matriculation in a frontier academy near Guilford, North Carolina, run by a Princeton graduate. A pious young man, he publicly declared his faith in Christ at the age of nineteen during one of several revivals then bursting out in the Carolina backcountry. In 1796, he was licensed to preach as a New Light Presbyterian. Five years later he was one of the principals who led in the great frontier revival that centered at Cane Ridge, Kentucky.[2]

Stone's experiences at Cane Ridge profoundly influenced him. He witnessed firsthand what he judged to be the work of the Holy Spirit, sometimes with strange manifestations (as in the case of the "jerks"). And he experienced a fervent sense of unity that transcended denominational differences. Stone put the two together and, according to historian Richard Hughes, concluded that the unity he observed among Christians at Cane Ridge came as a result of a direct intervention of the Holy Spirit, "which moved scoffers to conversion and Christians to holy life."[3]

This vision of a practical Christian unity prompted Stone and five of his Presbyterian brethren to organize the Springfield Presbytery in 1803. Sensing, however, that the faith and practices of their own community were promoting denominational division, they acted to dissolve the presbytery on June 28, 1804. In *The Last Will and Testament of the Springfield Presbytery*, Stone and his colleagues directed "that this body die, be dissolved, and sink into union with the body of Christ at large" so that its members could "betake themselves to the Rock of Ages, and follow Jesus for the future." The historic but very American frontier document declared that every Christian should be free of the restraints of man-made confessions of faith and able to "taste the sweets of gospel liberty."[4] Thereafter Stone and his colleagues did not think of themselves as Presbyterians, but as a community of Christians free of human traditions in religion and committed to achieving unity by restoring the primitive gospel they found described in the New Testament.

According to Hughes, the Great Revival also had a dramatic impact on Stone's theology and religious practices.[5] Most significantly, Stone developed a "profoundly apocalyptic worldview"—that is, he gave his allegiance to the kingdom of God, not to the kingdoms of this world, and lived as if the final rule of God's kingdom were present in the here and now. This belief "drove him to advocate simple, ethical living" that would "separate himself from the prevailing values of his culture, and . . . hold him . . . aloof from militarism and even from politics."[6]

The apocalyptic perspective, the promise of freedom, and the expectation of religious unity resonated with thousands of Americans—sometimes labeled "New Light Christians"—residing in Alabama, Tennessee, and states bordering the Ohio River. Stone solidified it through his preaching, but also through publishing the *Christian Messenger*, issued monthly first from Georgetown, Kentucky, and then Jacksonville, Illinois, between 1826 and 1844.[7]

Thomas and Alexander Campbell

Born in 1788 in County Antrim, Ireland, Alexander Campbell (1788–1866) was homeschooled by his father, Thomas (1763–1854), an Argyle Scot and pastor of the Ahorey Presbyterian Church. Alexander also spent some three hundred days in intensive study of Greek, French, literature, and Common Sense philosophy at the University of Glasgow. He came to the United States in 1809, arriving two years after his father, who had preceded him in an attempt to improve both his health and, as a minister, the family's fortune.[8]

Alexander found his father residing in southwestern Pennsylvania and no longer associated with the Seceder Presbyterians, a group that had withdrawn from the General Assembly of the Presbyterian Church and was splitting again over the role of the state in determining true religion. The Seceders had issues with Thomas's preaching and had tried to discipline it. Moreover, Thomas had already penned the famous *Declaration and Address*, a fifty-six-page pamphlet that called for Christian unity though a restoration of primitive Christianity.[9] Alexander was enthusiastic about the document, which, historian Hughes notes, came to chart the course for the movement that the Campbells would lead.[10]

The son quickly emerged as the central figure of the effort. After months of careful study, he saw new potential in his father's vision. Not only would the restoration of primitive Christianity lead to unity, but the reality of unity would simultaneously usher in the millennial era, the final age of human history when peace, justice, and righteousness reigned under the rule of Christ himself. Put differently, the promise of restoring New Testament Christianity had profound eschatological implications.[11]

Alexander Campbell exercised his leadership in the movement through widespread preaching and strategic debates, and as an educator, author, and editor of religious periodicals. In the latter capacity, he edited the *Christian Baptist* from 1823 to 1830 and its successor, the *Millennial Harbinger*, from 1830 until his death in 1866. His early editorial work, especially in the *Christian Baptist*, would become particularly important to Churches of Christ in Oklahoma and elsewhere. During these "aggressive years," Campbell the iconoclast assaulted "creeds, clerics, and denominational systems" that he believed "must collapse before the millennium would dawn."[12] Christian unity remained his principal objective, but it did not always sound that way.

Commonalities

The Campbell and Stone movements had much in common. Each was uncomfortable with the diversity of religious sects and denominations (or pluralism) on the frontier, which they both hoped to escape by returning to primitive Christianity. The two groups also embraced America's passion for social and political democracy, seeking freedom from religious constraints by abandoning creeds, clerics, and church controls. Each, therefore, organized themselves congregationally, without the control of a bishop or clergy-led presbytery. Over time, therefore, the two movements gravitated toward each other and formally united in Lexington, Kentucky, in 1832.[13]

But the merger was not without challenges. Stone was a pietist while Campbell was a Baconian rationalist. Stone believed that a return to "apostolic holiness" was the quickest route to Christian union. Campbell held that it would come by the induction of facts taken from the Bible, in a manner akin to today's scientific method. Unity derived as well from an understanding that the New Testament was the constitution and blueprint of the church. Stone's worldview left him pessimistic about his culture and age; Campbell was optimistic about the potential of primitive Christianity as a religious plea, not to mention the promise of science, technology, and American civilization.[14] Indeed, Campbell was so positive about American civilization that he defended American Protestantism in a widely discussed debate with Catholic bishop John Baptist Purcell in 1837. And there was the problem of a name for the movement. Stone preferred "Christian"; Campbell was partial to "Disciples." Members of the movement identified specific congregations as "Christian Churches" or "Churches of Christ." To avoid the confusion associated with the name, like recent historians, I will use the descriptor "Stone-Campbell Movement" for the united effort from 1832 to 1906.[15]

The Movement Divides

Since a decade earlier Campbell had found little commendable among Protestants in general, the position he advocated in the Purcell debate confused many of his brethren. From their perspective, he seemed to be accommodating the prevailing culture, rather than fighting it. In the post–Civil War years, others in the brotherhood, better known as "progressives," took the same approach, especially as they utilized parachurch organizations to expedite evangelism and instrumental music to contemporize worship services. The "traditionalists," "conservatives," or "antis" strongly objected to the "innovations," which they insisted were not practices of the primitive church. As a consequence, over three or more decades the Stone-Campbell unity movement pulled apart. In 1906, the religious census of the U.S. government finally recognized the obvious: the restoration movement had divided into (1) Disciples of Christ/Christian Churches concentrated in urban areas and midwestern states and (2) Churches of Christ concentrated in rural areas and southern states.[16]

The division of the Stone-Campbell Movement complicates the telling of its history. With which segment (progressive or conservative; Disciples of Christ or Churches of Christ) is a historian to associate a particular person or group? Before and after 1906, more than just a few Stone-Campbell adherents stood with feet in both camps, insisting on their freedom to fellowship with either side. That was certainly the case of R. W. Officer, an early missionary among the Choctaws, and Meta Chestnutt Sager, an educational missionary among the Chickasaws. Accordingly, historian Stephen J. England included both as integral parts of his story of Christian Churches in Oklahoma.[17] That is certainly defensible, but given Officer's and Sager's life experiences, extensive writings, and religious practices, they could just as easily be associated with the history of Churches of Christ in Oklahoma, and in this telling they are.

Faith and Practice of Churches of Christ

According to historian Hughes, four factors influence the faith and practices of Churches of Christ today.[18] First, they are committed to the restoration of primitive Christianity, or "to a replication of the beliefs and practices of the church of the apostolic age" as described in the New Testament. Professors Gary Holloway and Douglas Foster would add that the purpose of restoration was to achieve unity among believers, rather than be legalistically correct about faith and practice. It is true, however, that, for some, correctness about worship practices and evangelistic activities was so key that it appeared that the entire movement considered fundamental Christian doctrines about God, Christ, the Holy Spirit, salvation, and end times of lesser importance. In fact, Stone-Campbell adherents agreed with other Protestants on those topics and saw little reason to question or defend them.[19]

Second, over time the movement adopted the characteristics of a sect—that is, a religious organization that insists that it—and it alone—constitutes the entirety of the kingdom of God and stands in judgment on both culture and competing traditions. The strong commitment to believers' immersion for the forgiveness of sin contributed to this development. The notion was that salvation required baptism. Thus many Stone-Campbell advocates found it difficult to deny that they believed themselves to be the only Christians, even though their founders had taught the contrary.[20]

Third, according to Hughes, there has been a slow abandonment of the sectarian posture associated with the Stone-Campbell movement, particularly among Churches of Christ, and a recognition of "many other Christian traditions—to some degree at least—as authentic expressions of the Christian faith." At the dawn of the twenty-first century, however, the transition from sect to denomination was far from complete, with circumstances in Oklahoma being a good example.

Finally, despite the reality of Churches of Christ as sect or denomination, they have generally denied that they were anything more than a replication of the New Testament church and, therefore, neither Catholic, Protestant, nor Jew, just "nondenominational."

A New Way of Discerning Truth

Whereas Richard Hughes finds four themes useful in understanding Churches of Christ over time, historian Leonard Allen calls attention to other things that are less visible. Among these was a particular hermeneutic, or methodology of discerning biblical truths, as championed by Alexander Campbell. The idea was to read the Bible as if it had never been read before, or without wearing the glasses of Luther, Calvin, Wesley, or some council of the Catholic Church. Readers should confine themselves to the plain declarations in the Bible, explain Bible things by Bible names, and understand that the Bible was a book of divine facts (something said or something done), not opinions. Those facts represented a constitution and provided a pattern for the kingdom of God on earth. To Campbell, this approach was nothing more than the scientific method championed by John Locke applied to the Book of Life, with the end result being truth.[21]

This "wholly new" approach to scripture yielded, inductively, the essentials of the original gospel (faith) and the ancient order of things (practice) within the primitive church. The elements of the original gospel were gospel facts (death, burial, resurrection, and ascension of Christ), faith, repentance, reformation, baptism, remission of sins, reception of the Holy Spirit, sanctification, resurrection, and eternal life. The preaching of these facts produced faith, which led a person to "obey the gospel," that is, to repent of sins and be baptized for the remission of those sins.[22]

The rational reading of scripture discerned the ordinances and order of the primitive church and apostolic community set down in the book of Acts and the

Epistles. This portion of the scripture codified the laws for the church, including congregational autonomy, a plurality of elders and deacons in each congregation, baptism for remission of sins, a simple pattern for worship, and weekly observance of the Lord's Supper. The ancient order as discerned in scripture was "specific and complete," so said Allen. Moreover, "any practice or organization [in the contemporary church] lacking an apostolic command or example was simply an illicit novelty."[23]

Results of the New Way

For those who embraced the rational approach to reading scripture, an awesome by-product awaited: Christian unity and the dawning of the millennial age. The Christian millennium would not come in some supernatural, catastrophic way, however, but gradually, progressively, and naturally, propelled by social and technological improvements derived from scientific and moral developments (including the restoration of the primitive church). Alexander Campbell could not imagine God working his will in the modern world outside of natural law.[24]

Nor could Campbell imagine God stepping outside his word as revealed in scripture to affect people's lives. With those words only did God communicate spiritual truth, and only by use of those words could the divine spirit influence the human spirit or one person exert power over another person. Since there was power in the revealed word and only the revealed word, biblical study was extremely important. That God's power seemed to be confined to revealed words only, however, opened Campbell to charges of "biblical deism."[25]

Stone's Apocalyptic World View

The rationality and millennial optimism of Churches of Christ, with which we associate the worldview of Alexander Campbell, is no less unnoticed than Barton Stone's apocalyptic worldview and sense of cultural pessimism. For Stone, sinfulness characterized the human condition, individually and collectively. Individuals could escape only through the power of the Holy Spirit. What happened at Cane Ridge, he believed, was proof of the fact that there was more to salvation than just belief in a certain set of propositions. And insofar as society was concerned, it could be redeemed only by the judgment of God, probably in a cataclysmic event.[26]

Given his perspective, Stone's views differed significantly from those of Campbell. Stone was open to God's direct, even miraculous, working in the world, whereas Campbell taught that God worked through secondary channels like natural law and the Bible. Since Christians were members of God's kingdom only, Stone had reservations about participating in a human government, whereas Campbell saw government as a means of ushering in the millennial dawn. Stone also had qualms about religious societies beyond the church (colleges, Sunday schools, tract societies, and Bible societies, among others), whereas Campbell did not. Stone was unlikely to accommodate the prevailing (American democratic) culture, whereas Campbell was more likely to do so, especially in his later years.[27]

Stone's worldview was particularly strong among Stone-Campbell congregations in southern States, where the Stone movement had achieved considerable traction. There the lack of confidence in human society was exacerbated by states' rights issues leading up to and following the Civil War, and of course the Civil War itself. Tolbert Fanning (1810–74) and David Lipscomb (1831–1917), the principal leaders of Churches of Christ in the South, had direct connections to the Stone movement. Lipscomb particularly had an abiding sense of the sovereignty of God's rule and a pessimistic view of human society. So strong were his feelings that he would discourage voting in elections and service in the military. R. W. Officer, James A. Harding, and J. N. Armstrong, Lipscomb's influential coworkers in Indian and Oklahoma Territories, held those opinions to one degree or another as well. And perhaps even Meta Chestnutt Sager.

Two Distinct World Views

Thus, by 1880, when the Stone-Campbell movement launched a sustained mission effort in Indian Territory, two distinct worldviews characterized it. One was optimistic about the course of American society and willing to accommodate it, while the other was pessimistic and reluctant to tolerate it. One saw potential in humanity, while the other saw sinfulness. One saw God's power operating through scripture and natural law, while the other saw that power not confined to scripture and natural law. One was concentrated geographically in northern states and urban centers, while the other was largely concentrated in southern states and rural areas. These different worldviews would impact the history of the movement in Indian Territory and, subsequently, in Oklahoma.

2

THE INDIAN MISSION
1857–1889

The different worldviews notwithstanding, the Stone-Campbell movement remained united in its essential plea: restore Christian unity by replicating the faith and practices of ancient gospel as found in scripture. That simple message, rather than the uncertain sound of conflicting worldviews, was the one that Stone-Campbell missionaries brought to Indian Territory beginning in the 1850s.

James J. Trott among the Cherokees

James J. Trott (1800–1868) was the earliest Stone-Campbell missionary of record. In 1830, he was a circuit-riding Methodist minister who preached among the Cherokees in Georgia. His Cherokee wife was a member of the prominent Adair family. Trott was an outspoken critic of the forcible removal of the tribe from its homeland. With other notables, specifically Presbyterian missionaries Samuel Worcester and Elizur Butler, he was imprisoned for his audacious support of the Cherokee people. During his time in prison, he had occasion to read widely, including some of the publications of Alexander Campbell. He found the restoration plea sensible and rational. When his sponsoring Methodist conference would not publicly condemn Indian removal, he resigned from it, was baptized by immersion, and thereafter identified his ministerial work with the Stone-Campbell movement.[1]

Trott did not remove to Indian Territory when the main body of the Cherokees relocated there after 1835. Instead he moved his family to Nashville, Tennessee, where he became a friend and co-laborer of Tolbert Fanning, one of the principal leaders of the Stone-Campbell movement in the South. Trott preached widely in Tennessee, Georgia, North Carolina, and Alabama, generally to non-Indian congregations. He was a strong advocate of mass meetings of the evangelists and leadership of Stone-Campbell churches. In 1852, he was a charter member and president of the Tennessee Evangelizing Association, the object of which was to educate and train ministers.[2]

Trott Goes West

Trott, however, did not forget his relatives in Indian Territory. No later than 1853, he accepted an appointment from the four-year-old American Christian Missionary Society (ACMS), probably the Stone-Campbell movement's first parachurch organization, as a missionary to the Cherokees. His departure was delayed, however, by unknown personal circumstances, the continuation of post-removal strife among the Cherokees, and the lack of adequate capital to finance the mission. In 1856, Trott traveled three thousand miles through Missouri, Arkansas, and the Cherokee Nation in an attempt to raise money for the mission as constituted by the ACMS. The economic, social, educational, and spiritual potential of Indian Territory impressed him greatly. Others whom he visited along the way were not quite so enthralled, however. They tended to sympathize with D. S. Burnett, one of the founders of the ACMS, who said that one could convert fifty American citizens for what it would cost to convert just "one savage Indian." Trott raised only $166 in support of the Indian Mission during the course of the trip.[3]

Despite the cool reception, Trott remained convinced that the Cherokee Nation was a fertile mission field. Absent any help from the ACMS, Trott received the assurances of adequate financial support from the congregation that met at Franklin College in Nashville, where Tolbert Fanning was president. On the basis of that pledge and $1,500 of his own resources, Trott and his family joined the Cherokees in November 1857, taking up residence near what is now Westville, Oklahoma. According to Trott, this was "the first Christian Mission [in the Stone-Campbell tradition] among the red children of the New World." By 1860, he had gathered up into a handful of churches some seventy-five disciples.[4]

But the glorious harvest Trott anticipated never materialized. The American Civil War brought division, strife, and devastation to the Cherokee Nation. Chief John Ross initially aligned the Cherokees with the Confederacy. Subsequently, when Union soldiers from Kansas pushed south to Tahlequah, the Cherokee capital, Ross and other "loyal" Cherokees met them with gladness, renouncing the Confederate treaty. Unfortunately for Ross and his supporters, the Union column considered itself exposed and retreated back to Kansas. They, including Trott, had no option but to go with the federal troops. In the process, Trott lost all of his possessions, and one of his sons was killed.[5]

The Cherokees loyal to the Union, along with remnants of other tribes, spent the remainder of the war in Kansas as refugees. Trott continued his ministry, in poverty and peril and with the loss of another child, this time a daughter. In 1866, he returned to the vicinity of his pre–Civil War work, although this time he took up residence on the Arkansas side of the border. It was not an especially joyful homecoming, for Trott's health had broken and his energy had been sapped. Nonetheless, he continued his ministry until 1868, when friends visiting from Tennessee insisted that he accompany them back to Nashville in an effort to regain his health. Trott made the journey back, but his health did not improve. He died in December 1868 and was buried near Gallatin, Tennessee.[6]

Other Missionaries among the Cherokees

Little of Trott and his mission among the Cherokees lasted. Six years after his death, two or more congregations apparently existed in the Fort Gibson area, but five years later, there was no memory of those islands of restorationism. In another five years (1884), the general wisdom was that Trott had carried on his mission work in the vicinity of Vinita, probably because some of his descendants had located there. The Vinita myth was so strong that the ACMS assigned W. B. Stinson there in 1889, apparently on the assumption that he could build a new ministry on the foundation of the old.[7]

Four years earlier, the missionary society had persuaded Isaac Mode to begin a work among the Creeks in the vicinity of Wetumka. Illness and unfamiliarity with the language caused the society to transfer him to the Cherokee Nation near Vinita in late 1884. His surroundings there, however, "were of such a nature that he did but little, and for some cause resigned."[8]

H. C. Collier, a Cherokee Indian by blood, preached regularly in the Muskogee area in the late 1880s and early 1890s. His colleagues appealed to him to move to Indian Territory from Arkansas and work as a full-time evangelist, an invitation Collier considered but did not accept. M. J. Simpson evangelized among the Cherokees resident in the Fort Gibson area. After not much more than a year, he left to work among the Sac and Fox Indians.[9]

J. Ellis among the Chickasaws

J. Ellis, a Stone-Campbell evangelist from Texas, was also active in Indian Territory, notably in the Chickasaw Nation. In the Spring, 1874, Ellis found that the "unsophisticated children of nature" liked his preaching "because . . . they say we have but one book and we tell them to go and do something instead of sitting down and feeling." He was able to organize a "very pleasant" congregation of both Indians and whites, which he named the "Chickasaw Christian Church." Among his congregants was B. F. Overton, whom he apparently baptized and rightly predicted would soon be governor of the Chickasaw Nation.[10] Ellis's work was short lived, but in less than seven years Robert Wallace Officer and others from the Stone-Campbell movement would extend it via the so-called Indian Mission.

R. W. Officer Envisions an "Indian Mission"

Officer (1845–1930) was a Tennessee native, Confederate veteran, and former Baptist preacher, who in 1880 at the age of thirty-five accepted the position of minister of the Gainesville, Texas, Christian Church. Almost immediately he was fascinated with Indian Territory situated just north of the Red River and dreamed of a full-fledged mission there involving both evangelism and education. He began work to implement those dreams as he ministered first at Gainesville, then at Paris, Texas, and finally in Indian Territory itself.[11]

Officer's vision of an Indian mission developed over time. While filling the pulpit at Gainesville and Paris, he made several trips into Indian Territory, specifically the Chickasaw Nation. On these journeys, he did little more than make acquaintances of its residents, learn something of Indian culture, familiarize himself with geography, and distribute religious tracts. Surely he also learned of the previous work of J. Ellis. Officer did not preach until February 1881, and then to an audience of thirty Chickasaws gathered around a campfire near present Madill. At this service, Officer met the then second-term governor of the Chickasaws, B. F. Overton (1836–84). Officer impressed Overton, who encouraged him to focus his Indian Territory preaching on the Chickasaws. Officer agreed to do so, a promise that gave some credibility to the notion of "our Indian Mission."[12]

Murrell Askew among the Chickasaws

Officer, however, was not thinking so much of himself as Murrell Askew (1811–84). Askew, a revered Alabama friend who had left the Baptist community with him, was seventy years old, a Choctaw by blood, and the father of adult children. He was not excited about moving to Indian Territory, but Officer helped Askew overcome his reluctance by reminding him that his Choctaw blood made him eligible for Choctaw-Chickasaw citizenship and use of tribal lands. Officer also promised financial assistance if necessary. Askew agreed to come; as promised, Officer helped with expenses; Askew established tribal citizenship; and Governor Overton gave Askew a horse and appointed him teacher at Burney Institute, a tribal school near present Lebanon, Oklahoma, with a salary of one hundred dollars per year.[13]

Askew, with Officer's support, was an effective missionary among his Choctaw and Chickasaw relatives. In less than thirty months, he established fifty-three active churches, with a membership that included Governor Overton.[14] Together, Askew and Officer attended the annual meeting of the Chickasaw National Council at Tishomingo, where Officer took the occasion to preach, submit credentials endorsed by the elders of the churches at Gainesville and Paris, and propose that Stone-Campbell churches organize an institution of learning for the Chickasaws. The council did not endorse the school proposal, but it did grant Officer and Askew the privilege of "locating preachers of the faith" in the Chickasaw Nation.[15] The missionaries could have asked for more, but for the moment what they got was enough. The council's action affirmed the reality of and sanctioned the work of the Indian Mission.

Mission Work According to the "Lord's Plan"

With Askew hard at work among the Chickasaws, Officer made some personal adjustments that would enable him to focus his attention on the Choctaws. In late 1883, he moved his family some ninety-five miles east to Paris, Texas, which had better rail access to the Choctaw Nation and better living arrangements for his family. He accepted the appointment of city evangelist as offered by the local Stone-Campbell church, whose leadership had agreed to sponsor the Indian Mission according to the "Lord's plan," that is, with resources from their own congregation and from freewill offerings donated by cooperating churches and individuals. There would be no relationship with the ACMS, a parachurch society that operated independent of a local congregation. For such an organization, the Paris church elders found no pattern in the New Testament. They were also willing to release Officer from his local preaching so that he could devote one-half of his time to mission work in the Choctaw Nation.[16]

The Indian Mission may have had willing workers and been organized according to the New Testament pattern, but that was about all. It had no funds to carry out its work. Success would require participation by other Stone-Campbell churches. After the Chickasaw council meeting, the Paris church elders announced the promising developments in Indian Territory through the pages of the *Gospel Advocate*, a periodical published by David Lipscomb, the esteemed leader/editor of the movement in Nashville, and a mentor and friend of Officer. They also suggested that each congregation dedicate one Sunday's contribution to help fund the construction of a small church building in the Chickasaw Nation. The response of less than forty dollars was disappointing but not deterring, although it probably should have been.[17]

A Heartbreaking Development

Just as Officer opened a new aspect of his mission work, the first ended dramatically. Murrell Askew died in early January 1884. Governor B. F. Overton died six weeks later. In the passing of these two coworkers, Officer felt a deep sense of loss. Askew's death, he wrote, left him lonely and sad, "with a heart that bled" and "eyes that could not be dried." Askew was "a true and tried soldier of the cross, who died the death of the righteous." Overton, a dear friend who had wept with him at Askew's funeral, was a leader with a "bold, liberal spirit" who did right "because it was right."[18] But the deaths of his coworkers did not leave Officer disconsolate or purposeless. His friends were in the hands of God, he believed, and he had work to do in the Choctaw Nation.

Launching Work among the Choctaws

After his relocation to Paris and for several months each year, Officer went by train, the Missouri, Kansas, and Texas (MK&T), and/or wagon north into Indian Territory. On these excursions, he always took with him a supply of religious books and pamphlets, generously provided by the readers of the *Gospel Advocate*. He believed that the distribution of Christian literature was an effective and inexpensive way to introduce the gospel in any mission field.[19]

He also preached, usually in the churches or schools founded by one of the Protestant denominations that had served the Choctaws since their removal to Indian Territory in the 1830s. Officer spoke in English, and, depending upon the audience, with the aid of an interpreter.[20] Among his listeners, he seldom found individuals who knew of or identified with the Stone-Campbell movement. Those who did know generally had a dim view of it. But the circumstances were different in Atoka, a county seat town for the Choctaw Nation and a stop on the MK&T Railroad line.

In Atoka, Officer met James S. Standley (1841–1901) and his family, widely recognized as one of the community's, indeed the Choctaw Nation's, most prominent families. A direct descendant of Chief Apukshunnubbee, Standley was Mississippi born, privately educated, a Confederate veteran, and an attorney by profession. In 1872, he had immigrated to the Choctaw Nation, established his citizenship, and made his permanent residence in Atoka. On frequent occasions, he represented the tribe in Washington, D.C. Of most importance, Standley had long been associated with the Stone-Campbell movement. Upon meeting Officer, he invited him to preach in his home. Subsequently, he convinced the missionary to spend every fourth Sunday in Atoka, an appointment Officer seldom failed to keep over the next few years.[21]

Through the agency of Standley, Officer made the acquaintance of a large number of Choctaw dignitaries. No doubt the influence of these men, and the commendations Officer received after speaking to the Chickasaw council the previous year, accounted for the Choctaw National Council inviting him to speak at its annual meeting at Tuskahoma in October 1884.

Components of the Indian Mission

For Officer, the invitation was a rare opportunity to draw attention to the Indian Mission as he envisioned it. He had a broad view of evangelization that included not only preaching the word but providing programs to care for orphans and to educate the rising generation. Officer had been touched by the number of orphaned or fatherless children he encountered on his trips into the Choctaw Nation. He had devised a program to place such children in individual Christian homes in the United States, where they would get care for their physical, educational, and spiritual needs. One of the first to take advantage of the program had been a ten-year-old Choctaw girl, Phoebe Anderson, who was placed in a home in Springfield, Illinois. Over a period of time, some thirty-six boys and girls took advantage of this program, often spending weeks or months in the Officer home before joining their "adopted" families in one of seven states plus Indian Territory. Officer considered these children to be members of his family and stayed in touch with them during the course of his life. Unfortunately, we know the names of only a few.[22]

Officer also envisioned an industrial boarding school for Choctaw children to be situated near Atoka. The institution would provide students with both liberal and vocational educations, and it would be staffed by members of the Indian Mission and built by donations from Stone-Campbell churches. All that he would ask of the Choctaws was a small grant of land and a tuition subsidy of ten dollars per student per month.[23] The facility that Officer had in mind would look like a number of other educational institutions in the nation either owned or operated by one of the Protestant denominations. These included Spencer Academy; Wheelock Academy; Armstrong Academy; New Hope Academy; Atoka Baptist Academy; and Tushka Lusa Academy.

As another component of the Indian Mission, Officer envisioned a complex of neighborhood schools. The Choctaw government itself funded day schools in tribal neighborhoods at two dollars per month per scholar. It made no provisions, however, for buildings or for non-Indian students. Officer and his associates saw this as an unusual opportunity to share the gospel. They envisioned constructing buildings in the neighborhoods where traditional schools would meet, as well as a Sunday school and a church. The success of the plan required teachers who had a strong Christian commitment and pedagogical competency, but it also required teachers who were self-confident women. Men need not apply, wrote Officer, for "women work with more earnestness than men, and as a rule, are more honest and unselfish in their efforts." Besides, the Choctaws wanted women teaching in their neighborhood schools.[24]

Getting Endorsed by the Stone-Campbell Movement

The Choctaw National Council was pleased to hear from Officer, but it wanted assurances that he represented the "denomination" he claimed. The council had learned from cruel experience that some of the missionaries among them asserted relationships that they did not possess, including individuals who identified themselves as being part of the Stone-Campbell movement. The rogues were more interested in themselves than the Choctaws and generated significant prejudice in the Indian and broader missionary communities against legitimate representatives of the movement.[25]

The endorsement desired by the council was fairly simple for Methodists, Presbyterians, Baptists, and Catholics to secure. But the congregational polity of Stone-Campbell churches made denominational endorsements of that kind problematic. Officer resolved the issue by asking the Texas state convention of the Stone-Campbell churches meeting in Bryan, Texas, in 1884, to affirm his qualifications as a legitimate representative to the Choctaw Nation. The request was granted, but only after an uncivil, if not un-Christian, debate. The elders of the church at Paris, Texas, at the request of the state convention meeting at Ennis the previous year, also certified him as "a worthy teacher of the Gospel of Jesus the Christ."[26]

With three companions, Officer traveled by wagon from Atoka to Tuskahoma to present his credentials. The Choctaw council itself, he believed, was filled with "novel, big-hearted . . . men, whom one could learn to love without much effort." For three evenings, he preached to them and their guests. During one of the council's formal sessions, he submitted his credentials as provided by the Texas convention and shared his vision of Stone-Campbell churches supporting a mission that would not only share the gospel but would care for orphan children, construct an industrial boarding school, and create neighborhood and Sunday schools. Presumably, he also spoke of the financial supplement that the mission would require from the Choctaws themselves.[27]

Although no known record of the Choctaw government confirms as much, Officer's written reports suggest that the Choctaws embraced his vision of an Indian Mission. George W. Harkins, a former chief of the Choctaws who was present, was sufficiently impressed that he pledged fifty dollars a year for three years to help implement the dream.[28] Doubtless the Choctaw delegates also affirmed his credentials, and it certainly flattered him by reacting positively to his preaching. The responses were all encouraging save two: the council allocated no land and appropriated no money for the industrial boarding school.

Support for the Work

Officer's appearance before the Chickasaw and Choctaw councils and his many reports of the ongoing work of the mission stirred the imagination and interest of members of Stone-Campbell churches, and especially editors of its periodicals. For editors like David Lipscomb of the *Gospel Advocate* and Daniel Sommer of the *Octographic Review*, Officer was proposing mission work according to the "Lord's plan," that is, with the management and support of the local congregation rather than through a parachurch organization like the ACMS. It was a distinction, along

with the use of instrumental music in worship services, that was then disturbing the unity of the Stone-Campbell movement. "Brethren," Lipscomb wrote of
Officer, "help him. He is a self-sacrificing brother, working for the up-building
and exaltation of a race long lost in ignorance of the gospel."[29] Sommer picked
up on the same theme, noting that Officer had never been "under the auspices of
any man-made society" and was laboring with a people "whose manners [were]
simple." He commended the Indian Mission "wholeheartedly" and hoped that his
readers would say "Amen" by sending a contribution to the Paris church elders.[30]

Officer, of course, hoped they would do the same thing. Finding "scriptural"
support for the mission was critical. Through his reports and sermons in the
Advocate and *Review*, and other church-related journals,[31] he encouraged his
readers to take "fellowship" with him in the Indian Mission, meaning make a
freewill gift. He often suggested that the congregations dedicate the offering of a
particular Sunday or divide a regular contribution, or that Sunday schools take up
a special collection. Whatever the source of the contribution, it should be sent to
the elders of the Paris church, to the editorial offices of the periodical publishing
the report, or directly to him. All gifts would be reported in the periodicals and
distributed only by the elders of the Paris church. Additionally, Officer dispatched
coworkers, generally women, to solicit churches for contributions to carry on the
work of the mission, especially as it related to orphans and neighborhood schools.[32]

The appeals generated just enough interest and gifts for Officer to remain
positive about the future of the Indian Mission. At least five young women agreed
to take charge of different neighborhood and Sunday schools. By late 1885, one
of the schools was operational with twenty scholars.[33]

The continuing interest of the Choctaw National Council also encouraged
Officer. In April 1885, he received another invitation to preach at its fall meeting.
He recalled that at the previous gathering, he "was first to thrust . . . the sword
of the spirit in [Tuskahoma]" and, with the help of the brethren, would build
there "the first house of worship in the name of the Lord Jesus."[34] The reception
he received in October was gratifying. He stayed in the new McCurtain Hotel,
and when he preached each evening, "all" came to hear him. More importantly,
six embraced the restoration appeal, and on the last Sunday of his stay the newly
ordered congregation celebrated the Lord's Supper "for the first time in the
history of the world."[35]

Whether Officer used the occasion of the 1885 council to broach the idea of
an industrial boarding school for orphan children is unknown, although it is
reasonable to assume that he did. It is also fair to conclude that, as in the previous

year, the council neither committed itself to support the school financially nor
to help it with a grant of land. But in Officer's mind, the prospect of assistance
remained, for he did not abandon his plans but merely recast them. He intended
to find property and financial support elsewhere.[36]

Officer Moves the Indian Mission to Atoka

Given the warm receptions of two National Council meetings, Officer could no
longer resist the call of his heart to move his family to Indian Territory from
Paris, Texas, and give the Indian Mission his full time and attention. But how
could he sustain his family in a destitute field? After prayer and discussion, he
and his wife, Lota Venable, decided that they would use the inheritance she
received from her father's estate plus what the two had been able to save over the
previous six years of ministry to get them established in Indian Territory. By the
time those means ran out, they had faith that the mission would have produced
congregations that could sustain them. To supplement and extend their own
resources, they would continue to call upon the churches in the states to divide
their means with them. And, if that were not enough, Officer, like the apostle
Paul, could work with his hands to support his family. It was a leap of faith to
leave Texas, but Officer and Lota had faith to spare.[37]

Will the "Lord's Plan" Work?

That faith was shaken and then restored in the winter of 1885–86. Because of Lota's
health, Officer took his family back to Winchester, Tennessee, where she could
get additional care and help. In December, he learned from the Paris church that
the response to their continued pleas for "fellowship" in the work of the Indian
Mission had been "feeble." He was dismayed. "I have thought a majority of the
brethren who read the *Gospel Advocate*," he wrote to David Lipscomb, "believed
as I do [about the ways and means of Christianizing the world] and that they
were only waiting for an opportunity to show their faith by their works." Is the
"Lord's plan to fail?" he asked. Officer reminded Lipscomb that "the brethren
who [were] in sympathy with the society suggested years ago that [he] consign
the work to them, with the promise that it would be supported." He respectfully
declined that opportunity. Yet in the present case, unless the brethren respond
more liberally, he would be "compelled to turn the work over to the first man
who [came] recommended by the Church of Christ." With irony and a touch
of bitterness, he concluded, "I have never called upon one of the brethren who
endorsed the society that I know of, who did not respond; but the rule is, in

almost every community, where the brethren endorse God's plan, I am turned away empty. What I have said is true, and it bleeds my heart."[38]

Officer's despair caused David Lipscomb to publish a ringing call to arms. If "we claim to be a missionary people on God's plan," he wrote, "let us all see [to it] that this mission is supported by the church of God. The church of God is Missionary Society enough, if we will only work." Substantial support at that point in time would "show skeptical brethren that the church [could] evangelize foreign lands without doing it through the Society."[39] Three months later, Lipscomb wrote another strong editorial in support of the neighborhood school program, endorsing the call for committed Christian women to serve as teachers.[40] For him, supporting the Indian Mission became a virtual test of fellowship.

Lipscomb's endorsement restored Officer's hope and rekindled his faith in the Stone-Campbell churches that upheld the so-called Lord's plan. There would yet be support for the mission, enough to supplement his own means and to sustain other evangelists, not to mention neighborhood schoolteachers, an orphans' program, and an industrial boarding school. Joyfully and expectantly, he determined to relocate to Atoka and trust that the Lord and the churches would provide. If contributions were limited, he was not above working with his hands. Either way, he and his family were casting their lots with Indian Territory. "I have loosed anchor from other fields," he wrote, and "pitched my tent in Indian Territory on the promise of support. I will . . . hold my grip till it thunders. I have made no arrangements to retreat."[41]

Resettling among the Choctaws

Officer and his family left Paris, Texas, by wagon in mid-June 1886 and arrived in Atoka, Choctaw Nation, at the end of July. During the six weeks in transit, he preached a series of "discourses" at Caddo, Oakland, and Lebanon; had his team stolen in Lebanon; and took advantage of the waters at Maytubby Springs (northwest of Caddo) to sooth his chronic rheumatism. Once in Atoka, he purchased a house situated on a 1.7-acre lot. Over time, he expanded the house "with his own hands," paying for the improvements with his wife's inheritance.[42] The result was a commodious home of multiple bedrooms that some thought was a bit too elegant for a missionary. Until 1900, however, Officer's house at Atoka was the headquarters of the Indian Mission.

Although Officer considered all of Indian Territory to be his field of labor, his initial point of focus was the community of Atoka, a commercial center for the Choctaw Nation and the site of the Baptist orphanage led by Joseph S. Murrow.

He had no more than arrived when he launched a two-week evangelistic effort that resulted in the "gathering" of a congregation of twenty members led by two elders, J. S. Standley and J. C. Pate. The fourth Sunday of each month he preached for the group. Since the congregation had no building of its own, it usually met in the new Methodist church chapel. By 1889, however, it had its own place of worship, a former commercial building where the Odd Fellows also met. Four years later, following appeals to Stone-Campbell churches in the southern states, the Atoka congregation, at a cost of $1,495, constructed a new building on the corner of First and South Delaware Streets that served the community, with some major remodels, until 1961.[43]

Simultaneously, Officer was active in Atoka community affairs. In 1889, for example, he was religious editor of the *Indian Citizen*, a weekly newspaper owned by J. S. Standley that circulated throughout Indian Territory. The front page of the *Citizen* was fairly inclusive when it came to local and national news, but its religious column had a distinct Stone-Campbell flavor, reproducing articles from the movement's journals, reporting on the activities of its preachers in Indian Territory, and suggesting topics for Sunday school studies.[44]

Despite his partisan approach, Officer's pithy column worked to elevate his standing within the community. In 1889 and 1890, city officials appointed him to delegations that represented the interests of the town to federal officers in Washington, D.C. On the last trip, the U.S. Census office asked him to gather data on Stone-Campbell churches in Indian Territory for the religious census of 1890.[45] Later, he chaired the Atoka Townsite Committee, which had responsibility for surveying and selling town lots as part of the general land allotment and dismantling of the Choctaw Nation.[46]

Serving as an Evangelist among the Choctaws

As he was establishing himself in Atoka, Officer preached elsewhere three of the four weeks of the month. In the first three months after settling permanently in Indian Territory, he had gathered up some three hundred souls who willingly "threw off human shackles and boldly . . . stepped out . . . on the Lord's side," embracing the restoration plea.[47] Among those communities where he found interest in his message, through 1890, were Oakland, Canadian, Stonewall, Prairie View [near present-day Kiowa], Caddo, Vinita, Bennington, South McAlester, Durant, Lehigh, and Leader. Most of these sites were easily accessible by railroad.

At some locations, Indian participants by blood were substantial minorities, and occasionally a majority. But those were exceptions. Of the total population of 177,000 within the boundaries of the Five Tribes, more than 120,000 were non-Indian, or 68 percent.[48] If they worked, it was as tenant farmers, ranch hands, coal miners, and railroad workers. A goodly number were outlaws. Some were in the Indian nations by permission; most were not. The non-Indians generally clustered around the towns and settlements along the railroads. Thus the evangelistic appeals up and down the line were generally to non-Indians. By 1890, therefore, of the 2,200 Disciples of Christ Officer counted in Indian Territory for the U.S. religious census, probably no more than 10 percent, if that many, were of Indian ancestry.[49]

In carrying out his evangelistic work, Officer preached what he termed the "simple gospel" of the New Testament unadorned by human additions. Those impressed by the message who had not "obeyed the gospel," he encouraged to do so. If they agreed, he would baptize them by immersion in some nearby stream or pond. If hearers said they wanted to "step out on the Lord's side" but that they had been baptized previously, Officer shook their hand and blessed them, explained that baptism had a purpose more important than just church membership but was actually essential for salvation, and counted them among his converts. He saw no point in rebaptizing the faithful, only in reeducating them, a position very much in concert with that of Barton Stone and David Lipscomb.[50]

Once the Disciples had been gathered, he "set in order" a congregation of the church of Christ. That meant that he appointed officers, generally elders but sometimes deacons too, and got pledges from congregants to meet thereafter the first day of the week to study scripture and partake of the Lord's Supper. Sometimes, Officer even initiated steps that would result in a house of worship for the new congregation.[51]

Finally, Officer stayed in touch with congregations he set in order. Those in communities along the railroad and relatively near Atoka he tried to visit once every month or two. More distant and isolated congregations he got back to only once or twice a year. To all he tried to send pastoral letters on a regular basis. And through the pages of the *Indian Citizen*, he provided to them curriculum and commentary for weekly Bible study.

Officer's evangelistic efforts were not always welcomed by the leadership of other faith traditions. At one time or another, Presbyterians, Methodists, and Baptists all refused to let Officer use their buildings to deliver his discourses. Officer would arrive at a community to begin a pre-advertised meeting only to discover that one of the denominations had just started a competing revival. This happened so regularly that Officer concluded that there was a preset "union of effort to spoil our efforts," especially in the railroad towns, forcing him to work in destitute and neglected places.[52] Regarding this harassment, he lamented, "I have had an experience here that no one need envy."[53]

Whatever his challenges, Officer had some success in his evangelistic efforts. In 1888, he baptized 137 individuals.[54] The response continued positive through 1889, when he baptized Grandmother Colbert of the much-esteemed Chickasaw family near Kiowa.[55] In addition to Atoka, he had organized congregations at Caddo, Canadian, Oakland, Lehigh, Prairie View, Leader, Bennington, Durant, South McAlester, and Vinita by 1890. Three of these met in good houses of worship.[56]

Other Evangelists in the Field

A number of Stone-Campbell faithful were in Indian Territory as farmers, merchants, or laborers but also felt compelled to share the gospel in their communities. Among these were Dr. C. P. Kelly in the Tishomingo area, M. L. Scott at Cowlington, B. B. Askew near Lebanon, M. J. Simpson at Muskogee, H. C. Collier at McAlester, M. L. Wilson of Kiowa and Leader, Dr. John T. Gilmore at Stonewall and later Allen, C. E. Prichard near Marlow, and D. B. Cargile at Dale. In more expansive moments, Officer included these men in the Indian Mission, reporting on their work in the *Gospel Advocate* and other journals. The men themselves probably would not have acknowledged the relationship, excepting perhaps H. C. Collier and B. B. Askew, the son of Murrell. (Both men were Native Americans, Cherokee and Choctaw respectively.)

Other evangelists had a more direct connection to the Indian Mission. Among the most important of these was W. B. Stinson. A native of Texas, Stinson held a commission from the ACMS to evangelize Indian Territory. By 1889, he centered his attention upon the area surrounding Vinita in the Cherokee Nation. Officer made several trips to Vinita to support Stinson in his work, even though he objected to the ways and means of the ACMS. Stinson returned the courtesy by serving as a nurse in Atoka when the entire Officer household was ill. In 1891, he left the mission field and returned presumably to local work in Texas.[57]

Well regarded by Daniel Sommer and the readers of the *Octographic Review*, M. Gorman came from Missouri to join Officer at Atoka in early 1890. His main responsibility was to work with the congregation at Atoka, which would provide some of his support, but also to serve other congregations "up and down the [MK&T] line." Whether Officer and the Indian Mission were to be responsible for some of his support is unclear, although Gorman apparently thought so. For a time, he and Officer worked together, but when the support he anticipated did not materialize, he became disaffected. In late May 1890, the Atoka *Indian Citizen*

announced that Gorman had apologized for circulating false reports regarding
Officer. The content of those false reports was never made clear, although they
probably related to the finances of the Indian Mission. Within months, Gorman
returned to Missouri, where he established a modest reputation as a writer among
Stone-Campbell churches.[58] Officer surely forgave Gorman for his disloyalty,
but he never forgot it.

M. L. Wilson came from Texas to join the Indian Mission, also in 1890. He and
his young wife located at Prairie View on twenty acres of land set aside by one of
the elders of the church, Charles Word. It was expected that Wilson would teach,
preach, and make use of the land as he pleased. He did not stay long, probably
because of the death of his wife. In time, however, he attributed his leaving more
to his unrealized financial expectations than his personal tragedy. He became a
lifelong critic of Officer and the Indian Mission.[59]

The Ever-Faithful C. C. Parker

Unlike Gorman and Wilson, C. C. Parker (1847–after 1907) knew nothing of
disloyalty. A native of Chattanooga, Tennessee, partly educated in Nashville, and
raised as a Baptist, he joined Officer and the Indian Mission in 1889. He had an
enthusiasm for evangelism that was unparalleled by Officer or any other Indian
Territory preacher. Located first at Brooken in Haskell County, Parker looked
to Officer for direction as to where to focus his energies, and Officer responded
by committing himself to sharing whatever means he had with Parker. Officer
supplied Parker with a horse and buggy and sent him north to Canadian to be
a full-time evangelist. Parker promptly lost both horse and buggy crossing the
Canadian River, whereupon he was reduced to walking to his appointments,
which were almost always destitute. Neither of those circumstances bothered
him much, other than the fact that he had a nearly blind wife and two small
children to provide for who were living in Canadian. Parker published pitiful
letters in the brotherhood journals appealing for support, but his solicitations
were considered the unseemly work of a beggar and were largely ineffectual.
Officer, however, did share what little support he received with Parker, who in
turn extended to Officer heartfelt gratitude and complete loyalty.[60]

Meanwhile, Parker's work in the destitute places of the Choctaw and Chickasaw Nations was having an impact. In the first four months of 1890, his effort
brought twenty-five additions to Stone-Campbell churches. Especially along the
Canadian River that productivity continued, aided perhaps by Parker's eagerness
to enter into religious disputes through formal debates. Seeking a better residence

for his family, he relocated to Oakland in 1892 and focused his preaching on communities in the Chickasaw Nation. Two years later his efforts alone brought about the addition of seventy-seven individuals to Stone-Campbell churches, but at the expense of one more horse.[61]

No evangelist pursued a more rigorous evangelistic schedule. There were not many congregations in southern and southeastern Indian Territory in which Parker did not preach. A goodly number of them he actually founded in the wake of spectacular revivals (Davis, where seventy were baptized, and Wynnewood, where ninety were baptized in 1891[62]). In 1893, he estimated that he had baptized over one thousand people in the territory.[63]

Parker was always in debt, and his family was always in crisis. In 1898, he lost his home in Oakland. His long-suffering wife died in 1899, leaving him to care for two small children. That challenge took him to Texas for a time, but by 1901 he was back in Indian Territory preaching at Allen. He was also an active debater and considered himself especially prepared to meet Mormons. In fact, he was the vice president of the American Anti-Mormon Association of Disciples of Christ. Over the course of his ministry, he became an effective writer, wrote a lengthy endorsement of Charles Carroll's virulent *The Negro: A Beast, or In the Image of God* (1900), copies of which he inexplicably sent to S. R. Cassius, "our colored evangelist." He even planned to publish from Noble, Oklahoma Territory, a small periodical, the *Star of Hope*. In 1906, however, fire, destroyed the press before an edition could be printed. Parker seems to have left Oklahoma shortly thereafter.[64]

A Notable Harvest

The evangelistic efforts of Officer and his coworkers yielded a notable harvest in Indian Territory, if self-reports are creditable. In 1887, they established five new congregations and baptized 163 converts. The next year they reported twelve solid congregations and 900 Christians. In 1890, they counted for the U.S. Census office 2,200 Disciples in fifty-four congregations, of which thirty met in schoolhouses, fourteen in private homes, and ten in dedicated buildings. To the 2,200, some 700 more were added over the next two years.[65] According to one observer of the Canadian River Valley, the Stone-Campbell churches were so thick in the region "that you can't turn over a chip without finding one."[66] The distinguished nineteenth-century chronicler H. F. O'Beirne remarked that they had grown more rapidly than any other faith community in Indian Territory.[67]

Of course, the Indian Mission was the poster child of those Stone-Campbell members who wanted to do mission work without the assistance of the "unscriptural" parachurch societies such as the ACMS. Periodicals like the *Gospel Advocate*, *Christian Standard*, and *Octographic Review* admonished their readers to support the mission, even agreeing to serve as a collection and forwarding agent.[68] And Officer published letter after letter requesting the "fellowship" of the churches in the work of the mission. All of these appeals had only limited impact through 1889; almost none thereafter.[69] Significantly, Officer never lost confidence in the preferred methodology of financing mission work. If the money did not materialize, he worked with his own hands to "keep the wolf from the door" and also curtailed his plans for the mission, in this case the orphans' program, the industrial boarding school, and the neighborhood school program. He and his coworkers would continue to evangelize, even if only on the weekends.[70]

So the preaching continued in Indian Territory, although less and less among Indian people per se. The populations of the railroad towns, the most accessible to Officer and his coworkers, were largely comprised of non-Indians, who were in the territory as tenant farmers, merchants, professionals, miners, and cowboys. Most did not see themselves as permanent residents of the community, but there only until a better opportunity for a free homestead developed elsewhere. Most of the congregations in Indian Territory, therefore, were composed primarily of non-Indian transients.[71] "The Indians do not attend any of our meetings at any place known to me," said evangelist John W. Harris, "and for ten years we have never seen but two Indians at church."[72]

Just how transient the population was became apparent in 1889. On April 22 of that year, the Unassigned Lands of what is now central Oklahoma opened for settlement in a fabled land run. Many of those who participated in that event, and others who would follow, were congregants of the Stone-Campbell churches in Indian Territory. Congregations so laboriously established and patiently nurtured were virtually wiped out by the mass exodus to Oklahoma Territory.[73]

The unexpected development disheartened Officer. Add the fact that financial support of the mission was diminishing, it was no wonder that he came to speak of withdrawing from the field altogether in late 1890. His published sermons spoke of pain and disappointment as being God's will and of the joy that comes through suffering. Had it not been for the encouraging work of Meta Chestnutt in the Chickasaw Nation near present Minco and the prospect of a robust mission among the Comanche, Kiowa, and Wichita Indians, Officer would likely have declared the Indian Mission defunct, retired from Indian Territory, and taken his family back to Tennessee.[74]

But he did not.

3

EVANGELIZING INDIAN TERRITORY
1889–1907

R. W. Officer was aboard the Santa Fe train on his way to Minco, Chickasaw Nation, on June 1, 1892. During a routine stop at Red Rock, a community northeast of Perry in Noble County, members of the infamous Dalton gang boarded the train with intentions of robbing the express car. First, however, they proceeded to hold up all of the passengers. Going from car to car, they ordered travelers to raise their hands and keep them up until they had turned their valuables over to one of the gang. In that process, Officer's arms began to ache, so much so that he finally told members of the gang that he had in his possession only a New Testament, a lunch, and seventy-five cents. He would gladly give them more in an IOU, he said, if they would let him put his hands down![1]

Organizing Indian Territory

Other than reflect the courage and feistiness of Officer, the incident demonstrated that Officer's mission field had undergone dramatic change since he began his work there in 1881. In addition to miles of new railroad track, the region had been especially affected by how the U.S. government had accommodated the perpetual quest of non-Indians for Indian land. In 1887, for example, Congress had created the Dawes Commission and charged it to negotiate with the Five Tribes to terminate their governments and divide their estates among tribal citizens, with any surplus land to be sold to non-Indians. Land-hungry settlers, some of whom may have been on the train with Officer, rushed to the territory to take advantage of the prospective bonanza. In 1890, Congress had also established U.S. district courts at Muskogee, Ardmore, and McAlester, effectively recognizing a formal Indian Territory.

Also, as already noted, the U.S. government had opened the Unassigned Lands for settlement in the famous horse race of 1889. In a matter of weeks, what is now central Oklahoma was home to some fifty thousand settlers.[2] The following year Congress created the Territory of Oklahoma, and thereafter would periodically add to its borders other tribal lands that had also been opened to white settlement. These successive openings, however, would wreak havoc for Officer and other Stone-Campbell evangelists, who worked diligently to build up congregations in Indian Territory only to have their members leave in search of free land in Oklahoma Territory.[3]

Meta Chestnutt as an Educational Missionary

When Meta Chestnutt (1863–1948) made her final decision to be an educational missionary among Indian people, she was not much troubled by the changing demographics of Indian Territory. Instead, she was realizing a childhood dream to serve Indian people as a teacher of matters both sacred and secular. Born in Lenoir County, North Carolina, on September 8, 1863, Chestnutt grew up in a traditional southern home on a plantation given to her parents by her maternal grandfather, Wiley Nobles, a physician, minister of the gospel, and friend of Alexander Campbell. She was baptized at the age of thirteen, a moment that she remembered vividly for the rest of her days and that she wanted her family, friends, students, and indeed everyone, to replicate it in their own lives.

Unlike many southern women, Chestnutt received a formal education, first at nearby Bethel Academy (1884) and Greenville Institute (1886). She did so well at Greenville that she won a scholarship to attend Peabody Normal School and the University of Nashville. She completed degrees at the two institutions before 1888. While in Nashville, she taught a young men's Bible class in a mission Sunday school that ultimately grew into the South Nashville Church of Christ.[4] She also had the occasion to hear and meet the noted educator and evangelist, T. B. Larimore, who made a lifelong impression upon her. Larimore was so taken with Chestnutt that he offered her a job at his college in Florence, Alabama, on the spot. Chestnutt declined the offer, but she took the occasion to share with Larimore her dream of ministering to Indian children. Larimore determined to help make that dream come true and referred her to his friends, Mr. and Mrs. W. J. Erwin, who were citizens and residents of the Chickasaw Nation.[5]

Chestnutt wrote immediately to the Erwins, who welcomed her inquiry. They reported that their local school at Silver City, on the south bank of the South Canadian River, where the Chisholm Trail crossed and one and one-half miles north of present Tuttle, had need of a teacher. If she accepted the position, she could live with them. Most of her students would be Chickasaw Indians, generally the children of white fathers and Indian mothers. Chestnutt was thrilled by the invitation, but deferred accepting until she could talk the matter over with her family and her fiancé in North Carolina. Her parents would have objected had they still been living, but her siblings did not. Her fiancé was heartbroken, but she argued passionately that she should pursue her dreams and answer the call of God to take the message of Christ to distant realms. He had little option but to let her go. Chestnutt was no clinging vine, but a woman of independent judgment, strength, vision, and purpose. And that purpose was clear: she was going to teach the word of the New Testament and found and develop a coeducational school, which was "God's plan for the human family," for Indians and for whites. Unlike others, she would later write, she was not in Indian Territory either to land hunt or to man hunt.[6] The latter must have come as a disappointment to many men, for she was a six-foot-two, attractive woman.

Mission Work in the Chickasaw Nation

After a long train ride, Meta Chestnutt arrived in Oklahoma City on September 4, 1889, barely four months after the great land run. The following day W. J. Erwin took her by wagon to Silver City. After the passing of only three days, the following Monday, she opened her first school, a day school financed by subscription, in a building that had been built from lumber imported from Denison, Texas, by wagon. She took up residence with the Erwin family, in a lean-to structure attached to the back of the house.[7]

In addition to teaching school, Chestnutt engaged in a ministry of the word. Two days after she arrived, she and Mrs. Erwin organized a Sunday school and "spread the Lord's table," or prepared communion, using a silver service and white linen that she had brought with her from North Carolina (and subsequently bequeathed to the First Christian Church in Chickasha). On later occasions, she was called upon to make appropriate comments at a burial ceremony. Although women had limited roles in Stone-Campbell congregations at that time, Chestnutt assumed these responsibilities "because there was no man to do it then." On her pastoral and, subsequently, business journeys over the prairie, she always carried her Bible with her, but also her pistol. The Bible she used frequently; the pistol she never used.[8]

Chestnutt had no more than arrived in Silver City than she petitioned T. B. Larimore to come and hold a revival. Larimore could not work it into his schedule, but he wrote to R. W. Officer in Atoka and invited him to supply the preaching. Officer accepted the invitation. In June 1890, following the South Canadian River, he went by horse and wagon to Silver City. Officer knew the location, for some nine years earlier just north of there he had preached to cowboys trailing their herds to markets in Kansas. His subsequent sermons were delivered to a small but enthusiastic audience. W. J. Erwin renewed his allegiance to the gospel, and Mrs. J. H. Bond, a widely admired full-blood Chickasaw woman, requested baptism, but at a later date when her health would permit. Chestnutt was thrilled with the results of the revival, not only in its harvest of souls but in the launching of a mutual admiration relationship with R. W. Officer.[9]

Meanwhile, the Rock Island Railroad extended its line southward across the South Canadian River and laid out the town of Minco as its railhead. Given the prospects of the new town and that it was only seven miles west, the community of Silver City moved en masse to Minco on July 4, 1890. This included Chestnutt and her school. The school building had been constructed with a dual purpose, as a day school, but also as a church, known as the "Sunny South Christian Church." The church, like the school, prospered almost from the beginning, with a membership that in time reached 120, met in its own wood-frame worship facility, was led by strong elders, and was served by notable evangelists, including D. T. Broadus of Wichita, Kansas. Said Chestnutt some years later, "I think that little church was the happiest church I have ever known."[10]

Organizing a Church-Related School

In 1892, with the help of Mrs. J. H. Bond, the Chickasaw and Choctaw tribal governments agreed to subsidize the children of their citizens enrolled in the Minco school at the rate of twelve dollars per student per term.[11] The prospects of this kind of support, in addition to support from a prospering and growing community, caused Chestnutt to think in terms of a much larger establishment, specifically a "college" for boarding and day students enrolled in primary, secondary, or collegiate departments. How to accomplish that goal was not clear, however.

S. E. Kennedy, an agent of the ACMS assigned to Oklahoma Territory, thought he knew how. Declare the school a "Christian University," he suggested, and place it under the leadership of the elders of the congregation at Minco, who, of course, would be sturdy males. Although the school had been her idea, Chestnutt would serve only as one of the faculty. Kennedy would then appeal to the ACMS and larger Stone-Campbell churches back East to support "our" school in Indian Territory. He felt confident that such an appeal, if properly framed, would be successful and assure the establishment of the college.[12]

And for a time it seemed promising. Appeals were published in both the *Christian Standard* and the *Gospel Advocate*. R. W. Officer commended the college to his network of friends and wrote of the college as if it were part of his Indian Mission. Members of the Minco church donated ten acres in the northwest part of the community as the site of the school building. They, along with other citizens, pledged some $6,500 of the $8,000 needed to construct a suitable building. In August 1894, construction on a three-story twenty-one-room building began.[13]

Meta Chestnutt had difficulty seeing herself as part of the institution Kennedy envisioned. She never made clear why, but it probably had more to do with who was to run the college than its envisioned relationship with Stone-Campbell churches. Kennedy apparently saw himself as the director. Chestnutt made her disappointment about the developing leadership known and left for a visit to North Carolina.[14]

By October, the project was struggling. Initial pledges were not being paid. Appeals for support from the ACMS, religious periodicals, and churches had yielded only sympathy. Absent the promised support, construction slowed down, with only the first floor of the building enclosed but not completed. Wind and dust made the much-promoted October 1 dedication ceremony a disaster, despite addresses by J. H. Hardin, president of the ACMS, and E. F. Boggess of Guthrie, both selected by Kennedy.[15] The dedication was something of an embarrassment, as well as a testimony that a formal arrangement with the Stone-Campbell movement did not exist.

Meta Takes Control

Through all of this, Meta Chestnutt remained at her post at Sunny South School. By January 1895, trustees and townspeople had turned to her to save the school. She agreed to assume personal responsibility for completing construction of the building and for paying the $12,000 debt incurred by the project along with all operational deficits. In return, she asked only for permission to name the school "El Meta Christian College," with "El Meta" being a tribute to her deceased mother, "Almeda." Thereafter, there was no formal connection with Stone-Campbell churches, although the college mandated daily chapel and Sunday morning services for all boarding students and employees. In 1902, Chestnutt dropped "Christian" from the college's name and retitled it "El Meta Bond College," with "Bond" being in honor of her benefactor, Mrs. J. H. Bond. There followed "most successful years" for the college, which afforded "an opportunity for the people of the Territory and the 'new country' to educate their children near home."[16]

There was a close relationship between the Stone-Campbell church at Minco and the college. The church first met in the Sunny South School building, which was relocated to the southeastern corner of the college campus around 1895. R. W. Officer, T. B. Larimore, and D. T. Broadus stopped by to preach and encourage.[17] Later, a baptistery was constructed and as many as 120 claimed membership in the congregation. It even planted a mission church at Brushy Creek just west of Minco, following a notable camp meeting in 1896.[18] In 1903, the Minco church building was burned following a strong sermon by D. T. Broadus against saloons and associated evils. The congregation then moved its place of worship to the college building. Unable to agree on whether to rebuild with wood or rock, the church had no permanent home thereafter. By 1920, the congregation was relegated to memory.[19]

Last Years in Chickasha

Meta Chestnutt remained at her post as president and founder of El Meta Bond College until 1920. That year she closed the college and with her husband, J. Alba Sager, who she had married in 1906, moved to Chickasha. Mr. Sager was a member of the music faculty at Oklahoma College for Women until he passed away in 1929. Chestnutt Sager then accepted an assistant cataloguer position at OCW, which she held until her death in 1948. She was elected to the Oklahoma Hall of Fame in 1939; eleven years later the University of Oklahoma named one of its residence halls in her honor. "My years," she wrote to her niece, "have been almost an unending prayer to God in the Master's name to help me to do all this, and now *it is done.*"[20]

Chestnutt Sager's lifelong commitment to the Stone-Campbell movement was apparent in her last will and testament. She left small but equal legacies to the Chickasha Church of Christ and the Chickasha Christian Church, where she had membership. She asked that not one cent of the money given the latter be used for church dinner parties, however. She also left legacies for her home church in North Carolina, a missionary in South Africa, and Johnson Bible College in Tennessee. Moreover, some of her personal possessions were donated to the orphans' home at Tipton, Oklahoma. Like her mentors, Larimore and Officer, Chestnutt Sager avoided taking part in the internecine strife that racked the Stone-Campbell movement at the dawn of the twentieth century.[21]

Reaching Out to the "Wild Tribes"

When Meta Chestnutt was trying to establish herself among the Chickasaws, R. W. Officer made several trips to Minco to help her. On those journeys, he also probed the possibility of establishing mission outreaches among what he called the "Wild Tribes," who were situated just west and southwest of Minco. He made the acquaintance of the Wichita chief, Tawakoni Jim, and contemplated leveraging that acquaintance into a full-fledged mission that would serve the Wichitas, Comanches, and Kiowas.[22]

In late 1890, Officer inquired of the U.S. Indian agent at Fort Sill as to the processes whereby he as a representative of "the disciples (Christian Church)" could be recognized officially by the federal government as a missionary.[23] That recognition was granted as of April the following year, although over the objections of the *Indian Missionary*, a Baptist journal published at Atoka.[24] With the endorsement of Horace Speed, the U.S. attorney for Oklahoma Territory, and J. W. Hadden, the superintendent of the Fort Sill Indian School, the U.S. secretary of the interior granted Officer and the Home Mission Board of the Christian Church the right to use 160 acres of the Kiowa-Comanche Reservation, assuming the consent of the tribe, for church and educational purposes in March 1892.[25]

It must have galled Officer to have to use the agency of a "human society," the Home Mission Board of the Christian Church (or the ACBM), to achieve formal recognition of the federal government. He was able to address that problem when the tribes in council considered the matter. They chose to grant the 160 acres to the elders of the Paris Christian Church, who would serve as a board of trustees for the property. The tribal councilors also stipulated that actual possession by the church depended upon its agents occupying the property and making improvements that would serve the permanent good of the Indians. Once occupied and improvements in place, the property would remain in the hands of the church even if the reservation was discontinued.[26]

For the next eight years, Officer made earnest efforts to realize the promise of the "Wild Tribes" mission. Through the pages of the *Octographic Review*,

Gospel Advocate, and *Firm Foundation*, he solicited Stone-Campbell churches to "fellowship" the mission in the amount of $1,000 per year, in addition to the cost of school buildings and teacher houses. The Methodists, Baptists, and Reformed Presbyterians all had similar facilities, so why not restoration churches? Officer enticed T. B. Larimore to meet government officials in Anadarko, and he actively recruited individuals to take control or be part of the proposed new school, including D. B. Cargile, J. W. Damon, Cora West (a Comanche woman educated in the states), and "brother and sister" Hadden of the Fort Sill Indian School.[27] Seemingly, G. S. Yates and G. W. Taylor, both residents of Comanche, actually agreed to take charge of the mission in 1896.[28] For whatever reason, they never did. Changing responsibility from the Paris church elders to the elders at Atoka, then Minco, and then Chickasha did not engender interest either. In 1898, Officer decided that he would just go himself. But that did not happen, in part because of a family tragedy but primarily because of the lack of means.[29]

Like Meta Chestnutt, Officer could not motivate Stone-Campbell churches to support a mission proposal that had objectives beyond evangelism. His many published sermons, appeals for fellowship, and reports on the life and times of Native Americans had little to no impact. The money never materialized, and as a consequence the promise of a Stone-Campbell mission among the Comanches, Kiowas, and Wichitas was not fulfilled.

Evangelization Elsewhere in Indian Territory

Although it had started with high hopes, Officer's work elsewhere in Indian Territory was no less challenging. By 1889, of course, his focus was largely evangelistic. He continued to preach regularly in Atoka and in other communities "up and down" the MK&T, including Muskogee, South McAlester, Savanna, Durant, Leader, Duncan, Purcell, Norman, Ardmore, and Chickasha, not to mention Minco. After the organization of the Red Oak church east of McAlester in 1891, Officer preached there on a regular basis. He considered it, with its mix of miners, railroad workers, and tenant farmers, as well as its school, one of the more promising congregations in Indian Territory.[30]

Red Oak was also the location of the first of Officer's four "discussions." Generally, he did not find debating a useful tool for evangelization in that the interactions changed fewer minds than they hurt. Still, he could see some value in them if conducted properly. Therefore, in August 1891 he debated N. B. Breshear of the Methodist Church before large audiences on the issue of justification of the soul by faith only, with Breshear affirming the proposition. It was a very civil debate, and Officer found his opponent "a very earnest, pleasant, good humored gentleman." Four were "added" to the "Lord's church" during the course of the debate.[31]

In the next twenty-four months, Officer conducted two more debates. One of these occurred in November 1893 at Cameron, just north of Poteau, and pitted Officer against John H. Milburn, a Baptist preacher from Fulton, Kentucky. The discussion topics were not recorded, but they probably had something to do with the permanency of the soul's salvation.[32]

In July 1893, Officer participated in his most memorable debate, in which he was paired against M. A. Smith, a Methodist minister widely respected in Indian Territory. The debate took place at Leader, a community south of Allen, and addressed issues of baptism for remission of past sins and whether the Holy Spirit influenced the hearts, minds, and lives of men only through the written word and other means of divine appointment, gifts, and miracles. Officer and Smith ended up agreeing on the propositions, even terminating discussion and shaking hands after one speech each on the second proposition. We reasoned "*together*, not apart," reported Officer.[33]

Six years later, in 1899, Officer participated in a written debate with W. J. Frost of Houston, Missouri, on the question of using missionary societies such as the ACMS to spread the gospel, as opposed to the individual congregation alone. Frost affirmed the use of such societies, while Officer denied it, a position that he had maintained since beginning his career as a missionary in Indian Territory. Efforts to publish the debate apparently failed; at least no copy of a printed tract survived to this date.[34]

In addition to debates, Officer found other evangelistic techniques useful in Indian Territory. Among these were camp meetings, so long as they were not bothered by exercises such as "fits and jerks"; union meetings, so long as participating groups did not try to divide up converts at the end of the service; extending public comfort to the grieving in the face of a disaster such as the mine explosion at Krebs in 1892; and locally publishing encouraging materials. He had the latter in mind when he set out to write *The Sower*, which he envisioned as a narrative of his own ministry. Unfortunately, he was never able to complete the book.[35]

Ministering to Former Slaves

Although more of an encourager than an instigator of the ministry, Officer had high hopes for an outreach to the African American population of Indian Territory.

These ex-slaves of members of the Five Tribes and citizens of former Confederate states comprised some 36,853, or more than 10 percent of the total population of Indian Territory, in 1890. In 1894, he recommended to Stone-Campbell churches David B. Bohannon, an educated African American from Texas, as an ideal head of a proposed private school for the children of freedmen and freedwomen. If the Presbyterians were cooperative, the school would actually succeed to the facilities of a similar institution long operated near Atoka. As it turned out, the Presbyterians were not obliging. It made no difference, however, for Officer never could get much support for Bohannon from Stone-Campbell churches.[36]

The same was true for D. C. Allen, also an African American. Allen was a capable preacher, also from Paris, Texas, who desired to work among his own people in Indian Territory, where there were few Disciples and no congregations. In 1897–98, Officer welcomed him as a member of the Indian Mission and appealed to Stone-Campbell churches abroad to contribute to his support at the rate of twenty-five dollars per month. Only a few responded, although enough did so that Allen could buy a tent in which to hold his evangelistic meetings. By 1899, Allen disappeared from the historical record, to resurface as a local minister in Oakland, California, in 1924.[37]

Demographic Instability

Despite some promising developments among the Comanche and Kiowa Indians and at locations like Minco and Red Oak, Officer found the 1890s in Indian Territory discouraging when it came to spreading the gospel. Present and prospective church members along his preaching circuit were transients, biding their time in Indian Territory until they could secure a relatively free farm in Oklahoma Territory in one of the sequential openings of reservation lands, or an inexpensive farm through the sale of surplus lands belonging to the Five Tribes in Indian Territory. Three hundred members of the Stone-Campbell churches participated in the opening of the Unassigned Lands in 1889. Officer and his coworkers found it virtually impossible to build a stable church when members were leaving for Oklahoma Territory every two or three years. This had been the case at Red Oak and Caddo, among others.[38]

A New Class of Evangelists Stimulates Change

A new class of Stone-Campbell preachers came with the increase in the non-Indian population in Indian Territory during the 1890s. Most came without support from their home or other congregations in the states, assuming that those in Indian Territory were strong enough to support them. That turned out not to be the case, however, and the newcomers became critical and cynical. Some also came to take charge of the congregations that did exist—that is, to enlighten, reorganize, and advocate especially as it related to music in worship and financing the work of the church. According to Officer, anguish and not liberty resulted.[39]

To circumvent such potential grief, the Atoka congregation under Officer's leadership took proactive measures. In advance of constructing a new building in 1893, the leadership agreed to exclude for evermore from the work and worship of the congregation "all things . . . not commanded by the Lord."[40] The next year, following a mini revival preached by Officer, they defined that which was to be excluded as instrumental music in the worship services and financing the work of the church via contributions not given "upon the first day of the week . . . as God hath prospered" his servants. Rather than embrace such "innovations" championed by some of the new preachers, the Atoka church intended to "'walk in the Spirit' on . . . matters pertaining to [its] wor[k] and worship," at least for the moment.[41]

Decreasing Financial Support

If Officer was disheartened by the threat of innovations in the 1890s, he was more discouraged by the declining level of financial support for his work. This despite an outpouring of lessons, reports, and appeals published in religious journals. By 1890, he was in debt financially. The following year his wife, Lota, was teaching fancywork to help ends meet. Two years later his finances were so bad that his son, Leon, took a day job, dividing his wage of $1.50 per day with his father. Officer himself found land and planted and harvested corn crops "to keep the wolf from the door." Such labor, however, became more and more difficult because of his health. Concerned, coworker C. C. Parker reported dramatically that Officer was living in abject poverty and confronting starvation. Officer's situation was not as dire as Parker reported, but his normal state of being was debt or deep debt. Only occasionally was he able to divide resources with Parker and other coworkers.[42] Did this diminishing support suggest that the Stone-Campbell churches had less interest in mission work? Probably so, at least as it related to Indian Territory and to congregations that supported missions with freewill offerings only.

Criticism from the Brotherhood

Most disappointing to Officer was that he found himself embroiled in controversy with his own brethren in the 1890s. The disagreements, which he generally tried to avoid, related both to practice and theology and came from both progressives and traditionalists within the Stone-Campbell movement. It was widely reported in Mississippi by supporters of the ACMS that Officer was supportive of the society, that his wife was a Baptist, and that he was personally wealthy and without need of outside support because of "the contributions of the brethren and churches." Those interested in Indian missions, therefore, would get more value for their money if it were invested with the ACMS rather than sent directly to Officer. The rumors had the potential of damaging contributions. They continued to circulate until John Stevens, state evangelist of Mississippi, visited Officer in Atoka and learned the fiscal realities of the Indian Mission. He disavowed the rumors and affirmed Officer's credibility, although the falsehood was slow to die.[43] Contributions did not improve, either.

Simultaneously, W. H. Horn, an articulate Kansas businessman, wondered in the pages of the *Primitive Christian* whether Officer's Indian Mission was justifiable. He read frequent and dramatic appeals from Officer, but especially from his coworkers, for financial support to stave off homelessness and imminent starvation of wives and families. There were also appeals to help erect church buildings, as in Atoka. The brethren, Horn believed, were weary of this "continual cant" from men "who would rather live upon the level with paupers and professional beggars than to rise to the dignity of true manhood."[44] Horn had crossed Indian Territory many times on the railroad and believed it to be no less prosperous than central Illinois or southwestern Kansas, where local Disciples sustained their own evangelists without appeals to the brotherhood at large. Why did that not happen in Indian Territory, he asked? Had Officer and his coworkers not organized their thousands of converts into sustainable congregations and taught them the cost of discipleship? Indeed, he inferred that Officer had never set a church in order in Indian Territory. Moreover, Horn asked, why would congregants want to build a $1,500 meeting house in which "unconverted Indians" could "play church?"[45]

Officer was taken aback by Horn's ethnocentricity and lack of understanding of conditions in Indian Territory. He tried to explain that there were self-sufficient congregations in Indian Territory. Admittedly, their numbers were limited, but that was due to the transient nature of the population rather than some methodological failure of the mission.[46] Horn was not impressed with the explanation. He did "not see that [Officer had] any more to contend with than brethren in other places."[47] Officer did not respond to Horn's second letter other than to say it was full of mistakes and that all should be "'slow to speak and swift to hear.'"[48] Horn was insulted and lashed out: "Whenever a man is compelled to take refuge behind a breastwork of sentimentalism and fire at an enemy from ambush, his cause must be in a very weak condition."[49]

The Horn controversy had important consequences. Thereafter, Officer was far less willing to appeal to the churches for support of the Indian Mission; he was even reluctant to encourage support for himself. As much as anything, the controversy explained why he planted crops for several years in the 1890s rather than petition for support among the churches. Certainly, it explains why he launched a special initiative to reteach the congregations he had organized in Indian Territory about their responsibility as workers in the kingdom. Before the controversy, Officer's recognized standing within the Stone-Campbell movement had prevented serious criticism of his work; thereafter, criticism was more frequent and more severe.

Officer Not Considered Sound

Most of that criticism related to Officer's views and practices on the issues then roiling the Stone-Campbell community. In addition to how missions were to be financed and administered was the question of instrumental music in worship services. Southern and rural churches had long considered their use an unscriptural accommodation to the prevailing culture. Officer held those views as well, insisting that instruments of music were not taught in scripture and therefore "should not be admitted into worship."[50] He considered them a temptation to abandon the purity and simplicity of Christian worship.[51] He was proud that the Atoka church did not use mechanical instruments or parachurch societies. At the same time, Officer was known to preach in congregations where an organ was used, in South McAlester and Washington, D.C., for example. He did not like it and would not work permanently with a congregation that utilized it, but he came to conclude that instruments were here to stay and whether they were used in worship or not was the choice of the local congregation.[52] That decision made his "soundness" suspect in the eyes of the conservative Stone-Campbell churches, although his course of action was not without precedent.[53]

Another controversial issue related to baptism. Stone-Campbell churches universally held that Christian baptism was by immersion and essential to the remission of sins. In other words, baptism was a condition of salvation. Other

Christian communities, primarily Baptist but certain Methodist groups as well, also practiced baptism by immersion, but it was not a condition of salvation, only admission into the local church. Following the lead of David Lipscomb, T. B. Larimore, Daniel Sommer, and other Stone-Campbell leaders in the American South, as noted earlier, Officer accepted the baptism of Baptists who "stepped out on the Lord's side," and then through instruction expected them to develop over time a "proper" understanding of baptism. This reluctance to rebaptize was strongly refuted by the publisher and readers of the *Firm Foundation* out of Austin, Texas. Initially supportive of Officer's work in Indian Territory, the *Firm Foundation* became his severest critic, especially as it related to his understanding of rebaptism and his persistent embrace of Barton Stone's apocalyptic worldview. According to the journal, Officer showed the signs of premillennialism, or a belief in the material manifestation of the kingdom of God on earth.[54]

Finally, Officer's critics charged him with being too cozy with the progressive segment of the Stone-Campbell churches. In 1896, he was listed as one of the organizers of the *Christian Union Record*, a short-lived journal published in Chickasha, Indian Territory, and he was identified as one of the participants in mass meetings designed to serve the interests of progressive churches in Oklahoma City.[55] Moreover, he was loose in his use of terms like "Pastor" and "Reverend" to denominate an evangelist, "Sabbath" as a substitute for "Sunday," and "Christian Church" to identify the "church of Christ" or "Church of God."[56] The *Christian Preacher*, published in Dallas, actually charged him with having "gone to the progressives" and was no longer "loyal to the truth" in 1900.[57]

Officer Responds to Criticism

To the consternation of his friends and the delight of his enemies, Officer said very little in response to this criticism. "The more we defend self," he wrote, "the more do we become interested in self."[58] It was far better to defend the gospel. Moreover, one could not heal a "carbuncle" by picking at it, nor did one make water in a bucket clear by stirring up mud on its bottom. Officer counseled periodical editors and columnists to verbalize more mildly, noting that it was quite possible to "speak the truth in the spirit of the devil." It was disgraceful, he believed, to spread family fusses before the world. With some exceptions, therefore, he held his tongue and kept the peace.[59]

Sadly, the mounting criticism took a physical toll on both Officer and his wife. For weeks, even months, at a time he was incapacitated by rheumatism, pneumonia, or broken bones, while chronic colitis turned Lota into an invalid.[60]

On January 30, 1900, after twenty-two weeks of intense suffering, Lota Venable died in the arms of her husband.

His wife's death closed a chapter in Officer's life and opened him up to other opportunities. After preaching for several months in southern Arkansas, he determined to leave Indian Territory and establish a ministry in West Texas at what is now Turkey, Hall County. Like Indian Territory had been and in places still was, West Texas was destitute and undeveloped. Above all, it was isolated; perhaps there Officer could find peace and appreciation once more.

Summing Up a Career

To Officer, twenty years of mission work in Indian Territory had terminated without much to show for it. During those years, by his count, seventy-two congregations had been organized. By 1901, however, "there [was] not a *peaceful* working congregation at one of the seventy-two points where once the cause prospered." They had been eviscerated by demographic instability, theological controversy, and campaigns of misinformation. Nor, of course, had anything come of the proposed industrial boarding school for Indians and freedmen, neighborhood schools staffed by women, or the mission to the so-called Wild Tribes. The only thing still standing was El Meta Bond College, which Officer claimed as a department of the Indian Mission although it was clearly not.[61]

But there was another way to assess Officer's work in Indian Territory—his faithfulness to Christian witness. T. B. Larimore described Officer as "a brave, generous, liberal, unselfish, consecrated, self-sacrificing man, who, *very meagerly supported*, is, 'without murmuring,' literally giving his life to *the cause*."[62] He, said Kansas evangelist D. T. Broadus, "is continually 'on the go.' He is working under the commission that said 'go.' He does not only go, but preaches the gospel as he goes." And despite discouragements, Officer is "fully determined to continue to go."[63] Simply put, according to coworker C. C. Parker, Officer "boldly, fearlessly, and gently [did] his duty as a brave-hearted Christian."[64] He was faithful, but he also inspired faithfulness, which according to one correspondent, was the real legacy of Officer's twenty years in Indian Territory: "Your faith and courage are a stimulus to many of us," she wrote to him, "and your strong brave words help us when we grow faint hearted."[65] Officer did not disagree, of course, but he put a slightly different spin on it: "I have fought a good fight, thank God I have kept the faith, and this leaves me striving for the crown."[66]

Officer was a beneficiary of the Stone-Campbell movement. From the beginning, he seems to have identified with Stone's apocalyptic worldview as embraced by David Lipscomb and other southern leaders. Yet he declined to make his understanding of scripture a test of fellowship. As the movement slowly began to divide, therefore, Officer often found himself with a foot in both camps, as did contemporaries of his like Meta Chestnutt Sager and T. B. Larimore. In Turkey, Texas, where he settled in 1901, he organized and served a congregation known to this day as a Church of Christ. Beginning in the mid-1920s, however, he ministered to the Christian Church in Nashville, Arkansas. In 1930, while visiting a granddaughter in Turkey, Officer died and was buried in the community cemetery. According to the *Nashville News*, he was "well known and loved" and "lived one of the most useful lives of any person ever residing here."[67]

Officer's departure from Indian Territory left a considerable vacuum among Stone-Campbell evangelists. This was especially true among those who were uncomfortable with accommodations to cultural change. Indeed, C. H. Kennedy (1861–1927) claimed that there were only eight "loyal" preachers in the Choctaw and Chickasaw Nations as of 1901, including himself. Born in Texas in 1861, Kennedy grew up as a Missionary Baptist but joined the Disciples in 1890, beginning to preach almost immediately. Five years later he moved to Connerville, Chickasaw Nation, as a full-time evangelist. Kennedy preached widely and successfully with hundreds of converts in what is now southeastern Oklahoma, often in the same towns as Officer, who he never mentioned once in his reports. Kennedy was an active debater. Around 1906 he moved his family to McKinney, Texas, but he continued to do evangelistic work in Oklahoma.[68]

Other loyal preachers included D. B. Cargile, John W. Harris, G. F. Whitley, W. D. Ingram, and, as already noted in the previous chapter, C. C. Parker. At the age of thirty, Cargile (1855–99) came to Indian Territory from Arkansas to practice medicine, operate a mercantile business, and preach in 1885. Officer considered him part of the Indian Mission and encouraged him to take charge of the effort to evangelize the Comanches and Kiowas. In due time, Cargile came to criticize Officer's views on rebaptism. The father of eleven children, Cargile did much of his preaching in Pottawatomie County, especially Dale. He moved to Florida, then Texas, and ultimately California.[69]

A native of Tennessee and a Baptist convert, John W. Harris relocated to Oakland, Indian Territory, from Texas in 1893, hoping to grow with the country. He was fifty-nine years old at the time. He also preached and or lived at Mannsville, Union City, Edmond, Russett, Ravia, and Dover. Despite ill health, he held seventeen meetings in 1903. He was always on the verge of starvation and wrote heart-wrenching but ineffective appeals for financial support from the churches in the states. Those appeals failing, Harris lashed out at the Indian Mission, which he thought had money and would not share it. At least two of his appeals were letters of farewell.[70]

G. F. Whitley was a blacksmith by trade, but after his baptism near Davis in 1883 he launched an evangelistic career. Surprisingly literate and articulate, he worked effectively with C. C. Parker, with the two of them suffering significant discrimination because of their message and methods. In addition to Davis, Whitley seemingly did good work at Johnson, Oakland, Palmer, and Stonewall. But he was always on the verge of starvation, continually begging the support of church-folk beyond Indian Territory, and when the support did not come he would infer that the brethren were stingy and withholding support due missionaries. In 1902, he also left Indian Territory for Texas.[71]

A native of Texas, W. D. Ingram (1867–1930) came as an evangelist to Indian Territory in 1895. He worked largely in an area that reached from Chandler to Madill and Boggy Depot to Lexington, which he proposed as a location for a mass meeting of Church of Christ evangelists and preachers in 1902. He engaged in few if any debates, although he did write extensively for the *Primitive Christian* and *Christian Leader and Way*. Ingram left Indian Territory for Washington State in 1904.[72]

By 1906 the Stone-Campbell movement was widely known in Indian Territory. R. W. Officer had taken leadership in bringing the restoration plea to the region, first to the Choctaws and then to non-Indian intruders. Other evangelists came to help, most notably the educational missionary Meta Chestnutt Sager. The work had been challenging, maybe even divisive, but there was confidence that the seeds that had been planted in due time would yield a bountiful harvest. That harvest, hopefully, would be even more generous because of the simultaneous work being done in Oklahoma Territory.

EVANGELIZING OKLAHOMA TERRITORY
1889-1907

As noted, what became Oklahoma Territory in 1890 was opened to non-Indian settlement with the famous land run of 1889. Over the next several years, four more runs, a lottery, and sealed bids opened up all the tribal reservations of central and western Oklahoma to settlement, which then became parts of Oklahoma Territory. In 1907, Congress would add Indian Territory to Oklahoma Territory and admit the Twin Territories as a single state to the Union. In Oklahoma's territorial era, Stone-Campbell evangelists were active there, just as they had been and were in Indian Territory. But there was a difference; divisions within the movement were apparent within Oklahoma Territory. R. W. Officer and his associates in Indian Territory were primarily conservatives who, as we have seen, objected to the use of mechanical instruments in worship and mission work done beyond the control of the local church elders. Other evangelists, who were particularly effective in Oklahoma Territory, were progressives who deemed parachurch groups and instrumental music in worship as positive innovations when it came to reaching souls with the gospel of Jesus Christ and in achieving religious unity. Of the two, the progressives were better prepared for the evangelistic task at hand in Oklahoma Territory, largely because of the foresight, resources, and effort of the parachurch agencies that backed them.

Evangelistic Strategies

Some Stone-Campbell progressives participated in the different land openings in Oklahoma Territory with the single objective of buying a town lot suitable for a church building. At the opening of the Unassigned Lands (central Oklahoma) on April 22, 1889, for example, Union Army veteran and evangelist J. M. Monroe took passage on a special car added to a Santa Fe train that went from the Kansas border to what would become Guthrie. There he located and obtained property for the first Stone-Campbell church in the territorial capital. Five years later under the aegis of the American Christian Missionary Society (ACMS), Edgar F. Boggess, then the minister of the Guthrie church, did the same thing at the opening of the Cherokee Strip, claiming land in the town of Perry. Still later, when the Kiowa-Comanche and Wichita-Caddo lands were opened by lottery and sale, the Board of Church Extension, a constituent part of the ACMS, purchased building sites in Anadarko, Lawton, and Hobart, which were held in trust for churches yet to be planted.[1]

Stone-Campbell progressives in Oklahoma Territory gave priority in their evangelization efforts to the county seat towns and commercial centers along the major railroad lines. There, they believed, audiences would be larger and presumably more open to a rational appeal for Christian unity through the restoration of the ancient order revealed in scripture. Moreover, the upwardly mobile townspeople presumably would embrace the work and worship practices favored by Stone-Campbell progressives and already employed by the Christian community at large. There too congregants would likely have the means necessary to support an evangelist.[2]

Board of Church Extension loans to purchase lots and to construct new church houses assured the success of the strategy. Between the opening of Oklahoma Territory in 1889 and the end of World War II in 1945, the board made 373 real estate loans totaling $11.8 million to Oklahoma congregations, more than to any other state in the union. Those loans, of course, all went to the Stone-Campbell progressives. According to C. M. Sharpe of El Reno, he did not know of a single progressive or Christian Church congregation in Oklahoma that had not received help from the home missionary fund.[3]

If a Stone-Campbell congregation already existed in a railroad town or the rural countryside, as was likely in Indian Territory because of the earlier work of Officer and his colleagues, it was largely ignored by the progressives.[4] Occasionally, it was reorganized and reconstituted by progressive evangelists. If the congregation proved to have growth potential, the Board of Church Extension would likely offer it a building loan. Acceptance of the loan, of course, announced that the congregation was progressive in its practices. Or as U. G. Wilkinson, a conservative evangelist from Comanche, put it, "The digressives never go into new fields but try to follow up the beaten paths and enter into the labors of others."[5] But the strategy worked. In 1908, J. H. Lawson, also a conservative evangelist, reported that three years earlier there was not a digressive congregation within thirty miles of Mountain Park, but "since that time the seeds of discord have been sown in many places and several loyal churches have been carried away."[6]

Settlement Patterns

Whether a congregation was progressive or loyal had as much to do with settlement patterns of immigrants in Indian and Oklahoma Territories as church-planting strategy. Stone-Campbell migrants to northern Oklahoma came via Kansas from midwestern, or Union, states where congregations were more likely to be progressive in faith and practice. In eastern and southwestern Oklahoma, migrants generally had roots in Southern, or Confederate, states and came to the Twin Territories via Arkansas and Texas. Their doctrine was more traditional. As a matter of course, therefore, Christian/Disciples of Christ churches prevailed in the northern part of the state, while Churches of Christ congregations dominated southern Oklahoma. The settlement pattern also explains why Phillips University, established by Stone-Campbell progressives, was located in Enid and Cordell Christian College, organized by traditionalists, was situated in Cordell.[7]

Evangelizing without Innovations

The evangelistic initiatives of the progressives were not celebrated by all Stone-Campbell leaders and preachers in Oklahoma Territory. The conservatives were increasingly offended by the parachurch organizations and other innovations used to carry out the "Lord's work" when they could find no example of those methods in scripture. But they were not ready to abandon the field. They too saw Oklahoma Territory as "the land of the fair god." Said one homesteader of the western one-half of the future state, "Anyone with energy and small capital can get him a home here and make money." And, more important, that region was open to an energetic mission effort.[8] Perhaps it was for these reasons that the congregation at Bethel, Kansas, as a group participated in the run for land on the old Sac and Fox Reservation in 1891, establishing both a settlement and a church near Kendrick in Lincoln County.[9]

But as a mission field, Western Oklahoma had its challenges. Evangelist J. C. Estes noted that it was "a droughty, windy country—a hard place to live in"; yet the quest for free homes had brought many hundreds of poor people to the region. "It is this class who want to hear and obey the gospel," he explained.[10] Indeed, wrote J. H. Lawson, Oklahoma Territory was "one of the most inviting fields for the church of Christ" he had ever seen. People "readily accept the gospel" and rapidly "demonstrate . . . Christianity," but sadly it was also a remarkably "destitute," or poverty stricken, field.[11] Consequently, said J. B. Nelson, only evangelists "willing to undergo hardships in the cause of Christ" should go.[12]

Indian Territory, the eastern one-half of the future state of Oklahoma, was even more of a challenge to the Stone-Campbell traditionalists. According to U. G. Wilkinson, "The people in many places are of a restless transient character." A congregation may be set in order, but within a year the principal members will have moved to other parts. Brethren "are generally in a lifeless condition and if a preacher happens to come along, the chances are they will put themselves to little or no trouble to go and hear him preach."[13]

The approach of loyalists to evangelism was less structured than that of the digressives. Typically, the process began when an evangelist or an area settler put out a call for neighbors familiar with the restoration plea for unity via scripture alone to gather for worship and communion at a particular cabin (homestead) or local schoolhouse, the latter most likely because it was often the first community structure built in a new settlement. At these initial gatherings, the evangelist was at pains to get the attendees to commit to meeting again on a regular basis, with or without him. With several steps in between, his goal was to set in order a congregation that would meet regularly and look and work like the church he believed was described in the New Testament.[14]

At subsequent meetings, if preaching occurred it came from a member of the community, generally a farmer or merchant. Periodically, the founding evangelist would return and in Sunday services exhort congregants to "obey the Gospel," have their sins remitted through baptism, and be granted citizenship into the kingdom of God on earth, or the church of Christ. (Presumably, the two were equivalent.) Typically, the evangelist's sermons were arguments and his prayers a proposition. He condemned human-made creeds and declared that the Bible was the only rule to faith and practice. According to historian Angie Debo, his beliefs and words, like those of his brethren, "followed a pattern as exact and rigid as though they had all graduated from the same Jesuit seminary." Preaching was always bookended by congregational singing led by men (sometime by women from their seats) with some sense of pitch and rhythm but unaccompanied by musical instruments. They sang of a beautiful land ("Beulah Land"); agricultural settings ("Bringing in the Sheaves"); and the sea ("Let the Lower Lights Be Burning").[15] There was little structure to the evangelistic process of this type, a fact not unexpected given the thoroughly democratic context of frontier Oklahoma, but it was surprisingly effective over time.[16]

Meetings and Debates

Conservative evangelists also sought to build up the kingdom through extended revivals. Known as "meetings," these events were sponsored by congregations already established or by a traveling evangelist eager to plant one where none existed. Almost always they were scheduled when crops were not being planted or harvested. After locating a place to meet (a barn, schoolhouse, brush arbor, or, later, tent) and advertising a date, the evangelist launched a two-week revival that emphasized the remission of sins through baptism by immersion and a weekly gathering of the saints. If the meeting went according to plan, the preacher was able to set in order a self-sustaining, independent congregation if none existed. He would follow essentially the same plan if the purpose was merely to build up an existing congregation.[17]

Conservative Stone-Campbell evangelists used debates as another tool to enlarge the boundaries of the kingdom. Alexander Campbell had participated in four such exchanges during his lifetime and had concluded that "a week's debating is worth a year's preaching . . . for the purpose of disseminating truth and putting error out of countenance."[18] His followers in Oklahoma agreed. Consequently, debates with representatives from other denominations or from within their own movement became quite common, especially among the traditionalists. Propositions under discussion ranged from the purpose of baptism, to the work of the Holy Spirit, to the errors of Methodism or Mormonism, to the necessity of a capella music in worship, to the righteousness of pacifism.

Steeped in Baconian rationalism, the men who argued in behalf of the restoration's worldview were deemed most effective in opposing denominational spokesmen who advocated a more emotional gospel. In the era of territorial Oklahoma and after, some of the more notable debaters were J. W. Chism, J. H. Lawson, D. S. Ligon, J. D. Tant, Joe Warlick (399 debates), and U. G. Wilkinson.[19] Like Campbell, they saw debates as a way to educate and convict large audiences at one time. There were others, however, who saw these events as opportunities to skin, mock, and make fun of their religious opponents. This "fighting style" was not designed to make friends within the denominational community, but it did make converts, at least in the short run.

Some Stone-Campbell debaters participated only if decorum was maintained, notably R. W. Officer, J. B. Nelson, and S. R. Cassius. Good speaking, Officer once said, "does not consist in rough and un-Christ like expressions. Unkindness and impoliteness in our dealings with those who differ with us is not one of the conditions in order to win them to Christ."[20] Nelson asserted that he was "a great believer in debates . . . but not in wrangles." It was his intention, he said, not to participate in such disputes no matter "what the opposite side may say or do."[21]

Evangelists

Among the thousands of settlers who rushed to Oklahoma Territory to claim free farms after 1889 were hundreds of Stone-Campbell adherents having embraced the movement while living in the states and Indian Territory. These included deeply committed farmer-preachers and shopkeepers who, much influenced by David Lipscomb and his intellectual heirs, held traditional views on the divisive issues confronting the movement. As already noted, they called themselves "Loyalists." These men faithfully reported their activities in Stone-Campbell publications, noting where they preached, the results of that preaching, and where they would preach next. The farmer-preachers especially active in Oklahoma Territory were Jeff Morgan at Ames (Major County), J. R. Shuff (1837–1904) at Mathewson (Canadian County), J. C. Glover at Stineton (Dewey County), E. C. Fakes at Meno (Major County), W. H. Horn at Perkins (Payne County), M. A. McPeak at Meridian (Logan County), S. W. York at Renfrow (Grant County), and John M. Harrel (1868–1949) at Cloud Chief (Washita County). Henry E. Warlick (1868–1948) was also much appreciated as a loyalist preacher, but he paid his bills with profits from mercantile establishments he operated in Cleveland, Greer, and Washita Counties.

From time to time, evangelists who lived in neighboring states had preaching appointments in Oklahoma Territory. Some of the most notable of these were out of Kansas and were contributors to the *Primitive Christian*. These included J. E. Cain (1846–1918) and D. T. Broadus (1852–1924). Cain, who also served as an editor for the *Christian Leader and Way*, out of Cincinnati, was especially active. A native of Canada and longtime resident of Illinois, he migrated to Kansas in 1876. There, he was a successful farmer and horticulturalist, as well as writer and preacher. As early as 1892, he was preaching in communities situated in the old

Sac and Fox Reservation (now Lincoln County). Cain developed a particularly strong attachment with the congregation at Meridian, located east of Guthrie, and for a number of years preached at its annual Grove Meeting on Bear Creek. In 1903, he helped dedicate the Meridian congregation's new church building.[22]

Born in 1852, Broadus was a native of Kentucky, where he received his education and worked as a teacher. He did not begin to preach until he was twenty-eight years old. Four years after, in 1884, he moved to Belle Plaine, Kansas, and made a name for himself by reporting regularly in the *Primitive Christian* and other Stone-Campbell newspapers. In Oklahoma Territory, he was particularly active in communities along the Rock Island Railroad, especially Minco and Chickasha. Broadus's sermon against liquor and saloons precipitated the burning of the Sunny South church building in Minco in November 1903.[23]

Evangelists living in Texas also preached in Oklahoma Territory. These included Jefferson Davis Tant (1861–1949), a Georgia native who took up residence in Texas in the 1870s, was baptized for the remission of sins in 1888, and became over the next half century one of the better known traditional Stone-Campbell preachers. Although he visited Oklahoma many times as a revivalist, he was best remembered for touring the territory by wagon for two months in a successful attempt to restore his small daughter to health in 1898, preaching all the while.[24]

Some preachers came to Oklahoma Territory to live and work as full-time evangelists. They assumed that the congregations they would establish would be able to support them and their families. Illustrative of those working in such a capacity were John H. Lawson (1866–1934) from Arkansas, William Franklin Ledlow (1877–1932) of Texas, Ulysses Grant Wilkinson (1863–1925) of Texas, and S. R. Cassius (1853–1931) from Washington, D.C.

John H. Lawson

Born in Arkansas in 1866 but a recent resident of Denton, Texas, J. H. Lawson began his evangelistic ministry in the former Comanche-Kiowa Reservation shortly after it opened for settlement in early 1902. "This is one of the neediest fields I have ever seen," he declared, filled with "brethren" who were "strangers in a strange land." Six months later he added, "I have never labored in a field where as much good can be done as in this new country."[25] For the first two years of his work, he was well supported by various churches in Texas. For him, the "Lord's plan" had been a success.[26] There were not many communities in southwestern Oklahoma Territory where he did not preach at least once. In his first year, he baptized 126 individuals and set 6 churches in order. The following year he conducted 18 meetings, baptized 160 people, and set 9 congregations in order. He also participated in three debates. Lawson was distinctive for emphasizing good congregational singing and organizing annual camp meetings.[27]

Lawson also found that the so-called Lord's plan had its limits. Because of the challenging economic conditions, the congregations he organized were unable to support him and his family. In 1904, he took his wife and children back to Texas, where financially sound congregations existed, although he continued to hold meetings in Oklahoma Territory. In 1907, he was named the first president of Cordell Christian College, a position he held for no more than five months. The next year, because of the continued lack of support, Lawson commenced the practice of law in Altus, a profession he followed for the rest of his life. For several years, he served as assistant state attorney general in Oklahoma City. He was also an active supporter of the anti-evolution legislation in Oklahoma in the 1920s.[28] His practice of law notwithstanding, Lawson never quit preaching. Over the course of his career, he baptized some 2,500 individuals, engaged in 60 debates, and organized 36 congregations of Churches of Christ. During World War I, he ministered to soldiers of the U.S. Army's Thirty-Sixth Division stationed at Camp Bowie, Fort Worth, Texas, through the Camp Bowie Christian Tabernacle.[29] Lawson died in Oklahoma City in 1934.

William F. Ledlow

A Texas native born in 1877, William Franklin Ledlow was just twenty-three years old when he took up residence at Lexington, Oklahoma Territory, in 1900. There, he met C. C. Parker, under whose influence he came to faith. He evangelized in both Oklahoma and Indian Territories with considerable success, wrote regularly for the *Primitive Christian* and *Gospel Guide*, and engaged in at least twenty-five debates. At Elk City, one of the elders described him as "a strong man in the Gospel, very strong indeed." As did other full-time evangelists in Oklahoma Territory, Ledlow found it difficult to support his family. In 1905, he left for Texas to further his education, which he pursued until he earned a doctorate. Subsequently, he served as president of Lockney Christian College and Thorpe Springs Christian College, both in Texas. In 1927, he authored *Jesus and His Methods*, which earned him a position on the faculty of North Texas State Teachers College at Denton the following year. Ledlow never wavered in his commitment to the Stone-Campbell tradition, although he became a strong critic of fellow evangelists who flirted with socialism, a movement that would find adherents in Oklahoma Territory.[30]

Ulysses Grant Wilkinson

Born in Missouri in 1863, U. G. Wilkinson grew up and was educated in North Texas, where he was also baptized. With his parents and siblings, he migrated to the Chickasaw Nation in 1887, settling between what is now Duncan and Comanche. He was the teacher of the first school opened in the region. During his tenure there, Wilkinson undertook a careful study of the Bible and kindred literature. Later, after his marriage and relocation nearer to Comanche, he studied the law, was admitted to the bar, and began a legal practice in Duncan. After several years as an attorney, however, he left that profession to devote full-time to preaching, which was the focus of his life thereafter. He was well known as a debater, especially against socialist advocates; as an editor of the Texas-based *Gospel Guide*; as an author of at least three books on faith and practice of the Christian community; and as a strong voice favoring Christian support of military action in World War I. He died in 1925 and was buried at Comanche.[31]

S. R. Cassius

S. R. Cassius was born a slave in Prince William County, Virginia, in 1853. He spent much of his youth and early manhood in Washington, D.C. In the early 1880s, he and his family moved to Indiana, where he was introduced to the restoration plea of the Stone-Campbell churches. He began to preach soon after his baptism. Pursuit of evangelistic and economic opportunity brought him to Oklahoma Territory in 1891. There was "no place in the United States that offers our plea such opportunities as are to be found in this territory," Cassius wrote. Moreover, it was the "purpose of God that the colored people should settle this country." Cassius spent the next thirty years trying to realize the economic and religious promise of Oklahoma to African Americans.[32]

Like Booker T. Washington, Cassius believed that economic improvement for African Americans depended upon education of both head and hands. He wanted to recreate in Oklahoma what Washington had done in Alabama, with a religious component. Accordingly, he set out to construct an industrial school for his race at Tohee, a community just south of Meridian in Logan County, where Cassius also served as postmaster. After great struggle, the school did open in 1899, but for only five months. Disappointed, Cassius took some consolation in his belief that what became Langston University was established and placed because of the brief existence of Tohee Industrial School.

Cassius's evangelistic work, although centered first at Tohee and then Guthrie, took him all across Oklahoma and Indian Territories. His message was one of unity to be achieved by restoration of first-century Christianity, but he included as an element of unity ethnicity as well as religion. He strongly opposed mechanical instruments in worship and objected to missionary societies, although less on theological grounds than because their white leadership preferred foreign to domestic missions. He established some forty or more congregations in his three decades in Oklahoma, including ones at West Guthrie, Boley, and Chickasha. By 1909, representatives of those congregations and perhaps even those planted by D. C. Allen in Indian Territory, were meeting together periodically at the call of the Executive Board of the Colored Disciples, of which Cassius was one of the founders.[33]

Disappointed by the Jim Crow racism written into the Oklahoma state constitution and manifested in riots like those in Tulsa in 1921, Cassius left Oklahoma in 1922. As historian Edward Robinson chronicles, the land Cassius had once seen as a heaven had turned into a hell. Moreover, his spiritual legacy was increasingly problematic in that no more than one-third of the churches he founded remained loyal, and most of those would soon disappear. He spent the next few years of his life in Ohio and California and his last years in Colorado. Cassius died in 1931. Robinson sees him as the first black national evangelist in Churches of Christ rather than the better-known Marshall Keeble.[34]

Tension Heightens

Cassius's work spanned the period of time when tensions within the Stone-Campbell community reached a boiling point. The social and theological cleavages that generated the heat nationally were also apparent in Oklahoma and Indian Territories, where congregations divided consciously or unconsciously along rural-urban, destitute-advantaged, southern-midwestern, and learned-unlearned lines. Congregations also divided over the question as to whether Christian work could be undertaken by means not specifically "authorized" in scripture. Could the faithful speak where the Bible had not spoken? The progressives, generally from urban congregations made up of economically and educationally advantaged midwesterners, said "yes." Consequently, they welcomed the use of parachurch organizations to carry out mission and youth work (the ACMS and the Christian Endeavor Society, the latter dedicated to training youth for service in the church), the convening of regional assemblies to organize and encourage the churches, and the use of mechanical instruments to modernize worship services. The loyalists, whom the progressives labeled "antis" and who tended to be rural, destitute, less educated, southern, and uncomfortable with the prevailing culture, generally said "no." From their perspective, the "digressives" were imposing so-called innovations that were without scriptural example.

The division between the antis and digressives was real and painful. It was so tension filled that when the church building at Mount Hope, a hundred-member congregation just southwest of Ingalls in Payne County and arguably the strongest loyalist congregation in Oklahoma Territory, blew up one night. The *Kansas City Star* did not think twice before attributing it to strife between the loyalists and progressives. One of the elders, Frank Pickerill, denied the connection, although not the explosion, and insisted that the congregation was at peace. Apparently it was, but clearly many were skeptical.[35]

The Plea for Unity Forgotten

If not at Mount Hope, tension within the Stone-Campbell movement certainly existed in numerous local situations in the Twin Territories. In Davis, for example, a seventy-five-person congregation organized in the wake of C. C. Parker's meeting there in 1893. For some time thereafter and with some opposition, George F. Whitley, a blacksmith by trade, preached regularly for the congregation, which was decidedly loyal. In 1897, S. E. Kennedy, the ACMS evangelist then in discussion with Meta Chestnutt about the school she hoped to build in Minco, reorganized the Davis congregation as the First Christian Church and secured a loan, probably through the Board of Church Extension, that enabled it to erect a new building that same year.[36] Under the leadership of O. M. Thomason, a convert to progressivism, the Davis congregation was seemingly content with its progressive cast, although not all members. In 1911, the discontented called a known loyalist preacher to conduct a revival meeting for the congregation. His condemnation of innovations irritated most of the progressive leadership. When they confronted the visiting preacher about his divisive message, he thanked them for their hospitality by leading forty-five loyalists out of the existing First Christian Church to organize a conservative Church of Christ, which would meet in city hall.[37]

A similar scenario played out in Holdenville. Early efforts by Stone-Campbell evangelists had resulted in a congregation of eighty-five meeting in a building valued at $2,000 in 1906. Under the influence of ACMS preachers, it held a progressive position on innovations. In May, upon the invitation of a loyalist member of that congregation, H. L. Taylor of Alabama launched a two-week meeting using the house of the Presbyterian Church. To his surprise, he encountered "fierce opposition" from the progressives. But he was able to reclaim thirty-three of the innovators and organize a congregation of Churches of Christ that met in the courthouse.[38] Taylor took some perverse pleasure in the fact that during the course of the meeting the preacher for the digressives resigned his position and left town.[39]

Taylor orchestrated a similar sequence of events in Henryetta. In 1906, he had organized a loyalist congregation there, only to learn the next year that a church splitter was at work.[40] He returned to Henryetta, where he went from house to house warning congregants of the dangers of innovations. He also debated the digressive preacher in a public forum. Taylor's influence was substantial, and, as a consequence of his actions, two-thirds of the "old" congregation (Christian Church) withdrew and organized a "new" congregation (Church of Christ). They immediately bought a lot upon which to construct a 60′ × 30′ church building, taking pains to insert their "creed in the deed," that is, stipulate in the deed language prohibiting incorporation into the work and worship of the new congregation the innovations to which they so objected. Moreover, Taylor agreed to move back to Henryetta and preach regularly for the loyalists.[41]

The scenario in Muskogee was slightly different. In 1891, if not before, R. W. Officer preached there. Later that year, H. C. Collier, a Cherokee by blood supported by the ACMS, conducted a series of discourses in the federal courthouse, reporting that a congregation had been set in order.[42] Three years later following a two-week meeting by W. C. Demmett of Texas, eighteen persons signed a declaration that "We, the undersigned members of the Christian Church, or Church of Christ, residing in Muskogee, Indian Territory, have on this 14th day of July, 1895, banded ourselves together as a Christian congregation to worship and serve God according to the doctrine and teaching of the New Testament of our Lord and Savior, Jesus Christ."[43] All of this notwithstanding, the following year in 1896 the ACMS reported that Alan G. Clarke of Texas had planted a congregation in Muskogee with fifty members and planned to construct a building.[44] Clearly, what was once a loyal congregation had been reordered by a progressive evangelist.

What happened in Muskogee mirrored the events in McAlester. R. W. Officer had preached in South McAlester regularly, but a Stone-Campbell congregation of some eighty members presumably did not organize until after J. Harry Barber of Texas held a revival meeting in 1893. To the consternation of some, Barber quickly pushed the progressive agenda and disassociated himself from Officer's work and doctrine.[45]

A similar sequence of events occurred in Chickasha. Officer preached in Chickasha as early as 1891, reporting the setting in order of a congregation the following year. S. E. Kennedy, the evangelist commissioned by the ACMS, began preaching in Chickasha in 1894, just as he was attempting to pull El Meta Christian College at Minco under the ACMS umbrella. Kennedy arranged for a loan from the Board of Church Extension to finance the construction of a frame church building on the corner of Sixth and Iowa. In 1896, L. B. Grogan, a committed progressive from Texas, assumed the pulpit. Despite visitations by Officer, D. T. Broadus, and other loyalists, the Chickasha congregation quickly embraced the progressive agenda. According to Broadus, who had great affection for the church and its leadership, the congregation made that decision because it openly wanted to be in step with other Christian denominations in the town.[46]

The Stone-Campbell church at Mangum had been meeting at least since 1900. J. B. Nelson, the Nashville Bible School–educated evangelist, located there in 1901. The next year he reported that the progressives had begun their "destructive work" in the community under the leadership of A. W. Putman, "a full-fledged digressive," who often tried to pass himself off as a loyalist. At the invitation of Putman and H. C. Sweet, ACMS missionary J. A. Tabor held a four-week meeting in which he championed the progressive agenda. The result was to split the congregation in two. Nelson felt compelled to warn loyalists about Putman and Sweet.[47]

In 1905, the Stone-Campbell church in Poteau was predominantly progressive in its work and worship. There were three or four disciples, however, who would not "bow to the ways of the 'digressives.'" They arranged for John T. Hinds of Arkansas, a well-known editor of the Gospel Advocate, to come and preach at the church building. After one or two discourses, he was uninvited by the leadership and had to close his meeting. But over the next two years he returned each summer to preach in a tent provided by the loyalists. The response to Hinds's preaching was so positive that the loyalists were able to buy a building and worship without instrumental music and parachurch organizations.[48]

In Henryetta, the tension between the loyalists and digressives would not go away. In May 1908, Texas evangelist J. W. Chism scheduled a meeting at the Church of Christ in Henryetta. Subsequently, he learned that the Christian Church had scheduled a meeting for two weeks earlier, which was to open with a "moving picture show." He rescheduled his meeting for late April, only to discover that the Baptists and Holiness had booked revivals simultaneously with his. Unable to compete with "human schemes" and "chicanery," Chism proposed that preachers of the Church of Christ, the Christian Church, and the Baptist church preach to a common audience each day over three days. When his proposal was rejected, he challenged the Christian Church preacher to meet him in debate on the proposition: "The Scriptures teach that the practice and teaching of the 'First Christian Church' in Henryetta is open rebellion against God." His challenge was not accepted, and the tension continued.[49]

In Indian Territory, audiences initially entertained Stone-Campbell evangelists without much attention to their views on instrumental music in worship or parachurch organizations doing kingdom work. This was true even if Officer, Parker, or their Indian Territory coworkers had "set them in order" as congregations. Consequently, when a respected ACMS evangelist like S. E. Kennedy appeared in the community, audiences saw no reason not to embrace his instruction on methods of work and worship. This was particularly the case in the railroad and county seat towns of the Twin Territories, where the ACMS by design had concentrated its efforts and had enjoyed its most enthusiastic responses. To the traditionalists, it seemed, therefore, that they had planted the restoration seed, but the innovators had stolen the harvest. They fought back by name calling, challenging debate, withdrawing, and putting their creed in the deed to the church building.[50]

Name Calling

For the progressives, the views and actions of the traditionalists helped explain the limited response to the Stone-Campbell plea for Christian unity in Oklahoma and Indian Territories. As J. C. Howell, minister at South McAlester, editor of the *Pioneer Christian*, and corresponding secretary of the Indian Territory Christian Missionary Cooperation, put it, the "Firm foundation, Christian leaders, Gospel advocates . . . [and] the irrepressible *Octographic Review* men came into this country because there was no other place to go; civilization's onward progressive march had driven them from among the intelligent, and other fields more congenial to their taste had to be sought. They have gone into our rural districts where our best, but uneducated brethren have moved to wait an opportunity to get a home for their loved ones" in lands opening for settlement in Oklahoma Territory.[51]

In the rural districts, Howell continued, the preachers who were "Anti Sunday School, Anti Endeavor, Anti Co-operation, Anti Missionary and Anti everything except anti up" preyed on these isolated brethren and kept them ignorant "of what was going on in the great religious world." But those who were trying "to clog the wheels of Zion" would not succeed "if we lift[ed] our voices in defense of

Primitive Christianity." As for the *Pioneer Christian*, Howell asserted, it would stand "boldly in defense and propagation of progressive Christianity . . . until every congregation in our beloved adopted homes [the Indian Territory] shall see that the only means of success is to move out into higher, broader and progressive fields of usefulness."[52] In other words, the restoration ideal would succeed only if the "antis" were left behind. And that did not seem to be happening.

L. B. Grogan, early minister at Chickasha and ACMS evangelist for Indian Territory, was a bit more generous when it came to explaining the lackluster response to the Stone-Campbell plea. He identified five "hindering causes." Four of those he held in common with R. W. Officer, whom he knew well. First, the Disciples who migrated to Indian Territory tended to take on the cultural traits of the people around them once they got there. Second, the religious neighbors of the Disciples who had been in the Territory for a long time and had made considerable capital expenditures were formidable opponents. Third, immoral preachers who claimed to be Disciples had done a great deal of bad work. And fourth, the Disciples had only a few church houses that they could call their own.[53]

The fifth hindering cause was Grogan's personal contribution to the list, specifically "the conditions brought about by the antagonistic spirit manifested in the preaching of our non-progressive brethren who had preceded us in many localities." Their congregations, especially before 1896 when he came to the territory, often "fell to pieces as organizations, or became too narrow and creed-bound to cooperate with the brotherhood in any organized evangelistic work."[54] Editor Howell agreed and added that the antis were "self-deluded" and "half witted" and that their "congregations [had] died an unnatural death and [would] soon be laid in the cold ground." That fate could be arrested elsewhere, however, if enlightened and aggressive congregants cooperated with progressive evangelists.[55]

The Results

Internecine squabbles aside, the standing of Stone-Campbell churches, both progressive and conservative, was impressive as the territorial era drew to a close in 1907. Of the 240,000 churchgoers, 10 percent belonged to that tradition. Only Methodists, Baptists, and Catholics had more.[56] In the first legislature after Oklahoma became a state, more members from the Stone-Campbell tradition, twenty-four altogether, served in that body than from any other denomination.[57] One of these, H. M. McElhaney from McAlester, sponsored the legislation that placed the penitentiary in his hometown. George W. Allen, whose mother was a Cherokee, also served in the first legislature.[58]

The turmoil within the Stone-Campbell churches during the territorial era was the mirror image of that experienced by similar congregations elsewhere in the United States. The hope of the founders of the movement to achieve Christian unity by relying on scripture alone in determining matters of faith and practice was floundering. The bright hope of the movement had dimmed with division. Two groups had emerged. One, composed of the "traditionalists," "loyalists," or "antis," identified themselves as Churches of Christ. The "old paths" they followed wound through the agrarian South and were curbed by noninstitutionalism and a capella music. The other group, composed of "progressives" or "digressives," denominated themselves as Christian Churches or Disciples of Christ. Its path meandered through the cities and prosperous countryside of the Midwest and was paved with cultural accommodation and biblical modernism and curbed by mechanical instruments and parachurch support groups.

In recognition of this reality, the U.S. Census Bureau listed the Churches of Christ and the Disciples of Christ as two separate denominations in 1906. The unity movement had divided. The bureau counted 159,658 members and 2,649 congregations of Churches of Christ nationwide, compared with 982,701 members and 8,260 congregations of Disciples of Christ. Over the next twenty years, Church of Christ membership would increase to 433,714 and congregations to 6,226. The number of Disciples would increase to 1,337,595, although its congregations would decline to 7,648.[59]

Of Churches of Christ in Oklahoma today, at least forty-seven were founded prior to 1906. Organized in 1883, the oldest congregation in what once was Indian Territory was at Allen. Under the leadership of John T. Gilmore, physician, postmaster, and mayor, the church first met in a schoolhouse, but after 1888 in its own building, which it has continued to do for the last 130 years.[60] In Oklahoma Territory, the oldest congregation was at Mangum, having been established when Old Greer County was part of Texas in 1888.

As the Stone-Campbell movement divided officially, the U.S. Congress joined Indian and Oklahoma Territories into one state, Oklahoma, and admitted it into the Union in 1907. That decision created precise geographical boundaries for the state, which in turn helped give more definition to political, economic, and social issues impacting the region. The same was true in the case of the emergence of the Churches of Christ as a distinct religious entity. Thereafter, the beliefs and practices that gave them specificity as a group were more easily discernible and their consequences more measurable. Describing and assessing the history of the Churches of Christ in Oklahoma, therefore, is a bit less complicated.

5

ESTABLISHING AN IDENTITY
1906–1920

Until 1906, Churches of Christ in Oklahoma had little identity as a religious community. They were recognized as a small group of dissenters within the Stone-Campbell movement who objected to the faith and practice of most religious groups, even those within their own tradition. In the U.S. religious census of 1906, as previously noted, the federal government recognized Churches of Christ at large as a freestanding, independent denomination separate from the Christian Church. Official acknowledgment at such a high level legitimized Churches of Christ as an independent religious institution and gave it an opportunity to define itself with greater clarity.

Oklahoma statehood offered a similar prospect. Prior to, Churches of Christ had operated on the margins of the mainstream religious community and more often than not in destitute places. Defining who they were was a struggle. Now, as members of a recognized church, free from the apostasy of their Stone-Campbell cousins, and resident of a brand new state, Churches of Christ were in a position to establish more fully their identity as a people. Above all else, they could reassert their message of Christian unity to be achieved by the abandonment of denominational creeds and the acceptance of the simple gospel message revealed in the infallible words of the New Testament. That declaration, as members saw it, would be the substance of their identity as a religious community.

The Social Context

Churches of Christ in Oklahoma did not live in isolation from the communities they served. The relationship was not wholly symbiotic, because Churches of Christ at least through 1920 tried to distance themselves from things of this world, everything from alcohol to military service. At the same time, what impacted the state of Oklahoma at large also impacted the church. To illustrate, Oklahoma's population increased from 1.4 million to 2 million between 1907 and 1920. Oklahoma's capital city tripled in population, from 32,452 to 91,295. The number of towns in the state with populations above 2,000 increased by almost 50 percent (from 46 to 63 percent) between 1910 and 1920.[1] This concentration of population caused church leaders to focus more of their evangelistic effort on urban centers, although Oklahoma remained essentially rural in character.

The creation of a public system of secondary and higher education by the state also shaped the Church of Christ community. Members were eager that their own children have access to an advanced education, but they desired that it be under the direction of people of their own faith. This desire became urgent after they learned that their recently separated cousins were organizing Oklahoma Christian University (subsequently Phillips University) at Enid in 1907. Church of Christ members saw need to replicate that development. The result was the formation of Cordell Christian College, also in 1907. Remarkably, El Meta Bond College with its impressive campus and curriculum was not deemed satisfactory to either group.

With and after statehood, racism impacted virtually every aspect of daily life in Oklahoma: political, economic, social, and religious. Like most other communities of faith, Churches of Christ felt its weight, which crippled efforts to share the gospel with people of color, both African American and indigenous. Racism impeded the ministry of S. R. Cassius and made Churches of Christ in Oklahoma virtually mute about the tragic conditions that spawned the Tulsa Race Riot in 1921. Outreaches to the state's Native population were equally limited, as the decades-long ministry of R. W. Officer predicted.

Low agricultural prices and consequent rural poverty also had an impact on Churches of Christ in the state. Those conditions produced a political radicalism in Oklahoma that infringed upon the peace and unity of the churches. There is little evidence that members were much involved with populism aside from admiring the Christian worldview of William Jennings Bryan, but as we will see they very much were engaged in the debate over socialism. Moreover, Oklahoma's promotion of and preparation for World War I forced Church of Christ members to evaluate whether they would participate given the apocalyptic theology of Barton Stone and David Lipscomb, that is, that Christians are citizens of the kingdom of God rather than a dominion of human creation.

Early Statehood Evangelism

Despite all of the different influences about them, the principal work of Churches of Christ after statehood remained evangelism. Most members attended small congregations in the small towns that dotted the countryside. Many did not meet in their own building, but in rural schoolhouses. Some even shared space belonging to a denominational adversary. These congregations were served by evangelists who fed their families as farmers, merchants, salesmen, teachers, and blacksmiths but preached on Sundays and held meetings during the summer months. Only a very few had what was called a "located" preacher.

Many of the evangelists who had served in Indian and Oklahoma Territories continued to do so after statehood. Among these were J. W. Ballard (1875–1959), a blacksmith; J. W. Chism (1865–1935), an insurance salesman, photographer, and artist who eventually entered into local work in Ardmore; and A. Leroy Elkins (1864–1945), a physician who denied the germ theory, objected to socialism, helped establish Tipton Home for children, and served in some ministerial capacity at Fort Sill during World War I.[2] Also notable were A. E. Freeman (1853–1944), an educator, farmer, and merchant who spent the later years of his life at Guthrie; D. S. Ligon (1866–1956), a business educator well known for his portraiture of famous Stone-Campbell ministers; and T. E. Milholland (1871–1942), who served the congregation at Madill as a located minister in addition to conducting summer meetings throughout the state.[3]

Other evangelists were primarily associated with the post-statehood era and lived and itinerated through south-central and southwestern Oklahoma. Among the more influential of these were faculty members associated with Cordell Christian College. On almost every Sunday, President J. N. Armstrong (1870–1944) and teachers B. F. Rhodes Sr. (1869–1947), R. C. Bell (1877–1964), Samuel Albert Bell Jr. (1879–1973), and William Webb Freeman (1887–1954), among others, preached somewhere in western Oklahoma. Their messages were noted for their rational approach to scripture, their emphasis upon the reign of God on earth, and their call for unity among believers. During the summer months, the Cordell faculty also conducted meetings across the state, their sermons helping to shape the Christian faith of an entire generation of believers in Oklahoma and surrounding areas.[4]

Ministerial Conferences

Given the congregational polity of Churches of Christ and the historic suspicion of human societies, evangelists in the early statehood era worked independently of each other. Any attempt to bring the preaching brethren together for fellowship and edification generated concern and suspicion among those who found no biblical precedent for such a gathering. From time to time, however, one of the evangelists would take things into his own hands and announce a gathering at his home congregation, arranging an agenda of speakers and discussion topics. Something similar had been done prior to statehood, but it occurred more regularly thereafter.

As we will see, initiative for many of the gatherings came from Cordell Christian College. Beginning in 1909, President Armstrong invited evangelists, parents of students, and friends to campus annually for a Thanksgiving celebration. Those who came enjoyed sermons and lectures as well as good fellowship. The Cordell Church of Christ followed suit and from time to time invited delegations from neighboring congregations to meet with them for special events. In December 1913, the Comanche congregation in Stephens County, with the encouragement of its local minister, young Dee Bills (1886–1946), organized a four-day gathering of evangelists, journal editors, and congregational leaders to discuss differences in theology and practice among the churches.[5]

The thirty or more who attended the meeting judged it a smashing success. Participants had come from different parts of the state with diverse points of view. Indeed, wrote J. N. Armstrong,

> There were present those that believed women should not even teach a class of children in one corner of the meeting house, while others believed they had the privilege of even offering exhortations to the Lord's day meeting when requested by the elders; then there were those who believed in the indwelling of the Holy Spirit only through the word, while others believed that the Holy Spirit 'actually' and 'really' dwelled in the Christian; then there were those who believed in using the lesson leaf in the Lord's day Bible school although others did not. These divisive issues were discussed calmly, creating an atmosphere of understanding.

To Armstrong, "it was one of the greatest blessings I have had given me in a long time." Leroy Elkins added that it was a "feast for the soul and an encouragement to those who are battling in the army of the Lord against the hosts of Satan." How could such a meeting be harmful, he asked?[6]

Some found that it was, however. They thought that the Comanche meeting looked very much like a convention where evangelistic programs were plotted, planned, and executed, all beyond the boundaries of the local congregation. To them, there was no indication in scripture that such a meeting had occurred in the first-century church. Lacking that precedent, such a tool was not available to those seeking to restore the New Testament church. The critics reminded their brethren that the digressives had used similar unbiblical institutions and had torn the Stone-Campbell movement asunder. Armstrong and subsequently U. G. Wilkinson countered that the meeting was all about mutual edification and had nothing to do with legislating for local congregations or infringing autonomy. Most accepted that explanation, but the controversy made clear that the fear of unscriptural institutionalization was part of the DNA of Churches of Christ in Oklahoma. It would remain so through most of the twentieth century.[7]

Congregations in the Early Statehood Era

Churches of Christ faithful experienced their greatest evangelistic successes after statehood in rural areas and small towns. In 1910, for example, Arkansan Andy T. Ritchie (1876–1950) baptized 117 during a four-week revival at Hastings in Cherokee County.[8] A host of other evangelists could have replicated Ritchie's report. But there were exceptions. Red Rock citizens were "cold and backward" when it came to hearing the gospel message, reported J. L. Wood.[9] At Coalgate, wrote Leroy Elkins, miners were beyond the reach of the gospel.[10] And the church at Rufe, said D. S. Ligon, suffered from an "acute attack of the quits."[11]

During the first two decades of the twentieth century, the county seats and railroad towns of Oklahoma generally welcomed all Stone-Campbell evangelists, whether conservative or progressive. But the reception afforded to the Church of Christ, or "loyal," evangelists often had more the appearance of Coalgate than Hastings. The greeting, however, was different for their kinsmen, who presented themselves as flexible in their faith and practices, open to urban lifestyles, and willing to embrace worship and organizational structures already in use by most Protestant communions. Probably for that reason Stone-Campbell congregations at Muskogee, McAlester, Ardmore, Chickasha, Edmond, and Norman established during territorial days by loyalists like R. W. Officer, embraced the innovations over time and denominated themselves as the Christian Church. In Ardmore, as a consequence, four hundred persons attended the Christian Church, while only nine identified with the Church of Christ. Those congregants who objected to the modernisms either joined the majority or melted away. Some congregations in railroad cities like Guthrie, Perry, Enid, and Oklahoma City were progressive from the beginning thanks to the work of the ACMS. Consequently, until the second decade of the twentieth century, the progressive Disciples dominated the principal cities in Oklahoma.[12] Nevertheless, by 1920 most of Oklahoma's towns and cities had congregations of Churches of Christ. The most successful were in Oklahoma City and Tulsa.

New Congregations

The organization of a Church of Christ in Oklahoma City dated from 1901, when Thomas P. Prickett and his family moved there from Indiana. Unwilling to worship with the digressives, he gathered a small group that met in a private residence on Harrison Street and quickly thereafter in a schoolhouse on West Twenty-Third Street. Byron E. Martin of Kansas assisted the infant congregation in making itself known to the community with a series of evangelistic sermons delivered in a meeting. About 1907, the group gathered in the basement of the Adventist Church building at Seventh and Robinson. A revival offered by H. H. Adamson of Indiana that same year doubled the size of the congregation to thirty-two. By 1913, the group was worshipping in the county courthouse and sponsoring yearly tent meetings to generate more interest in the primitive gospel. E. A. Bedichek held a thirty-five-day meeting in 1914, while Thomas E. Milholland held a successful meeting the following year despite competition from a meeting of the Shriners, an exhibition by boxer Jess Willard, and lectures by Adventist founder Charles T. Russell.[13]

Notwithstanding opposition from some congregants but encouraged by economic and population expansion spawned by World War I, church leaders purchased property on the northwest corner of Tenth and Francis Streets in 1918. The congregation worshipped in the small house on the property until 1921, when a larger, more commodious frame building with a seating capacity of six hundred was erected. Membership totaled 430, with 350 attending Sunday school. During the transition, the congregation selected its first full-time minister, B. U. Baldwin, who served for only a year. John Allen Hudson (1893–1962) succeeded Baldwin, facilitating the final move into a new building.[14]

The church at Tenth and Francis in Oklahoma City quickly became the largest congregation of Churches of Christ in Oklahoma. Led by strong elders and served by talented ministers, it committed itself to vigorous evangelism in Oklahoma City and to lending encouragement and help to other churches in the state.[15] Accordingly, Tenth and Francis hosted periodic public debates and biannual meetings that attracted thousands to the Municipal Auditorium, the Oklahoma City Coliseum, and large tents. From this activity came at least four additional congregations in the Oklahoma City area: Capitol Hill, Twelfth and Drexel, Southwest, and Culbertson Heights (now Mayfair). It also brought new members to the mother church, swelling their number to nine hundred by 1935. Four years later the Tenth and Francis congregation built a 1,300-seat auditorium at the cost of $44,000 and dedicated it with a revival that attracted 1,500 people. The weekly contribution averaged almost $14,000 per week.[16]

What the Tenth and Francis church was to Oklahoma City, the Tenth and Rockford church was to Tulsa. The progressive churches of the Stone-Campbell movement organized a congregation in the small village of Tulsa in 1902. It grew with the city, and within a decade it had 1,100 members. Loyalists, if there were any, worshipped at the First Christian Church, if they worshipped at all. Economic growth associated with an oil boom and the onset of World War I brought additional population to the city, often from the rural countryside. These migrants brought their religious preferences with them, including the simple gospel of Churches of Christ. By 1916, a small group was meeting together at Whittier Elementary School. A year later with attendance at fifty, the congregation moved to the Tulsa County courthouse. By the end of another year, one hundred persons were attending. Under the guidance of a very young W. L. Oliphant (1900–1947), a minister from Oaks, the congregation appointed elders and deacons in 1919. The next year it appointed its first located minister, R. D. Henley. The group quickly purchased property at Tenth and Rockford Streets on the eastern edge of Tulsa and began constructing a building in 1922, which was completed six years later.[17]

Over the next several decades, the Tenth and Rockford church enjoyed sustained development. By 1926, there were 190 members. A succession of located ministers served it well, including James E. Laird (1890s), Lee P. Mansfield, John Allen Hudson, L. R. Wilson, W. R. Yowell, W. Curtis Porter, and L. O. Sanderson. The congregation also sponsored annual gospel meetings that reached out to residents of Tulsa and occasional lectures that looked very much like an assembly of Church of Christ preachers. One of the most notable of these was held in 1938 and addressed topics like "Restoration Principles" and "The Music Question." Participants included musician L. O. Sanderson, Harding College president George Benson, and Abilene Christian College president Don Morris. The Tenth and Rockford congregation also planted other congregations in the Tulsa area—for example, the one at Fifteenth and Delaware, but most of that work would be post–World War II. In sum, the Tulsa congregation made a big mark in its community, although not quite as big as the mark of the Tenth and Francis congregation in Oklahoma City.[18]

Other Congregations

Other congregations of Churches of Christ were organized in Oklahoma's principal towns in the first two decades of the twentieth century. Among these were Elk City (1901), Sentinel (1902), Hollis (1902), Tipton (1903), Lawton (1906), Hobart (1908), Frederick (1910), Enid (1913), Hooker (1913), Clinton (1914), and Chickasha (1915) in the western part of the state, and Healdton (1904), Wayne (1905), Holdenville (1905), Fort Gibson (1905), Idabel (1907), Shawnee (1907), Maysville (1907), McAlester (1908), Ardmore (1909), Wewoka (1913), Colcord (1913), Muskogee (1915), Okmulgee (1915), Pauls Valley (1915), Miami (1916), Drumright (1917), and Seminole (1920) in the eastern part.[19]

Their stories were similar to the Sixth and Arlington Church of Christ in Lawton. That congregation began meeting in a rural schoolhouse (1906), then the Methodist Church building (1907), and then the county courthouse (1907–19). The congregation built its first small building in 1920, which it soon outgrew and replaced on a larger lot at Sixth and Arlington Streets in 1926. In the meantime, the Lawton church, as elsewhere, arranged summer protracted meetings that brought noted evangelists to town, in this case J. H. Lawson, E. A. Bedichek, B. U. Baldwin, and Leroy Elkins.[20]

What happened in Muskogee was somewhat different. The legacy of R. W. Officer lived on in the First Christian Church. His spiritual heirs, however, did not meet in a sustained effort until 1913 or obtain a permanent home on East Okmulgee Street until six years later. This congregation became the Central Church of Christ over time and in 1931 moved to new facilities on Spaulding Street. For reasons that have been lost to history, a second congregation opened at Kankakee and C Streets about 1920. Both served Muskogee for the next fifty years.[21]

Upon statehood, the vibrant Christian Church in McAlester also owed its genesis in part to the good work of R. W. Officer. Moreover, progressivism was so strong that no conservative church existed there at the onset of Oklahoma statehood. Indeed, there were only three individuals faithful to "the old paths."

Not long thereafter enough loyalists were identified so that a small group could meet in the Odd Fellows Hall in North McAlester. In 1924, the congregation of sixty-eight members constructed its own building on South Third Street. Over the next ten years, the membership quadrupled, and the congregation expanded into the Busby Opera House in 1935. Built in 1907 for $175,000, the ornate and acoustically perfect theater was surely the most unique place of worship among Churches of Christ in Oklahoma.[22]

The situation in Ardmore for Churches of Christ was not much different than in McAlester. As early as 1893 there was a self-sustaining Stone-Campbell congregation in the community, where without a lot of trauma it accepted the innovations championed by ACMS preachers. At the time of statehood, the progressive church numbered 450, while the loyalists totaled no more than 7 and were meeting house to house. In January 1909, the tiny minority began worshipping regularly in a storehouse on the outskirts of Ardmore. Over the next eighteen months, noted evangelists C. H. Kennedy, J. D. Tant, and C. R. Nichol held protracted tent meetings that were "crammed with success." During Nichol's June 1910 meeting, fifty-two individuals were added (through baptism or membership transfer) to the Ardmore Church of Christ.[23] By 1912, the congregation purchased and paid for a building on Broadway, putting a restrictive clause in the title (its creed in the deed) that banned organs and bazaars from the building in perpetuity. When Sunday school attendance reached one hundred in 1920, the elders of the congregation purchased property at Fourth and A Streets NW and built a colonial styled red-brick building. Later, it would move to a new building on McLish Avenue, where it still worships.[24]

In general, the number of church plantings during the era was not over-whelmingly impressive, but it did reflect a vitality that after World War II would explode, making Churches of Christ, the fastest-growing denomination in the United States.

Sustaining A Capella Music

One of the foremost identity markers of Churches of Christ in Oklahoma was its use of a capella music in its worship services. In the post-statehood era, evangelists, elders, and editors exhorted members to make their singing as melodic as possible. In that way, they could demonstrate to both friends and critics that musical instruments were unnecessary when it came to worship ascetics, not to mention acceptability to God. To this end, talented musicians frequently taught singing schools of one to two weeks in duration that were attended by entire congregations as well as community members. Among other things, the teacher gave instruction on how to sight-read shaped notes, pitch and lead a song, and sing in four-part harmony. There was also a lot of practicing of old hymns and introduction of new ones. The better instructors were also competent hymn writers, who would publish their work and that of others in a collection of tune books that would be used as texts in the school and available for sale to students. The instructor also made himself available to lead the singing in protracted meetings.[25]

In the early twentieth century, some of the more notable singing school instructors, hymn writers, and song leaders in Churches of Christ at large had Oklahoma roots. Most notable of these was William W. Slater (1885–1959), who claimed the Sallisaw-Stigler area as his home. During the course of his life, he published more than thirty songbooks, selling some 500,000 copies. His best-known hymns were "Walking Alone at Eve" and "There's a Home for the Soul"; equally well known was his arrangement of "Angry Words." During the course of his career, Slater also served as a full-time minister at Muskogee, Henryetta, and Elk City.[26]

Albert E. Brumley (1905–77) was more of a songwriter than a song leader, but he too was a frequent music school instructor. A native of Rock Island (near Pocola), he grew up in the midst of poverty and faith. Early in life he determined to be a gospel songwriter. His first tune was not published until 1927, but in the next half century he was probably the most successful gospel songwriter in the United States, publishing over seven hundred tunes. Among his most noted hits were "I'll Fly Away," "I'll Meet You in the Morning," "Jesus, Hold My Hand," "Turn Your Radio On," and "He Set Me Free." He would be recorded by Elvis Presley, Charlie Pride, George Jones, and the Ray Charles Singers.[27]

L. O. Sanderson (1901–92) was just as prolific, writing more than five hundred hymns. Among his more noted tunes were "Be With Me Lord," "The Lord Has Been Mindful of Me," "Buried with Christ," "Bring Christ Your Broken Heart," and "Take Me Home, Father." But of more impact on the church was his participation in the publication of the hymnal *Christian Hymns No. 1* (1935). An Arkansas native, Sanderson did serve as minister of the Tenth and Rockford Church of Christ in Tulsa and the Central Church of Christ in Norman. He also studied music at the University of Oklahoma. On numerous occasions, he led the singing in protracted meetings and served as singing school instructor throughout Oklahoma.[28]

Less notable as songwriters than music teachers and song leaders were J. H. Lawson (1866–1935), Ira Y. Rice Sr. (1882–1968), Austin Taylor (1881–1973), and Mrs. J. N. Armstrong (1879–1971). Lawson, the dedicated evangelist in the first decades of the twentieth century, generally made improved congregational singing a secondary objective of his gospel meetings.[29] Ira Rice migrated from Arkansas to western Oklahoma around 1908. A gifted tenor who had studied music with private teachers, he gave full time to singing schools and evangelistic singing until 1929. Through midcentury, a substantial percentage of song leaders among Churches of Christ had studied with Rice.[30] Austin Taylor was a singing school instructor and song leader from Texas well known for such tunes as "Do All in the Name of the Lord" and "Closer to Thee." In Oklahoma, he made his name by leading singing during the Foy E. Wallace Jr.–E. F. Webber debate held at the Oklahoma City Coliseum in 1937. The eight-thousand-person audience on that occasion probably represented the largest single gathering of Church of Christ people in the history of the state to that point in time.[31]

While the men would improve congregational singing by training and technique, Mrs. Armstrong, the music teacher at Cordell Christian College and the wife of the president, emphasized singing "with the spirit, and . . . with the understanding." When individuals sang, she believed their minds often were not on the song at all, and thus they missed the depth and beauty of the composition. To her sorrow, she admitted, "Many of our songs have no depth of meaning, and, hence, can inspire no depth of feeling. . . . Their words are light and the music is light—so light that, instead of filling the souls of the audience with a spirit of worship, they create a kind of irreverence in the hearts of the young, at least." She had "actually known boys approaching manhood to jig to the accompaniment of the invitation song." Mrs. Armstrong cautioned congregational leaders to select songbooks that were "filled with songs in which both sentiment and music [were] worthy."[32]

The notion that singing "sacrifices of praise" a capella made worship acceptable to God lent force to the congregational song service. Its level of importance did not always make the service musical or inspiring, for there was only so much that tone-deaf farmers could do, but it did impress members with the importance of good singing and instilled a desire to improve their own skills. Hence, formal singing schools, evangelistic singers, composers of gospel songs, and use of songbooks were traditional Church of Christ characteristics. So, too, was the ubiquitous Sunday afternoon songfest where singers from several congregations gathered to sing new and old hymns, support young men who were just learning to lead songs, and listen to congregational singing groups that often included women. Those experiences also explain why many choral teachers in Oklahoma high schools wanted Church of Christ youngsters in their choirs.

Problematic Doctrinal Issues

With 1906, Churches of Christ were recognized as a distinct Christian community. That did not mean, however, that unity prevailed in faith and practice. There was general agreement that musical instruments did not belong in worship services and parachurch agencies should not undertake the work of the local congregation. About other issues there were fewer consensuses. Among these were the questions of pattern theology, Sunday schools, rebaptism, special providence, materialism, millennialism, and pacifism. Living in democratic Oklahoma and convinced that when it came to things religious every man was a priest, most church members had strong opinions regarding the various issues.

Pattern Theology

Pattern theology, a hermeneutic embraced by Alexander Campbell, presumed that scripture provided a constitution for Christ's church and that the obligation of the twentieth-century Christian was to replicate that church. If the biblical pattern did not include this or that activity, it was to be excluded from current practice. It was for this reason that members of the Churches of Christ had objected to the "innovations" of musical instruments and missionary societies. On that basis, others objected to Christian colleges, Sunday schools, located preachers, cooperative mission work, the study of literature other than the Bible, and multiple cups in communion. Those practices too, argued critics like *Octographic Review* publisher Daniel Sommer, were not part of the biblical pattern. These objections looked like legalism to some church leaders, and thus "Sommer-ism" was deemed an "awful malady" that could impede the work of a given congregation, disturb the peace of the church as a whole, and even divide it. After World War I, it did just that.[33]

Sunday Schools

Although they had developed independently, Sunday schools were long a staple of Protestant churches in the United States. Progressive Stone-Campbell congregations, or Christian/Disciples of Christ churches, incorporated them into their practices readily. But since they were not mentioned in scripture as part of the New Testament pattern, some members of Churches of Christ had considerable reservations about adopting them. It had not been much of a problem in pre-statehood Oklahoma and Indian Territories because congregations seldom met in their own buildings. But when they did, the Sunday school was a matter for discussion in church periodicals, preacher assemblies, and local gatherings. There was great concern that the Sunday school with superintendents and Endeavor groups would become institutions separate and apart from the local church, which in New Testament times had the only responsibility for spiritual instruction. The same fears caused reservations about using extra-biblical helps (published quarterlies and commentaries) and Bible translations other than the King James Version in Sunday school classes.[34]

Baptism

How to receive into fellowship persons of faith who had previously been baptized by immersion was also a troubling issue for Churches of Christ in the post-statehood era. They held that baptism was essential to salvation, while their Baptist friends held that it was essential only to church membership. This was not a significant dilemma for evangelists like R. W. Officer or church leaders like David Lipscomb, who welcomed Baptists with a handshake and a promise to teach them "the way of the Lord more perfectly." However, others like Oklahoma-based D. B. Cargile and Leroy Elkins, Texas revivalist J. D. Tant, and *Firm Foundation* publisher Austin McGary insisted that rebaptism was necessary. If the purpose of immersion was not remission of sins, from their perspective, it simply did not count. Judging from reports published in Church of Christ periodicals, most Oklahoma evangelists preached that one had to get their baptism right to be saved, and insisted on rebaptism.[35]

Scripture and Special Providence

Given their Baconian mindset, many members of Churches of Christ believed that God had revealed himself fully in his creation and that thereafter he governed the universe according to predictable patterns known as natural law. In this realm, God worked the same everywhere at all times to all people. He did not differentiate between saints and sinners. Church of Christ members, therefore, were skeptical of modern miracles executed by "special providence." They acknowledged a Divine Power (the Holy Spirit), of course, but that power was active only if it was in concert with natural law and did not exceed teaching revealed in scripture. What seemed like reducing the God of Israel to a Deist God troubled men like J. N. Armstrong and R. L. Whiteside, respectively president of

Cordell Christian College and Abilene Christian College. They therefore called for more faith and "less religious philosophizing."[36]

Materialism

Materialism as a religious doctrine was associated with William Miller (1782–1849) and Charles T. Russell (1852–1916), considered the founders of the Adventist and Jehovah's Witnesses churches in nineteenth-century America. It assumed that humans were wholly material and that the soul was mortal—that is, that the soul did not exist out of the body. With death, the soul merely went to sleep, to be awakened when Jesus physically returned to earth and established a millennial kingdom. Thus the dead did not exist, nor did hell, nor did heaven. Judging from the number of debates between Church of Christ evangelists and "infidels," materialism got a hearing in Oklahoma. T. B. Wilkinson, a younger brother of U. G. Wilkinson flirted with it, for example, until he listened to a debate between evangelist-salesman J. W. Chism and an infidel, when he lost all of his "taste for Russellism." Others within the fellowship did not lose their taste, however.[37]

Millennialism

The attraction to millennialism, both positive and negative, had as much to do with Russell's interest in the millennium as his conviction about the absence of heaven and hell. Stone-Campbell churches, for example, had long embraced the reality of the kingdom of God on earth, or the millennium, leaving open to question only the matters of agency and time or place the kingdom on earth would appear. Many, especially in Christian Churches, tended to see it coming at the end of a thousand years of human progress (post-millennial); others saw its occurring as an act of God at a time of spiritual darkness, which would cast Satan "into a bottomless pit" and through the rule of Jesus enshrine peace, justice, and righteousness for a thousand years (pre-millennial); still others saw it as a yet-to-be realized kingdom, imperfectly reflected in the church, to which believers nonetheless gave their allegiance in the here and now rather than to the kingdoms of this world. The latter view, which historian Richard Hughes defines as "apocalyptic," characterized much of the leadership in the Churches of Christ in Oklahoma in the first decades of the twentieth century. And if those leaders tilted toward one of the other two, it would have been the second rather than the first. It was this propensity that gave William Miller and Charles Russell a hearing in the pews of the church.[38]

Pacifism

Many Church of Christ members in Oklahoma still viewed the world through an apocalyptic lens as World War I approached. Barton Stone's conviction that this world was not the Christian's home had been reinforced by David Lipscomb's treatise on *Civil Government* (1913). Most Church of Christ members, therefore, rejected politics as a solution to worldly tribulations.[39] That meant, explained well-known evangelist J. E. Dunn (1867–1932), "We must not take life. We must not fight in an earthly kingdom. Our Kingdom is a spiritual kingdom. Our sword is the 'sword of the Spirit, which is the word of God.'" Not only must Christians not fight, he urged, but they must not even vote lest they unknowingly support a candidate for the U.S. Congress who subsequently would vote for "carnal warfare."[40]

Dunn was only one of the notable church leaders who embraced the pacifist tradition as the United States embroiled itself in World War I. Most notable was J. N. Armstrong, president of Cordell Christian College, but his colleagues on the faculty were equally committed. B. F. Rhodes Sr. (1869–1947) urged an alternative: rather than carnal warfare, Christians should gird themselves for spiritual warfare, the kind where one led a soul to Christ, the definition of true heroism, rather than send many to eternity on the battlefield. He did see a silver lining in the turmoil: evidence of the "hastening end" of this world and the beginning of the next one.[41]

A review of postings in denominational periodicals would suggest that church members in Oklahoma who did not hold the pacifist position outnumbered those that did. Typical of these, of course, was J. H. Lawson, the respected evangelist and public servant who ministered to soldiers training at Camp Bowie.[42] U. G. Wilkinson of Comanche was a strong voice in support of the war. And two of the periodicals that circulated widely in Oklahoma, the *Firm Foundation* and the *Octographic Review*, both supported it.

As we will see in the next two chapters, there were varying shades of pacifism among church members in Oklahoma as the nation prepared for war against Germany. There were those who would refuse any action that could be seen as contributing to the war effort. Others sought exemption from military service on the basis of conscience. And some accepted the draft but sought noncombatant service. All three of the strategies were employed by one or more of the draft-age male students at Cordell Christian College. It is not clear how Oklahoma socialists responded individually to the draft, but their opposition to the war was doubtless even louder and tinged with talk of revolution.

So, by 1920 Churches of Christ in Oklahoma had developed a clearer identity. They had new congregations across the state, including Tulsa and Oklahoma City; they had established a college in Cordell; they had debated doctrinal issues to clarify their teachings and practices; and they had survived the "war to end all wars." As a consequence, they had a better understanding of who they were and for what they stood.

6

CORDELL CHRISTIAN COLLEGE
IN PEACE AND WAR
1907–1918

The eleven years (1907–18) after Oklahoma entered the Union were formative for the "brand new State." The state implemented a constitution that was considered a model of progressivism, established an impressive system of public education, constructed public buildings, and prohibited the consumption of alcoholic beverages. Moreover, the petroleum industry demonstrated great economic potential. Not everyone, however, had access to all of the privileges provided by the state, particularly those of color. Also, most rural residents and many townspeople barely wrested a living from their farms or jobs, given persistent droughts and economic recessions. And more than just a few Oklahomans were offended by the nation's and state's decision to support involvement in World War I. All of this induced political, economic, and social turmoil that reminded residents of Oklahoma's populist heritage, although at the moment was defined as socialism.

More than a few present-day folk would say that the Churches of Christ in Oklahoma were anti-intellectual. As we have seen, however, members in fact embraced Baconian rationalism, a worldview that encouraged detailed Bible study in order to discern the plain facts of "God's Plan" for themselves, the church, and the world. For that reason, the Stone-Campbell movement at large had a rich tradition of establishing institutions of higher education. Among these was Franklin College, which became Nashville Bible School, the latter founded by David Lipscomb, one of the principal spokesmen for conservative Disciples. In Oklahoma, this accounted for the El Meta Bond College in Minco and what would become Phillips University in Enid. It also explained Cordell Christian College in southwestern Oklahoma. There, they considered themselves as being engaged "in the greatest work in the world."[1]

In the Beginning

Like most others taking up claims in the old Cheyenne-Arapaho Reservation in 1894, John M. Harrel (1868–1949) was a Texan. Like many Texans, Harrel strongly embraced the Stone-Campbell plea of Christian unity through the restoration of the New Testament church. He was also a farmer-preacher, and as soon as he completed a sod house on his claim he started looking for other loyalists. That quest, and others like it, was the beginning of Churches of Christ in Washita County. One of the congregations established, Cordell, became one of the stronger congregations in all of Oklahoma.[2]

John Harrel's brother, James, was one of the founding fathers of the town of Cordell, as well as a schoolteacher, entrepreneur, merchant, and church leader. Whatever would promote the growth and prosperity of the community found support from James Harrel. This was especially true when it came to education. In 1898, he organized an effort to build a private academy in Cordell.[3] When that institution closed several years later and the property was deeded to the Church of Christ, he was receptive to other possibilities. One of those came from local and regional leaders of Churches of Christ, who desired to establish a "college" that would begin with precollegiate work (grammar, secondary, and high school) and grow into collegiate work.[4]

Early Leaders

The vision of an educational institution in Oklahoma associated with Churches of Christ had its beginning in dinner conversations involving evangelist J. D. Tant and Granite merchants O. H. McGavock (1907–77) and W. D. Hockaday (1888–1958). Texas preacher Tant's evangelistic circuit often took him through Oklahoma Territory. He was widely known as a preacher who delighted in "skinning" the digressives and other Christian denominations in both sermons and debates.

A native Tennessean who was familiar with Nashville Bible School and Lockney Christian College, McGavock was a merchant-preacher who had resided in Granite since 1902. Hockaday, also from Texas, was a successful hardware merchant who was widely respected as an elder of the church at Granite. In search of a Christian school in which to educate his six children, McGavock commiserated both with Tant and Hockaday about the absence of one locally. All agreed that it was time for the brethren to organize one. After all, at least five such schools existed in Texas.[5]

In early 1906, McGavock took the matter up with James C. Harrel (1866–1911) and G. A. W. Fleming (1877–1966) in Cordell. One in insurance and the other in loan financing, Harrel and Fleming were close friends, Cordell boomers, and committed members of the Cordell Church of Christ. The idea of a college captivated their imagination. Indeed, in May when McGavock and others called a region-wide meeting at Hobart to discuss plans for the college, the two showed up with a specific offer to locate the desired school at Cordell.

Whether the proposal came from the city per se, as reported by the Oklahoma City press, or from Harrel and Fleming as city boomers is unclear. At any rate, the proposition was that, in return for establishing a Christian College at Cordell related to Churches of Christ, Cordell boosters promised a capital fund of $10,000 for college buildings and ten acres for a campus. They proposed to raise the money by subdividing an adjacent 150 acres into residential lots and auctioning them off to potential patrons of the college. Harrel and Fleming were confident that revenue from these sales and gifts from interested individuals would pay the $10,000 pledge. There was no thought of soliciting funds from individual congregations of Churches of Christ, incidentally, for all or virtually all would have agreed that using the "Lord's money" to make such a contribution had no precedent in scripture, and thus was not allowed.[6]

Influence of Daniel Sommer

Unlike Tennessee and Texas, in Oklahoma there was a strong sense that Christian education was the responsibility of the home rather than the church. Daniel Sommer, editor of the *Octographic Review*, which circulated widely in Oklahoma, concluded as much in part because he could find no evidence that the first-century church ever spent money on anything other than evangelization and benevolence. Moreover, such institutions developed a "clergy" attitude among preachers and fostered the idea that a person could not preach unless he went to college. Sommer found both perspectives offensive and unbiblical, positions he would articulate in rancorous debates with two men who had leadership roles at the college, J. N. Armstrong and B. F. Rhodes. Given the influence of Sommer in Oklahoma, it was no wonder that McGavock looked to individuals and the community for financial help rather than the different Churches of Christ.[7]

Harrel and Fleming's offer was too good to turn down. McGavock and friends quickly accepted, naming an eight-member board of trustees to give the envisioned college legal status. Hockaday was named president and James Harrel secretary and treasurer.[8] Articles of incorporation would soon be written, although they were not filed officially until some three years later.

Thanks to the management of Harrel and Fleming, the lots sold quickly, some above the asking price because it was known that all proceeds would go to the college. With $10,000 in hand or in sight, the board authorized construction of a large building that would house administrative offices, classrooms, and an auditorium with a full stage and seats for three hundred, as well as a dormitory for boys. It also set the opening of the first term as September 17, 1907, a very optimistic announcement inasmuch as construction of the main building did not get under way until May.[9] A new college in a new state seemed appropriate.

The College Opens

As the three-level main building with bell tower and the boys' dormitory rose slowly from the ground, the board was busy finding a president for the college. It finally settled on J. H. Lawson, one of the best-known evangelists in Oklahoma Territory, then a resident of Denton, Texas. Since Lawson could not move to Cordell until September 1, he asked the board to assume responsibility for appointing the new faculty, which it agreed to do. The board also discharged the responsibilities of setting the curriculum, with input from Lawson, and of recruiting the first class of students.[10]

The first term of Cordell Christian College began on schedule with seventy-eight students. Unfortunately but not unexpectedly, the main building on the campus was not completed, and classes had to be held in the Cordell church building, but for the first semester only. There was also an outstanding $6,000 debt. Even more troublesome was confusion over administrative authority. Who was in charge? In the preopening phase of the college, Harrel, as the board secretary, and Fleming, as the college's business manager and business teacher, had done virtually all of the necessary planning, from preparing the initial proposal, to raising $10,000, to organizing construction, to finding a president and appointing a faculty. Once the college opened, it was logical that the two friends would expect to be at the center of decision making. Whether that reality bothered President Lawson is unclear, but for it or some other reason he tendered his resignation at the end of the first term to return to full-time evangelism, then to pursue a career in the law.[11]

The Coming of J. N. Armstrong

In August 1908, the board appointed J. N. Armstrong (1870–1944) to succeed Lawson as president. A thirty-eight-year-old Tennessee native, Armstrong was, according to historian Norman Parks, "a tall, spare man with a visible stoop to his shoulders" who was "eloquent in speech" and had "a warm outgoing personality." Most important, he had had rich experiences in Christian college work. As a student, he had attended West Tennessee Christian College (currently Freed-Hardeman University) and Nashville Bible School (currently Lipscomb University), and as a teacher he had taught at Nashville Bible School and Potter Bible College at Bowling Green, Kentucky. In September 1905, he and three of his colleagues at Potter opened the Western Bible and Literary College in Odessa, Missouri. From there, after a year in New Mexico to recover his health, Armstrong agreed to come to Cordell.[12]

Surprisingly, at the end of his first year as president, Armstrong submitted his resignation to the board. At issue was, again, the question of who was in charge. Harrel, from the board, and Fleming, from the faculty, continued to make most of the day-to-day decisions. A hands-on and experienced collegiate administrator who, Parks wrote, "tended to make any college over which he presided become inescapably a projection of himself," Armstrong was uncomfortable with that arrangement. He wanted to select his own faculty and to manage his own budget. Chairman Hockaday urged the board to reject the resignation. Armstrong said that he would continue if Fleming's role was eliminated and Harrel's role constrained. Fleming promptly resigned his position at the school, although only after the board had reimbursed him for his investments in the institution. He remained a friend of Christian education for the rest of his life, although not necessarily of Armstrong.[13]

Harrel was less cooperative. He believed that no one had given more to the school than he and that Armstrong was wrong in trying to manage all aspects of the college. When the two could not be reconciled, the dispute, as often happened among church-related colleges, spilled over into the local Church of Christ. The leadership of that congregation withdrew fellowship from Harrel, who took a minority of the members and organized a second congregation in Cordell.

Thanks to the mediation of A. E. Freeman (1863–1944), the two congregations, after a meeting of "confessions and forgiveness," later reunited, and Harrel was restored to full fellowship. In the meantime, the college board dropped Harrel from membership.[14]

Retiring the Debt

Beginning with the fall term of 1909, Armstrong was in full control of Cordell Christian College, launching a period he later described as the happiest and most productive of his entire life as a teacher and administrator. Almost immediately he addressed attention to the physical facilities of the campus, finishing out the main building, remodeling the boys' dormitory, laying sidewalks on the campus, and constructing a house for his own family that included rooms for students. The ever-present debt was whittled down by selling student scholarships and stock in the college corporation, by gifts from members of Cordell's Commercial Club, and by faculty members forgoing salaries when they were able to draw compensation from churches for weekend preaching. Money that Armstrong received during the summer months for his meeting work all went to pay the debts of the college. The same was true of the fees Mrs. Armstrong, the daughter of the revered James A. Harding, received from her private lessons in music and expression. By 1915, the college was debt free.[15]

The Faculty and Student Body

Much of the success of any educational enterprise depends on the quality of the faculty. Armstrong was quite aware of that axiom and did his best to recruit the finest faculty available. To do that, he often drew upon personal friendships, as in the case of B. F. Rhodes (1869–1947) in history, R. C. Bell (1877–1964) in English, and S. A. Bell (1879–1973) in mathematics and science. All three had been with Armstrong at Potter and/or Odessa. He also encouraged some of his best students to get additional training and then return to the college as teachers, the most notable being Cline Sears, his son-in-law and biographer. Because of the fine arts curriculum and the primary department at the college, Armstrong was able to incorporate strong and talented women into his faculty, whom he often featured in college publicity. All of his colleagues, men and women, were committed members of Churches of Christ and considered teaching their Christian vocation.[16]

The college opened with a student population of seventy-eight. In Armstrong's first year, it totaled 112. Thereafter, it grew annually until it reached 288 students in 1916, vying with Thorp Springs Christian College in Texas for honors as the largest of all Church of Christ–related colleges.[17] Extant figures are skimpy, but it is fair to assume that at any one time at least 50 percent of the students were in the primary and junior high departments and 25 percent were each in the high school and collegiate departments. Most, of course, came from southwestern Oklahoma, but a few did come from out of state—indeed, as far away as Tennessee. The big majority of the students were from families associated with Churches of Christ, but not all.

Students paid modest tuition and board/room fees. In 1909–10, tuition ranged from nine dollars per year for first graders to thirty-six dollars per year for collegiate students. Instruction in special departments—instrumental music, voice culture, and business—required additional fees. Board and room either off or on campus was $12.50 per month. Depending upon special instruction, the academic year cost somewhere between $160 and $200.[18]

The Prescribed Curriculum

In matters of curriculum, Cordell Christian College stood in the tradition of the Nashville Bible School. All students, for example, studied the Bible each school day, even in the primary departments. In Bible and other studies, students did not dig for answers to a particular question, but for the "whys" and "wherefores" of those questions. It was not a seminary where only preachers were trained, but it was an institution devoted to the education of *all* believers, whatever age or interest. For that reason, Cordell's "college" included primary, junior high, and high school departments, with an emphasis on basic skills of reading, writing, and calculating. Significantly, it also included music, expression, and dramatics, thought of as fine arts today. Available to students as well were classes in the practical arts—namely, penmanship, typewriting, commercial law, spelling, and letter writing. And women students were encouraged to enroll in Greek, Hebrew, and Latin classes alongside the prospective preachers. Clearly, education at Cordell was for all believers, whatever their disciplinary interests or gender.[19]

Of course, the college offered courses traditionally associated with collegiate education. These included English literature, history, and science, but not government. In the tradition of David Lipscomb and the Nashville Bible School, there was no need to study worldly governments because Christians did not hold citizenship in them, only in the kingdom of God. The college's individualized approach to learning and the thoroughness with which it was done was so effective that the University of Oklahoma agreed to give Cordell graduates three years of credit toward a four-year bachelor degree. Although that level of accreditation exceeded the two years allowed sister institutions in Texas and Tennessee, it represented only a milestone for Cordell. The ultimate goal was a four-year accredited bachelor degree.[20]

The Cocurriculum

The cocurriculum was as broad based as the academic curriculum. All students attended daily chapel, which was considered a worship service. Along with patrons of the college, all could take advantage of the lyceum, which was a program of cultural presentations (musical and dramatic) by students as well as visiting artists, public figures, scholars, and preachers. Students could also attend the Thanksgiving lectures, which brought together large numbers of preachers and friends of the college. The lectures generally raised needed funds for the institution. The school also scheduled regular Monday night meetings, where any religious question could be raised, with faculty responding. Older students always attended this gathering since it was one of the few times young men could sit with their dates. Students also participated in one of two literary societies, with one society giving special emphasis to debate and the second to popular programs such as musical and dramatic presentations. Faculty also arranged intramural baseball games, but only among their own students. No football games were allowed; they were considered entirely too rough for Christian men and women.[21]

The Relationship with the Church

Cordell Christian College was associated with but not owned by Churches of Christ. Given the congregational polity and democratic nature of Churches of Christ, there was no synod, diocese, or convention to own the school. The relationship between the two was premised wholly upon the individual commitment to the church of the college's board of directors, administration, faculty, staff, and students. The force of that connection was critical to the college when it came to identifying itself to the public, in recruiting students, and in funding capital projects. It was to the advantage of the institution to nurture the tie.

President Armstrong used several strategies to achieve that result. Among other things, he worked to make the Cordell Church of Christ, the "college church," where students could find a home away from home and members could identify with the college in a personal way. Students and staff attended worship services at the church twice on Sunday and once on Wednesday evening.

Armstrong actually walked with the students from the college campus to the church building each Wednesday (on Sundays he was preaching elsewhere). As the college church, the Cordell Church of Christ grew in size and in influence and was widely recognized as one of the strongest congregations in Oklahoma.[22]

Armstrong also encouraged his faculty and students preparing for the ministry to preach on Sundays as often as possible. It not only provided students with experience and faculty with a small source of additional income but also strengthened the tie between the college and the church community in which they were preaching. The same was true of summer meetings.

Armstrong organized the annual Thanksgiving lectures at the college as another service for the church. He invited ministers, elders, and members of his faculty to present informational lectures, inspirational sermons, and thoughtful lessons on controversial topics. An estimated one hundred or more preachers, professors, students, and townspeople participated in these annual lectures, which lasted as long as a week. Most participants left Cordell with a high opinion of the college and renewed energy to spread the gospel in western Oklahoma.[23]

Little that Armstrong did to strengthen ties with Churches of Christ was as influential as the school's publishing the *Gospel Herald*. A weekly journal printed on the campus in the interest of the college, the first issue of the *Herald* came out on October 31, 1912. James A. Harding and R. L. Whiteside were editors, while J. N. Armstrong was managing editor and J. F. Smith was field editor. The initial articles addressed the topics "The Road to Happiness" and "Peace and Unity" and the question "Is Undenominational Christianity Possible?" They were thoughtful and irenic pieces, completely unlike the debating mentality of "my way or the highway" then appearing in the *Firm Foundation*, *Octographic Review*, and *Gospel Advocate*. Subsequent issues had the same spirit and were welcomed into at least one thousand homes each week, perhaps as many as three thousand, throughout the nation. With frequent references to the college, it put the Cordell school on the map and, no doubt, helped account for the record enrollments in 1917–18.[24]

Dealing with Carnal Warfare

The promising future of the increasingly distinguished school terminated abruptly when the United States entered World War I. The declaration of war on Germany on April 6, 1917, and passage of the Selective Service Act on May 18 caused a sizeable minority of Church of Christ students to reflect deeply upon whether Christians could be involved in taking human life, or participating in "carnal warfare." Certainly the president and most of the faculty at Cordell Christian did not think so, although Armstrong added the caveat that it was possible for conscientious objectors to wear the military uniform provided that they engaged in noncombatant service such as hospital duty and Red Cross work. Held by the *Gospel Advocate* and its longtime editor, David Lipscomb, a more radical view insisted that any war service while in uniform aided the war and hence was wrong.[25]

The Pacifist Tradition

As already noted, the pacifist tradition ran deep in the heart of Churches of Christ.[26] It held that human government had "usurped the role of God and therefore was foreign to the Christian life." Christians were obliged to obey laws that did not violate God's law, but they were not called to go out of their way to assist the "foreign" government, as in the cases of voting or holding office. For that purpose, there was no real reason to study that alien government in a college curriculum, sing the national anthem in a college program, or fly the nation's flag in a church building. According to historian Parks, upon the declaration of war, "the first response of almost every Church of Christ journal . . . was that 'Ceasar' could not demand of Christians the killing of men because Jesus himself was a pacifist and his redeemed ones must follow in his steps."[27]

The *Gospel Herald* strongly supported President Woodrow Wilson's early efforts to keep the United States neutral in the European conflict and was reassured by Wilson's reelection to a second term as president in November 1916. Its editors were deeply disappointed with Wilson's subsequent declaration of a war to end all wars, but they were heartened when Secretary of State William Jennings Bryan resigned in protest. Unlike the *Gospel Advocate*, which under government scrutiny went from opposing to supporting the war almost overnight, the *Herald* did not. That decision would create huge problems for Cordell Christian College.

Washita County Council of Defense

Upon declaration of war, the U.S. government launched a massive propaganda campaign to sell Americans on the war and to get them to register for the draft. Coordinated by the National Council of Defense, the promotion was effective, perhaps even too effective. In Oklahoma, the oversold war, mixed with the Green Corn Rebellion (a farmer/laborer demonstration against the war) and the rhetoric of socialist dissidents like O. E. Enfield, produced a "tar and feather patriotism" that fueled acts of persecution and intolerance. This was especially the case with the Washita County Council of Defense, an affiliate of the Oklahoma Council of Defense, which was in no mood to accommodate German sympathizers or "slackers"—that is, conscientious objectors.[28]

Already irritated by opposition of local Mennonites to military service, the Washita County council lived fitfully with the conscientious objection position of Cordell Christian in the early months of the United States' involvement in the war. The college dining room, after all, had joined other patriotic institutions in serving cornbread six days a week so that wheat flour could be shipped to the war front. It also had observed the meatless day protocol. Mrs. Armstrong produced a play that raised money for the Red Cross, and faculty and students bought war saving stamps and Liberty bonds. Students and teachers went into the fields to chop and pick cotton. As many as thirty-six Cordell students and three teachers entered the U.S. armed services either through the draft or by volunteering, Armstrong's nephew among them. And the positive moral influence of the college on the town of Cordell was widely acknowledged.[29]

But these evidences of support did not mitigate the fact that some Cordell students were registering for the draft and claiming conscientious objector status. Some chose not to register at all. One, Ben Randolph, registered but refused to accept noncombatant service. Just carrying a stretcher on the battlefield, he believed, would aid the war effort. For this act of "defiance," a super patriotic Washita County Draft Board sent him to the federal penitentiary in Leavenworth, Kansas, where he stayed for the duration of the war. At least two other Cordell students (Leroy P. Epperson and Levi Kendrick Wilmeth) joined him there.[30] From the defense council's point of view, the administration and faculty of Cordell Christian College were directly responsible for the students' decisions. If any question about culpability remained, it evaporated after the *Gospel Herald* published faculty member S. A. Bell's article in mid-May 1918 on whether a Christian could do noncombatant work in the military. His answer was "no."[31]

Randolph's reaction to World War I was typical of members of Churches of Christ in Oklahoma, given the strong apocalyptic views of founders of the tradition such as Barton Stone and David Lipscomb. But for Randolph, the reaction was more extreme than most. More common was the view that Christians could not kill another human being in carnal warfare, but they could serve as noncombatants. And there were many who had no reluctance at all to answer the call of the country for military service. Most of Randolph's classmates at Cordell Christian, for example, fell into this category. Some of Oklahoma's more notable preachers in Churches of Christ also held this view, including

U. G. Wilkinson of Comanche, J. W. Crumley Sr. at Sentinel, and the widely esteemed J. H. Lawson, who served as chaplain through the YMCA program at Camp Bowie near Fort Worth, Texas.[32]

A Conspiracy Unfolds

At the suggestion of some of the college's local enemies, the Cordell postmaster sent a copy of Bell's article opposing noncombatant service to his superiors in Washington, D.C. The U.S. Post Office judged the essay to be seditions and thus a violation of the Espionage Act of 1917. After Armstrong expressed regret for some of the radical statements in Bell's article and announced that the *Herald* would cease publishing altogether, both the Post Office and the Bureau of Investigation considered the matter moot.[33]

But not the Washita County Council of Defense. Perhaps seeing an opportunity to settle some old scores with Armstrong, former Cordell College board members G. A. W. Fleming and James Harrel, evangelist J. W. Crumley, and Clinton Cook, all Church of Christ members, agitated the local defense council and its chairman, Alvin Bingaman, to take another look. It did, twice, once with Armstrong alone and once with the board of regents, confirming to its satisfaction that the school taught the doctrine of "absolutism," or opposition to any military duty whatever.[34] The next day, July 24, 1918, the Washita County council issued an order to Cordell Christian that the board of regents and faculty "be so re-organized as will unreservedly conform to all military policies and requirements of the government in the present war." Moreover, "doctrines or teachings" in the school must comply with the military policies of the government. The reorganization required the withdrawal of Armstrong and the regents who agreed with him and replacements with individuals who "henceforth [will] stand for constituted authority in all its dignity and power."[35]

Armstrong and the regents appealed the order to the Oklahoma Council of Defense, who sent Supreme Court of Oklahoma judge Thomas Owen to investigate the situation. Upon learning of the investigation, Bingaman announced that it made no difference what Owen found because the community was organized in opposition to the school. He even threatened Hockaday, calling him a criminal and telling him to get out of town. Bingaman issued his threat on Cordell's courthouse square, in front of a fifty-person mob that included an approving Fleming, Crumley, Harrel, and Cook.[36]

Later that same day, after telling Bingaman pointedly that he wanted no roughhousing, Judge Owen opened his hearing. Armstrong made a complete explanation of his position. He believed in "war in self-defense," the kind of war in which the United States was currently engaged. He also reviewed historically and theologically the pacifist stance of Churches of Christ, that it was wrong for Christians to take part in carnal warfare. He insisted that "90% of the preachers of the Gospel . . . stood for th[at] doctrine." He admitted that he had advised all draft-age students to take noncombatant duty, but he denied that he ever discouraged anyone from enlisting, citing his own nephew as an example.[37]

While Owen questioned Armstrong judiciously and thoughtfully, Binga-man did anything but. He was loud and accusatory. Prodded and prepared by J. W. Crumley, Bingaman tried to connect Armstrong with events that he knew little of or were beyond his ability to control. His line of questioning told more about him and his advisors than about Armstrong. Accordingly, Judge Owen exonerated the school completely and announced, according to Cline Sears, "While the position of the faculty and board was unfortunate for them in time of war, many good people in the state held the same position and that they were free to proceed with their work if they wished."[38]

President Armstrong Concedes

But by that time, Armstrong and the board did not wish it. They were worn out defending their consciences and their actions. With Judge Owen and the board in agreement, Armstrong resigned as president and shuttered the school in August 1918, some three months before Germany surrendered and the Great War ended. Armstrong and other members of the Cordell faculty moved to Harper College in Harper, Kansas. The following year he became president of that school, which subsequently moved to Morrilton and then Searcy, Arkansas, where it morphed into Harding College.[39]

Historian Norman Parks believed strongly that Armstrong closed Cordell Christian College unnecessarily. The county council had no legal authority to enforce its demands. The more appropriate course, he argued, would have been for Armstrong to have hired an able lawyer, as socialist minister O. E. Enfield would do. However, given Armstrong's views that government was the instrument of the devil and that Christians did not go to court, it was not likely that he would have sought the advice of an attorney. Moreover, he had little to no understanding of government, constitutional law, civil rights, or state and local government. He, therefore, was without defense; what would be would be.

Nor did Armstrong have a sense of modern history. In August 1918, rudimen-tary knowledge of Europe and its past would have suggested that World War I was in its waning stage and that economic prosperity would doubtlessly follow. Cordell Christian, debt free and anticipating the 1918–19 academic year to be its best, was well positioned to benefit from a postwar world. The school had been exonerated by the state defense council, and it was strongly supported by Cordell's business community. Armstrong, however, saw the school as a projection of himself, and since he was done, so too was the school, "a martyr for the convictions of its faculty and board." He even acted upon that premise, when, with the permission of the board, he removed the science equipment and library books to Harper College the following year. And he never visited Cordell again.[40]

The Influence of Cordell Christian College

During Cordell Christian College's eleven years, the institution had a profound impact on the history of Churches of Christ in Oklahoma. Clearly, it established the tradition of institutionalized Christian education in Oklahoma, now carried on by Oklahoma Christian University at Edmond. Also, the reflective, rational and irenic theology of Armstrong and his faculty—apparent especially in the *Gospel Herald*—shaped numerous congregations in western Oklahoma known for their unity, sympathy, studiousness, good works, and apocalyptic vision of the kingdom of God. Cordell College also prepared scores of preachers and leaders who impacted the kingdom locally as well as globally, including S. J. Tipton (founder of Tipton Home), Dow Merritt (a missionary in Africa for fifty years), and O. D. Bixler (missionary to Japan and cofounder of Ibaraki Christian College).[41] The college, moreover, contributed substantially to the evangelization of western Oklahoma. The weekly and summer preaching of Armstrong and his colleagues encouraged and enlarged established congregations and helped plant new ones across all of Oklahoma, but especially in the west.

Finally, Cordell College's response to U.S. involvement in World War I spoke to a divided Church of Christ constituency on the issue of pacifism. In many Stone-Campbell churches, it was deeply engrained in their souls. After all, of the 1,060 objectors to the war assigned alternate service by the U.S. government, only five denominations, known as "peace churches," claimed more persons than Churches of Christ (31).[42] But as the enlistment decisions of the student body demonstrated, not all members took that position. The same was true of a significant number of Oklahoma church members, including such notables as U. G. Wilkinson, widely known for his objection to theological modernism, socialism, and evolution, and for his political patriotism. Of World War I, he said, "There is no alternative but to carry the war . . . to a successful termination."

At least, he argued, "let us cease our opposition to the wise policies of the lawful rulers of our country, and find some way . . . to do our part in assisting in the struggle for human rights and liberties."[43]

Another notable preacher, J. H. Lawson, would minister through a private agency for soldiers stationed at Camp Bowie near Fort Worth. The widest circulating church periodical in Oklahoma, the *Firm Foundation*, held a non-pacifist view toward the war also. So too did a sister college, Abilene Christian, at least to the extent that it hosted a company of the Student Army Training Corp, an early ROTC program, on its campus. It was no surprise, then, that most draft-age Church of Christ men in Oklahoma registered, went into the military, and fought for their country.[44]

Robert Wallace Officer (1845–1930), a native of East Tennessee, took the Stone-Campbell movement to the Chickasaw and Choctaw Nations beginning in 1881. His Indian Mission continued through 1901, when he retired to take up a different mission in West Texas. *Photograph from F. D. Srygley, ed.,* Biographies and Sermons: A Collection of Original Sermons by Different Men, with a Biographical Sketch of Each Man Accompanying His Sermon [1898].

James S. Standley (1841–1904), Choctaw by blood, was a graduate of the Kentucky Military Institute, an officer in the Confederate Army, and a member of the Mississippi bar. Standley and his family removed to Indian Territory in 1872. Subsequently, he settled in Atoka, where he practiced law, published a weekly newspaper, represented the Choctaws in Washington, D.C., and was a leader in the Stone-Campbell church. *Photograph courtesy of Atoka County Museum, Atoka, Oklahoma*

Opposite, top. Meta Chestnutt Sager (1863–1948), a native North Carolinian, went to Indian Territory as a Stone-Campbell educational missionary in 1889. At Minco, Chickasaw Nation, she organized a community school and then El Meta Bond College. *Photograph courtesy of Marilyn McGinnis, Glendale, California*

El Meta Bond College, Minco, Indian Territory, was constructed in 1894–95. The imposing central building of the college was three stories tall and housed the school's administrative offices, classrooms, and dorm rooms through 1920. *Photograph courtesy of Marilyn McGinnis, Glendale, California*

Sunny South School awards ceremony, ca. 1892. Under the watchful eye of Meta Chestnutt, R. L. Officer (*right*) and T. B. Larimore (*left*) present awards to scholars attending the Sunny South mission school, then located in Minco. *Photograph courtesy of Marilyn McGinnis, Glendale, California*

Opposite, top. S. R. Cassius (1853–1931) and his family embraced the Stone-Campbell movement in the early 1880s. Born into slavery, Cassius came to Oklahoma Territory in 1891 and spent the next thirty years trying to realize the promise of the "Land of the Fair God," most notably by establishing Tohee Industrial School for African Americans east of Guthrie. *Photograph courtesy of Disciples of Christ Historical Society, Bethany, West Virginia*

Opposite, bottom. John H. Lawson (1866–1934), a native of Arkansas, began his evangelistic ministry in the Comanche-Kiowa Reservation in southwestern Oklahoma following its opening to white settlement in 1902. Subsequently, he practiced law, served a few months as president of Cordell Christian College, accepted an appointment as an assistant attorney general for the state of Oklahoma, and served with the U.S. Army as a chaplain. *Photograph from Harriett Helm Nichol and C. R. Nichol, comps.,* Gospel Preachers Who Blazed the Trail *(1911; Reprint, Austin, Tex.: Firm Foundation, 1950).*

J. N. Armstrong (1870–1944), a native Tennessean, was highly educated and widely respected as a preacher. An experienced administrator, Armstrong served as the second president of Cordell Christian College between 1908 and 1918. *Photograph courtesy of Sweet Publishing, Austin, Texas*

Opposite, top. The Tenth and Francis Streets Church of Christ was first organized in 1901. This initial Oklahoma City Church of Christ congregation worshipped in a frame building located on the northwest corner of Tenth and Francis Streets. In 1935, the congregation constructed an adjacent Bible school building of buff brick, and then four years later replaced the frame building with a buff brick auditorium that seated 1,300, as seen here. *Photograph courtesy of Seminole Pointe Church of Christ, Edmond, Oklahoma*

Opposite, bottom. The Tenth and Rockford Streets Church of Christ in Tulsa was organized by 1916, but it did not begin construction of its own building at Tenth and Rockford until 1922, and it was not completed until 1928. The current building enjoys subsequent additions. *From the author's collection*

Cordell Christian College campus after it reopened as Western Oklahoma Christian College in 1921. Housing the administrative offices, classrooms, and auditorium, the three-story building on the left was completed in 1907. The wood building on the right was constructed simultaneously as a dormitory first for boys and then for girls. *Photograph courtesy of Oklahoma Historical Society, Oklahoma City, Oklahoma, 2012.201.B1404.0171*

Irene Young Mattox (1881–1970) and her family moved to Oklahoma from Texas in 1914, taking up residence in Oklahoma City in 1920. A highly respected teacher of women's Bible classes among Churches of Christ, she was also active in PTA, WCTU, and myriad child health and welfare programs. In the 1930s, she served as director of the Bureau of Social Services for Oklahoma County and was a political associate of gubernatorial candidate General William Key. *Photograph courtesy of the Helen and Norvel Young family*

Opposite, bottom left. O. E. Enfield (1882–1961) and his family moved to Day County, Oklahoma Territory, in 1897. Following his baptism, he became a much-respected Stone-Campbell evangelist. Enfield also embraced socialism, opposed participation in World War I, was judged guilty of espionage, and ran for public office in Oklahoma on the Socialist ticket. Over time, he abandoned his Christian faith. *Photograph courtesy of Barbara Enfield Patterson*

Opposite, bottom right. U. G. Wilkinson (1863–1925) migrated with his parents and siblings from Missouri to the Chickasaw Nation in 1887. He settled between Duncan and Comanche, where, for a time, he taught school before passing the bar and practicing law in Duncan. He soon gave that up for full-time preaching among Churches of Christ and writing books in which he strongly criticized socialism and pacifism. *Photograph from Harriett Helm Nichol and C. R. Nichol, comps.,* Gospel Preachers Who Blazed the Trail *(1911; Reprint, Austin, Tex.: Firm Foundation, 1950).*

The Wallace–Webber debate was held at the Oklahoma City Coliseum in 1937. The five-evening debate drew a daily audience of eight thousand from seven states. *Photograph courtesy of Center for Restoration Studies, Brown Library, Abilene Christian University, Abilene, Texas*

Oklahoma Christian University campus. Established first in Bartlesville, OCU moved its campus to Oklahoma City in 1957. Since then, little has had more influence on Churches of Christ in Oklahoma than the school. *Photograph courtesy of Oklahoma Christian University Archives, Oklahoma City, Oklahoma*

Opposite, top left. Foy E. Wallace Jr. (1896–1969) was probably the most noted evangelist, debater, and editor among Churches of Christ of his generation. After 1935, he considered Oklahoma City his home and the Tenth and Francis Church of Christ his home church. He was particularly offended by the doctrines of premillennialism and pacifism. *Photograph courtesy of Gospel Advocate Company, Nashville, Tennessee*

Opposite, top right. Marshall Keeble (1878–1968) was one of the most notable African American evangelists among Churches of Christ in the twentieth century. His work helped establish the black church in Oklahoma in the 1930s. *Photograph courtesy of Disciples of Christ Historical Society, Bethany, West Virginia*

Marian Guinn sued the elders of the Collinsville, Oklahoma, Church of Christ in 1984 for withdrawing from her for what they considered to be unbiblical behavior. The Tulsa County District Court ruled in her favor. The state supreme court, however, modified that decision and remanded the case back to the trial court for further adjudication. Rather than take that route, the parties settled out of court. *Photograph courtesy of the Tulsa World.*

Opposite, top left. James O. Baird (1920–98) served as president of Oklahoma Christian University from 1954 to 1974 and thereafter as chancellor. Baird made the college a bastion of conservative politics and religion. *Photograph courtesy of Oklahoma Christian University Archives, Oklahoma City, Oklahoma*

Opposite, top right. Hugo McCord (1911–2004) was a much-respected preacher and teacher who served Oklahoma Christian University as an administrator and Bible faculty member from 1954 until his retirement in 1980. *Photograph courtesy of the Oklahoma Historical Society, Oklahoma City, Oklahoma, 2012.201.B0421.0013a*

Opposite, bottom. George S. Benson (1898–1991) was born in Day County, Oklahoma Territory. A missionary to China, president of Harding College, and chancellor of Oklahoma Christian College, Benson sought to fund the colleges with which he worked by promoting the free market economy and conservative political programs. He is seen here addressing Boeing Company executives. *Photograph courtesy of Center for Restoration Studies, Brown Library, Abilene Christian University, Abilene, Texas*

⑦

ORVILLE E. ENFIELD AS A
CHURCH OF CHRIST SOCIALIST

Between 1914 and 1917, socialism was a major political force in Oklahoma. Per capita, the Socialist Party had more members in the Sooner State than in any other state in the Union. According to historian Jim Bissett, several factors helped to explain this phenomenon. The severe agricultural crisis that gripped the South was clearly an issue, but that alone did not account for the unique power of socialism in Oklahoma. Of more relevance was the previous experience of party leadership in cooperative activities, as in the cases of the Farmer's Alliance and the Populist Party. But lending special force to Oklahoma socialism was its ability to use the communitarian principles of Christianity, those of the "Upside Down Kingdom," to make Marxian truths sensible to Oklahoma farmers.[1] As a result, socialism within the state was essentially a rural movement that incorporated many of the practices, including the camp meeting, and the language, if not the faith, of zealous Christianity.

As a general rule, members, ministers, and editors of Churches of Christ kept political and social issues beyond the pulpit and pages of the press. Influential in this practice were the views of Barton Stone and David Lipscomb, who, as we have seen, taught that Christians were not citizens of any worldly kingdom, only of God's kingdom. Members were free to concern themselves with worldly issues on their own time, as it were, but that concern was to stop at the door of the church building. Even the flag of the United States was excluded.

Socialism's Appeal

Despite the established tradition and the best efforts of the theological descendants of Stone and Lipscomb, socialism with its economic, social, political, and religious agenda invaded Churches of Christ in Oklahoma. That should not be a surprise, for the movement appealed especially to the economically deprived, and, with rare exception, Church of Christ members were among the rural poor. In old Indian Territory, that meant that one in two of its members would have been tenant farmers, their income would have averaged only two hundred dollars per year, food would have been insufficient, housing would have been poor, and their health would have been problematic.

Oscar Ameringer, a socialist organizer from Oklahoma City, left a powerful image of these folks. In 1907, he visited parts of southeastern Oklahoma and wrote of "toothless old women sucking infants on their withered breasts"; an "hospitable old hostess . . . [with] her hands covered with rags and eczema," who apologized for the quality of her biscuits because she could not knead the dough as it ought to be; youngsters "emaciated" by hookworms, malnutrition, and pellagra, "who had lost their second teeth before they were twenty years old"; and tottering old men holding infants of their fourteen-year-old wives.[2] No wonder these rural poor found the socialist message so promising, especially when it was presented as compatible with their preferred understanding of Christianity. Among them was a strong belief that a man could not "be a Christian and oppose Socialism."[3]

Woody Guthrie certainly felt that way. Born in 1912, Guthrie grew up in Okemah, Oklahoma. One of the state's most noted sons, he was grounded in the agrarian legacy of protest manifested by Ameringer, but he also embraced the millennial Christian tradition that Jesus would drive the money changers out of the temple and that the poor and meek would inherit the earth. In the early 1930s, Guthrie was baptized by a Church of Christ preacher, Eulys McKenzie, in Pampa, Texas. He was never much of a churchgoer, but he read deeply in scripture, often quoted it, and put his take on the biblical message to music. His song "They Laid Jesus Christ in His Grave" made the Savior a rural radical who rallied working people until "the bankers and the preachers and the rich men and the soldiers" nailed him to a tree. Once when asked to name the people he most admired, he said, "Will Rogers and Jesus Christ" (the response of a true Oklahoman).[4]

More representative of Oklahomans who embraced Christian socialism was Orville E. Enfield of Ellis County. Born in McPherson, Kansas, in 1882, Enfield moved with his family to Ochiltree, Texas, when he was five years old.[5] There, they lived in a sod house in a country dominated by ranches and cows. Two years later, the family returned to southeastern Kansas to a homestead in Cherokee County. Enfield's father found work in the strip coal mines near Weir; he himself worked in those same mines for some five years.

In January 1897, the family relocated to Day County, Oklahoma Territory, now Ellis County, Oklahoma, taking a quarter-section homestead on Packsaddle Creek near Grand, the county seat. These were hard times for the family, with Enfield and his six siblings forced to gather buffalo bones to sell in Woodward for cash to buy essentials like flour, salt, beans, and sugar.

In October 1901, at the age of nineteen, Enfield eloped with sixteen-year-old Margaret (Maggie) Mercer. Maggie's father had disapproved of the proposed union. The young couple went to Texas for their wedding and returned to Enfield's parents' home to set up housekeeping. The following year, their first child was stillborn, a traumatic event from which Enfield and Maggie never really recovered. Through 1924, seven other children were born to the union.

A Baptized Believer and Preacher

The death of their first child caused the Enfields to seek comfort among people of faith. In October 1902, he and Maggie were baptized at Higgins, Texas. Eighteen months later he was set apart to preach the gospel by the Christian Church at Enon, Texas. Shortly, he had baptized his parents and siblings and went "far and wide" preaching the "glad tidings of great joy." He was recognized as one of the most promising young evangelists in Churches of Christ in western Oklahoma.

To sustain his preaching, Enfield took a position as a teacher of a one-room school in the Grand community of Ellis County at a salary of twenty dollars per month for three months. He had passed the teacher-qualifying examination after no more than three months as a student in a country school and some serious independent study. Yet, at the age of twenty-five, he later recalled, he did not know the difference "between an adverb and a proverb." He determined to do something about it. In late 1907, Enfield loaded his young family and brother in a wagon with several months of provisions and journeyed to Weatherford to attend Southwestern Normal School. There followed five months of serious study, during which he also preached for the Weatherford Church of Christ. The birth of a baby, the death of his mother, and serious financial difficulties, however, caused him to terminate his studies and to take his family and brother back to the Packsaddle farm. There, and across the state line into Texas, he resumed his position as a "flogger of urchins," he said, using the words of Ichabod Crane, for eight years.[6]

Enfield also became a noted agriculturalist. Over time, he and his family accumulated several quarter sections of land in Ellis County. On them, he ranged a sizeable herd of hogs that, once fattened on shin-oak acorns, his children drove to market in Gage. Subsequently, he exchanged the Packsaddle property for some on nearby Pony Creek. It was on this land that the Enfields developed terraces, built stock ponds, set shelter belts, erected "post lots" (holding pens), and constructed rock retainer walls. He also planted noncash soil-building crops and experimented with salt brine and thistles.[7]

Enfield's ability to double task won him the admiration of many in Churches of Christ. Some leaders did not believe that a farmer-preacher could do the gospel justice. According to D. T. Broadus, the noted Kansas evangelist, Enfield easily gave the lie to that assumption. He demonstrated very effectively that a man could "live on a farm and do very efficient work as a preacher."[8]

A Busy Evangelist

Indeed, Enfield was very busy as an evangelist. He not only preached almost every Sunday but also had a fall and winter meeting/revival schedule that took him into Texas, Kansas, Missouri, and Arkansas, not to mention Oklahoma. He also was an active debater, engaging agnostics, Adventists, Baptists, and anti-socialists in spirited discussion. In 1914 at Arapaho, he defended the Bible as of divine origin so well that the *Gospel Herald* labeled him as one of the coming defenders of the truth. Moreover, it was also impressed by his debating style, which did not respond in kind to ridicule and mud-slinging.[9]

Enfield also frequently published reports and mini-sermons in brotherhood periodicals. In the *Gospel Herald*, where he appeared most regularly, his articles challenged the tendency of some to substitute a social lodge for the church, showed concern over the growth of agnosticism, and compared and contrasted in a four-part piece the responsibilities of the evangelist to the church and the church to the evangelist. Enfield, who had real talent as a poet, also published several poems, the subjects of which were generally love and death.[10]

Since his ordination as a minister in 1904, Enfield had taken his religion and relationship with Churches of Christ very seriously. Nonetheless, he lived in some tension with his faith community. This was especially apparent during his student days in Weatherford, when resources ran short and food was scarce. The congregation of Churches of Christ where he preached each Sunday demonstrated little sensitivity to the crisis, although some ladies did call upon the family with food baskets, especially when his baby was born. That was not sufficient, however, to keep the wolf from the door. Enfield was offered a position at the First Christian Church in Weatherford at the regular salary of fifty dollars per month. He declined the offer, however, in part because of the differences between the two communions (Sunday schools and instruments of music) and his loyalty to Churches of Christ. But most importantly was his belief that regular salaries would commercialize preaching, and thus prostitute the work of the true evangelist. He wanted none of that.[11]

Although Enfield later admitted that he had not made the needs of his family known to the Weatherford church, he left with hard feelings against the congregation. Ignorance of his situation and "avarice," or the congregation's love of money, had held it back. The lack of concern for social issues within the church he also attributed to avarice rather than to doctrinal purity. What happened to him at Elk City was a case in point. There, a biblical and closely reasoned sermon on the evils of usury led to a reprimand by the elders and an injunction to preach only the gospel.

A Socialist Partisan Too

Given the ambivalence of Churches of Christ toward social issues, Enfield's reading of *Utopia* by Sir Thomas Moore and *Looking Backward* by Edward Bellamy exposed him to a world of possibilities not considered by the church. But a close reading of the apostle Luke, especially Acts 2:44–45, suggested that congregants should be open to such things as sharing of possessions. As he concluded, the church of the New Testament had a significant social agenda, concerned as it was with the poor, the powerless, and the peacemaker. In winter of 1912, while teaching in a school south of Higgins, Texas, Enfield put all of this together and determined to identify himself as a socialist, much to the consternation of his father, in addition to a Church of Christ preacher. He saw absolutely no contradiction between the two roles, for in both he acted as an evangelist, speaking to protracted gospel meetings and to revival-like socialist encampments. Moreover, the essence of his message to both audiences was not all that different—love and compassion, responsibility to one's fellow man, justice and peace, this world and the coming world.[12]

For a time, Enfield's blending of the two roles worked reasonably well. Churches of Christ in western Oklahoma continued to receive him as both a speaker and writer, but also as something of a curiosity.[13] This was fairly remarkable in light of the growing opposition within the church to socialism as a godless heresy. The influential Henry Warlick spoke of socialism's "direful influences" and its "strong delusion" and concluded that it was not true that Christians could be good socialists.[14] U. G. Wilkinson, who lived less than two hundred miles from Enfield, was just as skeptical. Published in 1915, Wilkinson's book *Why I Am Not a Socialist* had circulated widely in Oklahoma and Texas. To him, socialism was like a comet, "a bright deformity on high, the monster of the upper sky."[15] Sensing that his welcome in Churches of Christ was increasingly problematic, Enfield read deeply in the law to prepare himself for a potential legal or lawmaking career. In 1915, he sat for the Oklahoma state bar exam and passed it with the second-highest score in his cohort.

The socialists were impressed with this additional qualification. But they were even more impressed with Enfield's knowledge of history and economics and his ability to speak of social issues using the rhetoric of Christianity. Consequently, the Socialist Party made him one of its principal organizers in western Oklahoma. In 1916, it even nominated him as a candidate for the U.S. House of Representatives from western Oklahoma (District 7).[16]

Churches of Christ in Oklahoma and World War I

Enfield's ability to walk the narrow line between Christianity and socialism became questionable the more the United States got involved in World War I. In 1914 when fighting broke out in Europe, President Woodrow Wilson worked diligently to keep the country out of the war. His success in doing so secured his election to a second term in 1916. In all of this, he found support from that Stone-Lipscomb segment of Churches of Christ that on principle opposed war and advocated pacifism, of which J. N. Armstrong, the president of Cordell Christian College and editor of the *Gospel Herald*, was notably representative. The Socialist Party, moreover, enthusiastically supported Wilson's position. In 1917, much of that support vanished when the reelected president reversed his position and committed U.S. resources—first materials and then men—to making the world safe for democracy.

The pacifist leaders of Churches of Christ, especially those who read and wrote for the Nashville-based *Gospel Advocate*, were critical of Wilson's policies. Commanded not to kill, they argued, Christians were obligated not to take up arms against another human being. There was no such thing as a just war. Christians might possibly serve in noncombatant roles, but to the pacifists no service at all was preferable. That position was the majority position among Churches of Christ in Oklahoma and other southern states until the *Gospel Advocate* almost overnight switched its editorial position to support the war in 1917. The reversal reflected practical rather than theological considerations. The U.S. attorney general for Middle Tennessee had threatened to prosecute the editors for sedition if they continued to publish articles that discouraged young men to sign up for the draft.[17]

Not all leaders and congregations of Churches of Christ lamented the change. The editors and readers of the *Firm Foundation*, which was published in Austin, Texas, and circulated widely in Oklahoma, had rejected pacifism and embraced patriotism. Less committed, if committed at all, to the notion of citizenship in an apocalyptic kingdom of God, the *Foundation* editors extolled love of country, active patriotism (including support of the draft), and theories of just war. Many important Oklahoma church leaders held similar views, including J. W. Crumley Sr., who played a significant role in the demise of Cordell Christian College over this very issue.

O. E. Enfield, so far as is known, never commented on this reversal of opinion, if not theology, occurring in Churches of Christ. Surely he knew of the pacifistic stream that ran deep in the Stone-Campbell movement, but he also had to know that many heirs to the movement in the face of war had adopted stances agreeable to men killing men in a European war. This surely offended his Christian as well as his socialist sensibilities. So in his role as a socialist organizer and a Christian evangelist he spoke out against it.

In May 1917, at the Church of Christ in Canadian, Texas, Enfield pleaded with his hearers to "obey God rather than men" and to remember the commandment "Thou shalt not kill." His message was not well received. The elders sent him a letter asking that he never come to the Canadian church again, which he never did. In August later that year at the Christian Church in Seiling, Oklahoma, he pled with his hearers not to be deceived and plunge into the false thing called "war to end all wars." He also argued, "If you are going to conscript the youth of the land to jam them into the hell holes and the shell holes of Flanders field[,] then in the name of all that is fair and just, conscript the wealth of the nation to pay the boys and to pay them well and do not bind the nation to defray the expense of the holocaust."[18]

Arrest and Trial

In the foyer of the Seiling church building after his address, federal agents arrested Enfield for his seditionist language, handcuffing him as if he were "a Dillinger" and whisking him away to a jail in Woodward, Oklahoma. Subsequently, the county attorney and the sheriff of Dewey County found great satisfaction "in not only lying" to his wife as to where he had been taken but in also telling her that they hoped that Enfield would be hanging from a telephone pole when she found him. On August 16, 1917, Enfield was arraigned in Woodward before a federal magistrate "for making anti-administration speeches." He waived a hearing and returned to jail absent a $10,000 bond. Friends ultimately raised the bail, and he was released pending trial.[19]

Resistance

What seemed like an ugly and irrational application of the wartime sedition laws, as applied both to Enfield and the faculty and students of Cordell Christian College, was partially explained by the hysteria generated by the Green Corn Rebellion then occurring on the other side of the state in old Indian Territory. Reacting to usurious interest rates charged by landlords and bankers and to ridiculously low prices received for corn and cotton crops, working farmers had, with the encouragement of the Working Class Union (WCU), utilized the courts and "night riders" to get some relief. Their extralegal activity intimidated authorities and local businessmen. Passage of the draft law on June 5, 1917, only exacerbated the tenant farmers' anxiety. WCU organizers told them that in addition to high interest and low prices they were now going to have to go to Europe to fight a rich man's war.[20]

Along the South Canadian River in Pottawatomie, Seminole, Hughes, and Pontotoc Counties, hundreds of impoverished farmers took matters into their own hands. Gathering arms and ammunition, they threatened to burn bridges, cut telephone and telegraph wires, destroy oil pipelines, and march on Washington, D.C. When asked how they expected to feed themselves on that march, the farmers said they would eat the green corn then ripening in the fields. Given the strength of Churches of Christ in the counties involved, it stands to reason that not just a few of their members numbered among the rebels. For sure one of their leaders was a minister of Churches of Christ. Local officials, however, quickly staunched the actual rebellion after a brief gun battle in Seminole County and by arresting 450 suspects and holding them at the Oklahoma State Penitentiary in McAlester.[21]

The Socialist Party, although very active in southeastern Oklahoma, had tried to distance itself from the Green Corn Rebellion, but with marginal success.[22] No doubt the officers who arrested Enfield saw a relationship between his message and the action of the rebels just two hundred miles away. If they did not, certainly the presiding judge, John H. Cotterall, made the connection when the case came up for trial in the federal court in Oklahoma City in June 1918.[23]

Enfield Tried

In the trial, Enfield was charged with conspiracy to resist the selective service law by force of arms in Ellis County. His lectures and sermons, many of which had been published in the *Arnett Leader* and *Ellis County Socialist*, evidenced his sedition, charged U.S. attorney John A. Fain. Enfield admitted speaking against the war, but he denied that there was a connection between his words and any presumed armed rebellion in Ellis County, dubbed "the Oklahoma Outbreak" by the press, which, if planned, never materialized.[24]

The case went to the jury on June 6, 1918. The panel of peers was unable to reach a decision after ten hours of deliberation. Fearing a hung jury, Judge Cotterall delivered an extemporaneous charge to the jurors the next morning, reminding them of the seriousness of the offense and the importance of a clear decision.[25] The directive worked, and the jury found Enfield guilty on two counts, on one of which the judge sentenced the defendant to twenty years and on the other six years in the federal penitentiary at Fort Leavenworth, Kansas. He also assessed a $500 fine. Finally, Cotterall set bail at $20,000, the terms of which Enfield's friends promptly met, thereby releasing him to prepare an appeal.[26] It also enabled him, incidentally, to campaign as a Socialist candidate for the U.S. House of Representatives, in an election that occurred in November. Opposition was stiff. The Socialists were audacious to nominate a "convicted disloyalist . . . in these critical times," said the *Clinton Chronicle*. "The loyal voters of this congressional district should make a special effort to see that this man is the worst beaten man ever presenting himself to the voters of Oklahoma." And that was pretty much what happened, with Enfield receiving just over 12 percent of the 18,757 votes cast.[27]

Attorneys H. D. Adkins of Amarillo, Texas, and Charles Swindall of Wood-ward, Oklahoma (a Republican who won a seat as U.S. representative from Oklahoma and later served as a member of the Supreme Court of Oklahoma), represented Enfield in the appeals process. Both believed in his sincerity of purpose although they did deplore his judgment. From the federal Circuit Court of Appeals in Saint Louis, the attorneys won a ruling reversing Judge Cotterall's decision and remanding the case for a new trial.

In 1920, the case went to trial for a second time in the federal court at Enid. On this occasion, the jury deliberated for only ten minutes and voted to acquit. For Enfield, a long, dark night had ended, accompanied by the restoration of personal integrity, faith in the human family, and confidence in the judicial system.[28]

Enfield as an Elected Official

Enfield remained a faithful Socialist for the rest of his life (1961). He ran on the party's ticket for the office of governor in 1922, an election that Jack Walton won. He ran a second time for U.S. Congress in 1934, but again without success. By that time, the Socialist Party in Oklahoma was all but dead, and had been for at least a decade. In 1936, he ran for county attorney in Ellis County and won with a plurality of votes, but as an Independent. He could not serve, however, until his membership in the Oklahoma state bar, which had lapsed, was reinstated.[29] He held the county attorney post for fourteen years, when he was elected, again as an Independent, as Ellis County judge, a position he retained for another ten years.

The Socialist Party may have weakened over time, but Enfield's commitment to socialist causes never waned. In the 1920s, for example, he spent time in at least two socialist-inspired utopian colonies, one in California and the other in Louisiana. In the 1930s, he was a board member and business manager of the Shadid Community Hospital in Elk City, which, with its famous prepaid fee structure, was an early-day HMO that the American Medical Association severely censured as socialistic if not communistic. And then in 1944 Enfield petitioned President Franklin Roosevelt to revoke his administration's decision to deport Mrs. Earl Browder, the wife of the leader of the Communist Party in the United States.[30]

Enfield Parts Company with Churches of Christ

Enfield did not hold his relationship with Churches of Christ as meriting that kind of commitment, however. By the end of 1917, he judged himself as no longer "orthodox" and terminated his preaching, debating, and evangelistic work among Churches of Christ. Sometime later he abandoned his faith in the Bible as the revealed word of God. By 1935, he believed that the God of the Bible was cruel, unjust, and untrustworthy, or so he wrote to Frank Winters, an old Elk City friend, who was then an elder in the Tenth and Francis Streets Church of Christ in Oklahoma City. Enfield would seem to have still believed in a deity, but that god was the creator of beauty and love as revealed in nature and poetry. He was even a minister of that deity, having been ordained by the Los Angeles–based Humanist Society of Friends in 1940. In 1954, a letter of his to one of the elders of the Reydon Church of Christ made clear that his views had not changed from those articulated some two decades earlier.[31]

It is not hard to understand why Enfield parted company with Churches of Christ. Its leaders and members found socialism and even their traditional pacifism as antithetical to biblical truth. Enfield did not. When he was in the dock for having preached peace and not war, few if any from Churches of Christ stepped forward to support him. Many socialists did. Enfield came to see truth as accessible beyond the pages of scripture. Members of Churches of Christ did not. And so they parted company, although that parting did not include all members of his family. Many of them retained their affiliation with Churches of Christ.

8

DEVELOPING A SENSE OF SELF
1920–1945

From statehood through World War II, Churches of Christ in Oklahoma desired little more than an identity as faithful servants of the kingdom of God. Their cousins in the Stone-Campbell movement, the Disciples of Christ, were slightly embarrassed by them; most of their membership lived and worshipped in rural areas; their theology promoted pacifism in wartime; their evangelism relied on contentious debates. The years between 1920 and 1945, however, marked a turning point for the Churches of Christ. The communion developed a sense of self as it struggled to live out the "simple gospel" in face of the social, economic, political, and religious challenges of the Jazz Age, the Great Depression, World War II, and theological modernism, all within a context specific to Oklahoma.

Post–World War I Oklahoma

Oklahoma had a population of 2 million in 1920; a decade later it counted nearly 2.4 million residents. Undergirding that growth was a booming economy based on oil production. New fields like those in Seminole and Oklahoma City pushed state production to 762,000 barrels per day, making it either the first- or second-highest producing state in the nation.[1] Agriculture remained important to the state's economy, but mounting surpluses depressed prices and forced farmers to view the future with concern. So too did the looming Dust Bowl, which in the 1930s ravished agricultural land in the western part of the state and contributed to an exodus of population from Oklahoma (some 300,000 from it and surrounding states) that took thirty years to regain. There was also a reshuffling of population within the state primarily from small towns to urban centers. This ebb and flow left its mark on every aspect of the state's economy, social structure, and church life.[2]

Oklahomans also wrestled with the social, intellectual, and political issues that dominated the national landscape. Among these were the overly flexible moral standards of the Jazz Age, particularly the consumption of alcoholic beverages, which the majority of Oklahomans opposed. Indeed, the state had entered the Union as dry and was quick to ratify the Eighteenth Amendment to the U.S. constitution, which was intended to make all states dry. Oklahomans spent the 1920s and later decades trying to keep bootleggers out of the state and make prohibition an effective law.[3]

Like the rest of the nation, Oklahoma suffered from political anxieties in the twenties and thirties. The Farmer-Labor Reconstruction League replaced the communists and the socialists, playing a significant role in electing Jack Walton as governor in 1922. Greatly disappointed with the election, the Ku Klux Klan launched a successful campaign to impeach Walton. The electorate was still roiling six years later when a large majority refused to vote for Al Smith as president of the United States, largely because he was Catholic.[4]

The troubled race relations of other southern states were also apparent in Oklahoma. Civil law had disenfranchised African Americans, relegated black students to schools that were separate and unequal to white schools, and imposed a Jim Crow social system of separate neighborhoods, lodging, water fountains, public transportation seats, and hospital rooms, among other things. And a large Ku Klux Klan roamed there to see that the laws were followed.[5]

Theological modernism, so influential nationally, impacted Oklahoma too. Of special concern was the Darwinian theory of evolution, which cast doubt on the traditional Genesis account of creation. So-called higher criticism was equally troubling in that it challenged the traditional view of biblical inspiration. Those who opposed modernism were known as "fundamentalists," the dominate religious group in the state.[6]

Of course, World War II had a major impact on the state in the 1940s. Some 193,000 Oklahomans enlisted in the armed forces, while an additional 300,000 men were included through Selective Service. Of that number, some 11,000 men were wounded and 6,500 were slain. Because of the war, twenty-eight army installations, thirteen naval bases, four air bases, and eight German prisoner-of-war camps dotted the state. Also, it brought to the state thousands of soldiers, sailors, and airmen who trained on Oklahoma bases. On the home front, Oklahomans produced weapons of war, performed vital services, and provided vast quantities of metals, fuel, grains, and meat. They also submitted to a comprehensive system of rationing and controlled prices and rents. All Oklahomans felt the burden of the war.[7]

So too did Churches of Christ. Congregations near military installations (Lawton, Altus, Clinton, Enid, Midwest City, Norman, Muskogee, and Tulsa) experienced vibrant growth, while the rural congregations contracted even further. Virtually all provided one or more servicemen for the armed forces, and many buried one or more of those men. At least two from Oklahoma Churches of Christ served as chaplains: Henry C. Dixon at Camp Gruber near Muskogee and John D. Boren at different locations in the United States and South Pacific. Boren was the first Church of Christ minister to become a chaplain in the U.S. military.[8] In all of this change, church leaders struggled to define and perpetuate Churches of Christ as a religious organization between the wars.

The Church of Christ in the Eyes of the WPA

During the Great Depression, the Works Progress Administration (WPA) organized surveys of the different religious institutions of most states. Churches of Christ were one of the communions surveyed in Oklahoma. The WPA estimated them to have had a membership of 40,000 in 1930. The largest number of their members resided in Muskogee County (1,289), Oklahoma County (1,196), and Tulsa County (1,142), at least according to the religious census of 1936.[9] The WPA surveyed 272 of the Church of Christ congregations in fifty counties. The surveyors found that the membership had no strong sense of self as an institution or a distinct religious organization.[10] Rather, they were merely a group of people who gathered weekly to engage in simple worship services patterned upon what they described as the New Testament example. They claimed, one surveyor wrote, "to practice what the apostles taught without addition or subtractions," and did not "believe in anything except Bible study and [the] Lord's Supper, and holding revivals."[11] Another wrote, "They have no pastor & anyone of them that wishes may talk at their services."[12] Their congregations were completely independent, answered to no council or assembly, and saw no strong reason to keep any records, even of membership. They clearly celebrated their democratic qualities.[13]

The survey also revealed that most Oklahoma Churches of Christ worshipped in modest buildings in the 1930s. Many still met in schoolhouses or other public facilities. If they had their own church building, it was generally wood-frame, painted white, with single entry doors at the front and rear. There were few exterior adornments on the buildings such as a bell-tower steeple. Roughly 10 percent of the buildings were constructed of brick, stone, tile, or concrete blocks, most of which were situated in urban centers.

Some of the practices of Churches of Christ struck the WPA surveyors as different, even quaint. Most notable was the use of a capella music. It caused one to report that the Berlin Church of Christ "did not believe in music," and another to comment that the Springdale Church of Christ had "no music just singing."[14] Surveyors also noted that Churches of Christ did not ordain their ministers and were "very particular about what their ministers [were] called," preferring "Elder" rather than "Reverend." Most of their preachers, the surveyors noted, were educated through "home study," although some had trained at schools like Cordell Christian College, Abilene Christian College, and Thorp Springs Christian College, the latter two in Texas. Also remarkable was that women did not exercise any leadership in the various congregations. Several surveyors found it strange that many congregations did not use printed literature to guide their Bible studies, only the scripture itself.[15]

In sum, the WPA surveyors found Churches of Christ in Oklahoma largely rural, fiercely independent, served by untrained ministers, called to restore the first-century church as revealed in the New Testament, students of scripture only, opposed to use of instrumental music in worship, and committed to a gospel that sought to save souls rather than reform society. Their portrait was not far off the mark.

Church Membership Increases

Oklahoma Churches of Christ were affected by the ebb and flow of the state's population between 1920 and 1945. Surely, the growth in the twenties helped fuel a 37 percent increase in church membership, from 21,700 to 34,645, double that of the state.[16] WPA conclusions notwithstanding, in the twenty-five years after World War I, Oklahoma congregations appear to have achieved a stronger sense of self and a measure of institutional maturity. The church benefited from rural to urban migration, planting in the 1920s permanent congregations in at least twenty-seven thriving towns where evangelistic work began for the first time and, in congregations of more than fifty members, survived into the twenty-first century,[17] twenty-eight more in the 1930s,[18] and thirty-four more in the 1940s.[19] The mass exodus from the state during the Dust Bowl, Depression, and world war did not alter the urban slant; indeed, it seemed to intensify the tilt. In Oklahoma City, one congregation became thirteen by 1945,[20] while in Tulsa one congregation became eight.[21] Sunday school attendance reflected the increase: the Tenth and Rockford congregation in Tulsa counted 410 and Tenth and Francis church in Oklahoma City counted 512 in the early 1930s.

But the U.S. government's *Census of Religious Bodies, 1936* reported a 25 percent decline in Oklahoma Church of Christ membership (down to 27,750) and a 46 percent decline in number of congregations.[22] Members of Churches of Christ in Oklahoma were part of the great exodus to California, and certainly that migration, as well as in-state relocation, explained the demise of many rural congregations and the rise of many urban churches. But the depopulation of Oklahoma by just 2.5 percent in the 1930s simply cannot explain a presumed 25 percent decline in membership in the same period. Doubtless, many Oklahoma congregations did not report data to the census bureau, and compilers did not incorporate into their analysis the data they had gathered.[23]

Part of the fellowship's vitality was due more to vigorous evangelism than demographic changes. The methods used did not vary significantly from those of previous decades. The eight-day, two-Sundays gospel meeting remained the technique of choice. Generally with the assistance of a talented song leader, evangelists spoke twice daily, trying to convict their audiences of sin and then provide an option for salvation via the instrumentality of baptism. Horace Busby, a Fort Worth evangelist, held one gospel meeting after another throughout Oklahoma with great effect. In 1931, at Tipton, for example, he baptized 107 and "restored" 40 more. Simultaneously, Foy E. Wallace Jr. was filling tents with as many as one thousand hearers and getting equally dramatic responses in Oklahoma City and Shawnee, to mention just two.[24]

Developing a Sense of Self via the Radio

Like other denominations, leaders and ministers of Oklahoma Churches of Christ also found radio to be an effective tool in explaining its practices. Radio came to the state in 1922 when WKY in Oklahoma City first went on the air; three years later what became KVOO in Tulsa started broadcasting. It is not clear which congregation initially utilized radio in its outreach—perhaps Ada with L. R. Wilson broadcasting over KADA as of 1932—but by the late 1930s there were not many stations in Oklahoma that did not carry a Church of Christ–generated program. These included stations at Oklahoma City and Tulsa, as well as Enid, Elk City, Ardmore, Lawton, Cordell, Ponca City, Norman, and Ada. The potential audience numbered hundreds of thousands. Even inmates at McAlester seemed to be listening: in August 1932, seventy-six of them were baptized by a Church of Christ minister.[25] Radio remained a vital element in the church's expression of self into the twenty-first century, best illustrated by the *SEARCH* program sponsored by the Edmond Church of Christ. Of course, after World War II television would become the evangelistic tool de jure.

Via Lectureships

Church leaders continued to use regional gatherings of ministers, leaders, and laymen to further develop their sense of self. Generally identified as "lecture-ships," these were small and large gatherings where participants exchanged ideas regarding ministry, enjoyed special expositions of scripture, and drew inspiration from each other. Organized by John Allen Hudson, the minister at Tenth and Francis, one met for four days in Oklahoma City in January 1922.[26] A. R. Holton of the Central congregation in Norman organized similar meet-ings on the university campus as part of the work of the Oklahoma School of Religion at the University of Oklahoma in 1929 and 1932.[27] In 1934 and again in 1938, L. R. Wilson arranged a multiple-day lecture at the Tenth and Rockford congregation in Tulsa.[28] Meanwhile, congregations at Mangum, Drumright, and El Reno hosted day meetings in 1937; Lawton, in 1943; and Durant, in 1944. John Banister at Culbertson Heights in Oklahoma City organized other multiple-day meetings in 1944 (with thirty speakers) and 1949.[29] In some congregations, such as Sixth and Arlington in Lawton, annual lectures came to replace gospel meetings.

Via Missionaries

To undertake the support of a missionary working internationally suggested that Oklahoma Churches of Christ had developed a clearer sense of self as well as a worldview that extended beyond the local congregation. Surely this was the case of George S. Benson (1898–1991), a native of Dewey County, who took his bachelor's degree at Oklahoma A&M College. He was the first missionary representing Churches of Christ at large—not just Oklahoma—to go to China beginning in 1925. His decade of service there coincided with a turbulent political era where U.S. citizens were viewed as "foreign devils." Despite the discrimination, Benson founded the Canton Bible School and the *Oriental Christian* periodical. He and his family returned to the United States in 1936 when he agreed to succeed J. N.

Armstrong as president of Harding College in Searcy, Arkansas. Benson would later serve as chancellor of Oklahoma Christian College in Oklahoma City.[30]

As we will see, Oklahoma churches would send other missionaries to Asia, Africa, Australia, and Europe in the post–World War II era.

Via Church-Related Education

To burnish the church's sense of self in Oklahoma, Church of Christ leaders were eager to return Christian education to Cordell. Men like G. A. W. Fleming had been critical of President Armstrong's pacifist views and were dismayed when Armstrong and the board of trustees closed Cordell Christian College in mid-1918. Given the end of the Great War and the dissipation of passions associated with the military draft, he thought he saw a way to get the school reopened. Accordingly, he persuaded the old trustees to sell the property to the city of Cordell for a nominal sum. The city fathers then offered the property to Church of Christ members living in Cordell if they would assume the responsibility of reopening the institution.[31]

Western Oklahoma Christian College

A thirteen-member board of trustees assumed the obligation of managing the revived college. A. W. Lee, a prosperous Oklahoma City oilman who served as an elder of the Tenth and Francis Streets Church of Christ, was elected chairman. Lee's appointment to the board was a calculated effort to draw support from the more populated and prosperous central part of the state. Under Lee's leadership, the board immediately named the reconstituted school "Western Oklahoma Christian College"; instituted primary, secondary, and collegiate (the first two years) curriculums; and appointed Ira L. Winterrowd (1884–1959) as president.[32]

A Texas native, Winterrowd was a graduate of Nashville Bible School and held a BA degree from Southern Methodist University and an MA degree from the University of Oklahoma. He also studied at the Southern Conservatory of Music in Durham, North Carolina. He was an experienced teacher at the secondary as well as collegiate levels, including appointments at David Lipscomb College and Lockney Christian College. Winterrowd was also a veteran preacher.[33]

The curriculum offered by Western Oklahoma Christian College closely resembled that of its predecessor. All full-time, enrolled students were required to take a regular Bible course each term; history was important; English and expression were emphasized; and dramatics and music were highly valued. All students attended daily chapel. The curriculum differed from Cordell Christian in that it included competitive athletics: basketball, baseball, and, ultimately, football.[34]

The close relationship of the college to Churches of Christ did not change. The school hosted forums on issues important to the church. Faculty preached in Cordell and neighboring communities, and students regularly attended the services of the Cordell Church of Christ. Distributed as they were across the state, members of the board of trustees demonstrated to an even larger audience that Western Oklahoma Christian College advanced the cause of the church.[35]

At first, enrollments in the college were encouraging. In the inaugural year, 161 enrolled, while in the second year, 250 enrolled. Of course, the largest percentage of the students were in the primary department, but the 31 college freshmen in the 1922–23 academic year reflected considerable interest in the collegiate department. The gross enrollment dropped to 185 in Winterrowd's third year (1923–24) and to 132 in his fourth year, with the decline attributable in large part to the absence of girl's dormitories, which made all students day students. The decline in enrollment, of course, had budget implications, to the extent that it was often difficult to pay salaries. In an effort of establish a broader basis of support, Winterrowd called for members of Churches of Christ to meet at Oklahoma City in the fall of 1924. There, he emphasized the importance of Christian education and of a college in Oklahoma to meet that need. Western Oklahoma Christian College, however, could not meet the need without the help of church members across the state. Moreover, if additional support was not forthcoming, he would have to resign the presidency at the end of the academic year.[36]

The necessary additional support did not materialize. Indeed, some things got worse. The thirteen-member board of trustees dwindled to four: A. W. Lee; T. E. Burch, a banker from Wewoka; J. J. McCurley, a Cordell insurance man; and B. W. Grozier, a Cordell farmer. Rumors raced through the town and campus that the college would close. That did not happen, of course, but President Winterrowd, faithful to his word but also out of concern for his health, resigned effective the summer of 1925.[37]

Oklahoma Christian College

The college at Cordell continued on but under a new name and new leadership. Probably for marketing purposes, the board of trustees renamed the college "Oklahoma Christian College." As the new president, they named W. Claude Hall (1883–1967), an alumnus of both Nashville Bible School and Peabody Normal School, who had just completed a two-year term as president of Freed-Hardeman

College in Henderson, Tennessee. Hall made few substantive changes in the curriculum, but he did authorize the organization of a football team and the initiation of a $150,000 capital campaign.[38]

As it turned out, the football team was more successful than the capital campaign, which netted pledges of only $20,000 to be paid over five years. Additional contributions from Cordell citizens enabled the college to add more than eight hundred books to the library. Gross enrollments, however, continued to decline, although, ironically, more students signed up for college work in 1925 than ever before—seventy-six. And many of those students were training for the ministry, including J. Harvey Dykes, Loyd Smith, Wilburn Hill, and Howard Casada. Few influenced these students more than Professor of Bible Carl L. Etter, later a missionary to Japan, but they were also shaped by the sermons and examples of prominent Church of Christ ministers and scholars who visited the campus regularly, especially during a three-day lectureship scheduled each February from 1926 on.[39]

President Hall stayed at Cordell for only two years, resigning to serve the Church of Christ at Altus as a full-time minister. In 1927, he was succeeded by Dean George A. O'Neal (1892–1978), a Cordell Christian College and University of Oklahoma alumnus. A man of commanding presence and an ever-ready smile, O'Neal ably and effectively fulfilled the responsibilities of both the president and the dean, able to live within a $20,000 annual budget. He did that until 1929, when he too resigned. Three of his faculty colleagues were so disappointed that the board of trustees had accepted the resignation that they also resigned.[40]

The trustees next appointed Oklahoman Ulrich R. Beeson (1893–1983), who had served as dean in 1921, as the new president. He reorganized the faculty and welcomed 107 students, but the revenue generated by those students hardly paid the faculty, much less other expenses. Discouraged, he resigned at the end of the academic year.[41]

As their new president, the board of regents selected Adlai S. Croom (1892–1985), at the time on the faculty at Washburn College in Kansas but with considerable prior experience at Harper College in Kansas, Arkansas Christian College, and Harding College in Arkansas. Croom held an MA degree in math from Harvard. For the 1930–31 academic year, he organized the faculty with only a few changes and set out to build a broader base of support from Churches of Christ across Oklahoma. Among other things, he invited four hundred churches and individuals to meet in Oklahoma City at the Tenth and Francis church building on December 28, 1930. On the appointed date, 150 people attended the meeting, representing only five different congregations. Croom concluded from the poor attendance and discussion that there was little statewide church support for Oklahoma Christian College because church members considered the school to be a project of Cordell's business community, which had failed to support it adequately. Presumably, churchgoers would do their duty, if Cordell citizens would first do theirs.[42]

Assuming that the businessmen were not in a position or of a disposition to open their wallets further, Croom recommended that the board of trustees close the school. Interestingly, the board took no immediate action, although the president announced that the college was dead in 1931. When local members of the board acted to prevent sale of the property to pay just debts, Croom brought suit in federal court to force bankruptcy. The court ruled in his favor, and the property was sold at auction. The three-thousand-volume library went to Cameron College in Lawton, and the well-stocked chemistry laboratory went to Phillips University in Enid. Oklahoma Christian College at Cordell was no phoenix, and this time it did not rise again.[43]

Bible Chairs

As the demise of Oklahoma Christian College illustrated, many college-age students from Church of Christ families were pursuing collegiate degrees at state colleges and universities. These students found it virtually impossible to study religion in these institutions because of the necessity of keeping church and state separate. To remediate this circumstance, Churches of Christ in Oklahoma organized Bible Chairs adjacent to college campuses and offered religion classes at the collegiate level. Traditional, pastoral services were also available, but the raison d'être was academic study of scripture. As often as not, classes were taught on campus but sometimes in facilities adjacent to the campus. Generally, the college gave degree credit for the courses.

Although Disciples of Christ/Christian Churches had organized Bible Chairs at six state universities between 1893 and 1910, Churches of Christ did not establish their first Chair until 1918 at the University of Texas. In 1929, following UT's lead, the Stillwater Church of Christ organized a Bible Chair at Oklahoma A&M College, now Oklahoma State University. Leroy Thompson, then the minister of the congregation, taught classes on campus in the religious education department, which were offered for college credit after 1931. Bible Chair courses, along with those from other denominations, were listed in the college class schedule each semester.[44] Other Oklahoma congregations helped support the Bible Chair work at Stillwater.[45]

Oklahoma School of Religion

How the Central church in Norman ministered to Church of Christ students at the University of Oklahoma looked much different that at Stillwater. At Norman, the outreach was folded into an interdenominational Oklahoma School of Religion (OSR), which had been organized in 1928 under the leadership of E. Nicholas Comfort. Located adjacent to the campus, the School of Religion was not part of the university per se, but the university's president did serve on its board of trustees, and the university's semester schedule did list OSR classes.[46]

A. R. Holton (1891–1964), former president of Thorpe Springs Christian College in Texas, served as minister of the Central church in Norman between 1928 and 1935. During that period, he organized the first Vacation Bible School among Churches of Christ in Oklahoma if not the United States. He also held an appointment as professor of religion at the Oklahoma School of Religion. Holton taught accredited courses on the New Testament and the letters of Paul. He distinguished between OSR and a Bible Chair such as existed at Oklahoma A&M College, a distinction of importance to Holton. OSR was more academic, more integrated into the university curriculum, less connected with the local Church of Christ, more interdenominational. Later historians did not recognize Holton's distinction and honored Norman as having the first Bible Chair in the state. That was an error; the honor belonged to the Aggies.[47]

Holton's successor at the Central church, John P. Lewis (1919–2018), who held degrees from David Lipscomb College and Vanderbilt University, continued the relationship with the OSR, serving as associate professor of religion, assistant dean, and acting dean. Lewis also had "several" weekly radio programs, one of which aired on Saturday and was intended to prepare listeners for the Improved Uniform Sunday school lesson series.[48]

Lewis first divided his time between the pulpit and his teaching responsibilities. In 1938, however, he determined to devote full-time to his educational ministry at the OSR. The Central church at Norman supported him to the extent of $200 per year, with congregations and individuals over the state supplying another $2,200. In 1943, Lewis incorporated the Church of Christ Bible Chair in the School of Religion at the University of Oklahoma with church elders Henry E. Warlick, Y. E. Jones, and himself as trustees. Lewis remained at the

OSR until it closed in 1948, when he then took a teaching position at Abilene Christian College.[49]

The close relationship between the OSR and Churches of Christ in Oklahoma was extraordinary. Not only were Holton and Lewis very active members of the faculty, but two of the most noted laymen in the state, A. W. Lee of Oklahoma City and G. A. W. Fleming of Cordell, were members of its board of trustees.[50] Through the auspices of the school, Lewis convened leaders of Churches of Christ in various workshops on the university campus.[51] The history and theology of the church were featured in the publications of the school, notably in the *Oklahoma Journal of Religion*.[52]

Most extraordinary about the church's relationship was that the OSR was wholly interdenominational. At one time or another, it had faculty representing Presbyterian, Methodist, Jewish, and YMCA communities of faith, not to mention Churches of Christ. Additionally, Congregational, Christian, Unitarian, and Episcopal communions had representatives on the board of trustees. The editorial board of the *Oklahoma Journal of Religion* included representatives from still other groups: Church of the Brethren, Reformed Church of America, American Baptists, Reorganized Latter-Day Saints, Mennonites, Lutherans, Nazarenes, and Southern Baptists. For Churches of Christ, whose leaders tended to think that cooperation with "the denominations" compromised scripture in both word and practice, this kind of collaboration came close to fraternization with the enemy.[53]

The church's relationship with the OSR was strong despite the controversy that swirled around Dean Nicholas Comfort. An advocate of the social gospel, Comfort objected to racial and social injustice, capitalistic greed, nationalism, and militarism. Both the U.S. House Committee on Un-American Activities and the Oklahoma State Legislature investigated him in the 1930s. Critics of Comfort seldom distinguished between him and the OSR and considered both guilty of disloyalty to God and nation. Despite this criticism, however, Churches of Christ remained supportive of Lewis's relationship with the school until it closed in 1948.[54]

What explains this apparent anomaly? Perhaps it was because the Stone-Campbell plea for unity among Christians remained viable, but probably not. Perhaps the answer lay in the continuing commitment of Churches of Christ to serious, rational examination of scripture, and the opportunity to engage in it within the state university was irresistible, but probably not. Perhaps it was because Oklahoma Christian College in Cordell had closed its doors and Churches of Christ were looking for other ways to provide biblical literacy in a higher education setting, however "suspect" the vessel, but probably not. Possibly,

it simply was because church leaders did not know about the controversy swirl-
ing about Nicholas Comfort and the OSR or were unaware of the connection
between the outreach ministry of the congregation at Norman and the school.
Clearly, Lewis was widely respected as an educator among Churches of Christ
in Oklahoma, and it would have been easy for church leaders and members
to disassociate him from the rumors of unorthodoxy coming from Norman.
Whatever the reason, the twenty years of support Churches of Christ gave the
OSR remains something of a paradox.

Clearly, the Churches of Christ in Oklahoma were not wholly insular in their
congregational life and practices, as was suggested by the WPA survey, and
had been changed by war. They continued to host gospel meetings and debates,
adopted new evangelistic tools (Sunday schools, radio broadcasts, and lectureships), displayed a degree of social consciousness, and supported outreaches to
higher education.

Soul Salvation Rather Than Social Reformation

How did Churches of Christ in Oklahoma respond to the quest for greater clarity
of self in the Jazz Age? Doubtless such issues as the prohibition of alcohol and
requirements for Sunday closing were important to individual church members,
but they seldom were seen as the stuff of sermons from the pulpits of the local
congregation. If they were to be mentioned at all, it would be in a congregational
bulletin or brotherhood periodical. The purpose of the New Testament church,
it was insisted, was to save souls rather than to reform society, to honor the
kingdom of God rather than a government that promoted "carnal warfare."
For the twentieth-century church to do any differently would compromise its
purpose of restoring the simple gospel of the first-century church. Besides, the
congregational structure of Churches of Christ made it almost impossible for
any single entity to speak officially for the church at large.[55]

Leadership

More so than in previous decades when evangelists provided most of the congregational leadership, male laymen came to provide it between the wars. These were
the elders, of whom there was generally a plurality. Some larger congregations
also had deacons. Located ministers and traveling evangelists continued to serve
the churches, but the elders bore the responsibility for the spiritual and even
physical operation of the local congregation. Consequently, the success of the
congregation often depended more upon the elders than the preacher. Many

elders struggled with their responsibilities, but some were remarkably successful. Illustrative of the stronger elders during the 1920s and 1930s were A. W. Lee, T. E. Burch, J. E. Wright, and Frank Winters.

A Texas native, A. W. Lee (1876–1960) moved to Oklahoma City about the time of statehood. He was soon in business for himself, becoming a self-described "oil merchant" by 1920. In time, he was a distributor for Champlain Oil Company and owned a string of six filling stations in Oklahoma City.[56] Relative to others in Churches of Christ, he was a wealthy man.

Lee associated himself with the congregation in Oklahoma City soon after his arrival and quickly assumed a principal role within it. The church recognized him as an elder by 1915, an office he held until 1952. With other leaders, he helped move the congregation from rented to permanent quarters at Tenth and Francis Streets in 1916 and to a new building in 1922. The church added a classroom building in 1930 and a new auditorium in 1939. For these capital improvements, Lee generally loaned the church much of the money and then over time canceled the debt.[57] Church attendance during his service as an elder went from a few dozen to more than eight hundred, while annual contributions grew from less than $500 to more than $28,000 per year. Lee's influence in Churches of Christ extended beyond Oklahoma City, for he served, as already noted, as chair of the board of trustees of Western Oklahoma Christian College in Cordell and as a member of the trustees of the Oklahoma School of Religion in Norman in the 1920s and 1930s.

As a leader, Lee was more pragmatic than doctrinaire. He was out to build a congregation that was strong in number, finances, and physical facilities. Given his support of Foy E. Wallace Jr., a relationship similar to that of a father and son, he clearly was a theological traditionalist when it came to the work and faith of the local congregation. On the other hand, his support of the Oklahoma School of Religion suggested a broad-mindedness that was unusual for Church of Christ leaders in the first half of the twentieth century. Surely it was that characteristic that put him at odds with a fellow elder, L. L. Estes, in the 1940s and early 1950s and led to his withdrawal from the leadership in 1952.[58]

T. E. Burch (1890–1974) was to the Church of Christ in Wewoka what Lee was to the Tenth and Frances congregation in Oklahoma City. Burch was a native of Arkansas, who came to Stuart, Oklahoma, in 1908 to live with his grandparents and to complete his high school education. Subsequently, he attended a business college in Tecumseh and entered the banking business in Wewoka. Beginning as bookkeeper and janitor, he came to own the Security State Bank, an institution in which he took great pride.[59]

Beginning with his baptism in 1909, Burch was an active churchman. In 1913, he helped organize the Wewoka church, which recognized him as an elder from then on, an unusual circumstance in that he was only twenty-three years old, newly married, and without children. The congregation prospered under his leadership. It met first in a rented building, which it later purchased, then in a new building on Mekusukey Street in 1929, which lasted for thirty-two years, when it was replaced by the current building. Membership totaled thirteen in 1913; forty years later it numbered three hundred and had an annual contribution of $20,000. Although preachers with strong egos and widely differing theological perspectives preached there, the Wewoka church never divided. Burch was a careful student of the Bible and conservative in faith and practice. Like Lee, he was called upon to serve Churches of Christ at the state level. Consequently, he too was a member of the board of trustees of Western Oklahoma Christian College in Cordell in the 1920s and Oklahoma Christian College first in Bartlesville (as Central Christian College) and then in Oklahoma City in the 1940s and 1950s.[60]

J. E. Wright (1892–1984) of Tulsa was another prominent Church of Christ layman. A native of Kansas and a trained sewing pattern maker, Wright owned and operated Sentinel Manufacturing Company, a manufacturer of valves used in the oil industry. He held membership first at the Tenth and Rockford congregation, then North Main Street, and finally Brookside. He served as elder at the last two. His energy and dedication prompted the Main Street church to organize and help sponsor a children's home at Turley, Oklahoma, just north of Tulsa, and the Brookside church to be engaged in active evangelism and to support retirement centers for the elderly and precollegiate education for youth. Grace-filled and with the heart of a servant, Wright was a diligent student of scripture, writing an analysis of *God's Progressive Plan* and commentaries on the books of Acts and Hebrews. As with Lee and Burch, Churches of Christ statewide called upon him to serve in various capacities, specifically as a founding member of the board of trustees of Central Christian College in Bartlesville and then Oklahoma Christian College in Oklahoma City.[61]

Frank Winters (1884–1963) was widely admired in Oklahoma as a layman church leader. Born in Missouri, he migrated to Elk City in 1902. He not only was a stalwart in the Church of Christ there but also served as principal of one of the public schools and subsequently became an active member of the bar. He moved to Oklahoma City in 1918, where he established a legal practice, developed real estate (Warr Acres), invested in grain markets, and bought and sold oil royalties. He became a man of significant financial means.[62]

In Oklahoma City, Winters and his family became part of the group that would establish the congregation at Tenth and Francis Streets. Indeed, he chaired the finance committee that was responsible for finding the money to construct the first building on the property. He also served as one of the elders of the congregation, as a song leader, and as a Bible school teacher. In 1937, Winters and other families from Tenth and Francis planted another Church of Christ congregation in the Culbertson Heights neighborhood of Oklahoma City, just east of the state capitol. Winters served as an elder there as well, as he would twenty years later at the Mayfair congregation on Northwest Fiftieth Street, a successor to Culbertson Heights.[63]

Winters was always eager to share the traditional restoration "plea" of the Stone-Campbell movement with men and women of goodwill and a Christian mindset. For them, he prepared some fifty "lessons," or ads, that the Culbertson Heights church then paid to run in the Oklahoma City newspapers and congregations elsewhere paid to run in their local papers. He then folded the message of those ads with additional commentary into tracts—one titled "The Restoration of the Spirit of Christianity"—that were widely distributed. Something of a celebrity within the church, Winters spoke widely in Oklahoma, was a member of the group of men that organized Central Christian College in Bartlesville, and played a significant role in bringing the school to Oklahoma City as Oklahoma Christian College.[64]

Lee, Wright, Burch, and Winters were recognized as men of stature within the community at large. All four were successful businessmen. There were others whose status derived from other professions. J. H. Lawson, as already noted, was widely recognized for his service to the state of Oklahoma as an assistant attorney general. Henry E. Warlick (1868–1948), merchant and farmer, who after thirty years in Greer County moved to Lexington in Cleveland County and then in 1930 to Norman, served as an elder at the Central church and as a trustee of the Oklahoma School of Religion. In recognition of past favors, Governor William "Alfalfa Bill" Murray, appointed Warlick as chair of the State Board of Affairs, in which capacity he was able to help the Tipton Home in an hour of need. Likewise, Gerald A. Hale (1904–67), a deacon at Tenth and Francis in Oklahoma City, helped invent the parking meter, the first one of which occupied the southeast corner of First and Robinson Streets in Oklahoma City. He was a generous contributor to the church and would later serve as chair of the board of trustees of Oklahoma Christian College at Oklahoma City.

Otis Durant Duncan (1897–1970) was an internationally known professor of rural sociology at Oklahoma A&M College and a deacon at the Stillwater Church of Christ. Born in Texas in 1897, he took degrees from East Texas State, Texas A&M, and Louisiana State University. He was on the faculty at Oklahoma A&M for thirty-four years, much appreciated nationally for his work on Dust Bowl migration to California in the 1930s. Duncan was a lifelong member of the Church of Christ. He was, he wrote to an academic friend, "the only sociologist I have ever known or heard of, who is, was, or ever could be a member of the Church of Christ, and I do not know how many thousands of times I have heard congregations being told that we [sociologists] are the Number One source of atheists, communists, whoremongers, hypocrites, and every sort of disturbance which the 'ELECT' should avoid as a plague, since we must shun the very appearance of evil." Even Duncan's mother was worried about his fate in the hereafter. "Needless to say," he told his friend, "my religious life is not easy, it is not happy, and it is not entirely gratifying, but it is interesting."[65]

Those reservations aside, Duncan was faithful to his church heritage. He represented Churches of Christ on the board of the Oklahoma School of Religion, and he wrote articles for the *Oklahoma Journal of Religion* that gave insights into the church.[66] Duncan accepted that his fellow church members were poor and country and that they survived by mutual aid. For that reason, he helped young preachers with their diction and sermon delivery.[67] According to him, the congregation he attended in Stillwater was the first all-white church "to have Negro members without the slightest idea of segregation." This was not the result of legalistic behavior derived from the hermeneutic of command, example, and necessary inference, he said. Rather, it was evidence of subjective reality based on faith that one passes from death to life "if you love the Brethren."[68]

The status of Lee, Burch, Wright, Winters, and Duncan was acknowledged statewide, even internationally, providing Church of Christ members with a greater sense of self. Not all of the men who served as elders or deacons in the pre–World War II era, however, were as equipped for the responsibility as these men. They were not only men of means and experience as real-world leaders; they were students of the scriptures, they were committed to the kingdom, and they possessed a strong sense of history. But that was not true of all elders or church leaders, the consequence of which was tension with peers and preachers when it came to theology and administration. What happened at the McAlester Church of Christ is an example.

Leadership at McAlester

As mentioned elsewhere, the McAlester congregation purchased the ornate Busby Theater and commenced worshipping in it in 1935, launching with a successful gospel meeting preached by Foy E. Wallace Jr. Within months, there was serious difficulty within the eldership, which included D. B. Killebrew, B. M. Strother, and A. C. Grimes. At issue was the appointment of an additional elder and deacon as nominated by Killebrew and Strother. When some members of the 150-person congregation raised "scriptural" objections to the candidates, Strother and Killebrew rejected the complaints and terminated all meetings of the church (including Sunday school), save for the Sunday morning service to curtail gossip. When Grimes objected to the procedures followed, Strother and Killebrew advised him to resign from the eldership and then threatened to withdraw fellowship when Grimes declined.[69]

By September 1936, matters at the McAlester church were at an impasse. Probably advised by Foy Wallace Jr., Strother and Killebrew invited C. R. Nichol and R. L. Whiteside, the acclaimed authors of the multivolume systematic theology titled *Sound Doctrine*, to help mediate the issues. Two church leaders from Muskogee knowledgeable of the situation at McAlester were not allowed to participate. When there was no resolution of the issues, the following Sunday Strother and Killebrew announced that the congregation was withdrawing fellowship from Grimes and others who had challenged the proposed new leaders. At this news, Grimes's supporters, who represented well over half of the congregation, "rose up in arms," signed petitions of protest, and locked the minority out of the building, or so their adversaries said. They then served notice on Strother and Killebrew that the congregation no longer considered the two as elders. They also selected additional elders and deacons who would be favorable to their leadership, appointed a preacher, and scheduled a full complement of services and programs.[70]

Very quickly the case gained national attention, probably through the influence of Wallace, who had kept a close watch on the troubles of the McAlester church. In an article on May 6, 1937, W. E. Brightwell, Wallace's successor as editor of *Gospel Advocate*, excoriated the majority as "sit-down strikers," a reference to tactics then in use by organized labor. Brightwell considered "the McAlester affair [as] a consummate disgrace upon the cause of Christ." He further declared, "It ought to be despised by every honest soul in the brotherhood." Wallace added the following year that a "mob spirit" reigned at the McAlester church, and he simultaneously dismissed assertions by an eyewitness that there were two sides to the story and that many of Brightwell's facts were wrong. For Wallace, it was a clear case of a "devil possesse[d] people" rebelling against God's plan for church governance, or elder rule, substituting in its place the chaos of unscriptural majority rule.[71]

Probably with Wallace's urging, Killebrew and Strother brought suit against Grimes and others to regain custody of the building early in 1938. The case was tried in the court of Judge R. W. Higgins of Oklahoma's Fifteenth Judicial District at McAlester. To testify in their behalf, the plaintiffs called C. R. Nichol, R. L. Whiteside, D. A. Kirk, W. L. Thurman, and M. E. Ewing. The defendants, represented by Allen D. Dabney, an elder in the Church of Christ at Eastland, Texas, called Robert M. Alexander, C. M. Stubblefield, Leroy Elkins, and George O'Neal. In the trial, the plaintiffs argued that the church was not a democracy and that the will of the elders must prevail, while the defense countered that the elders had a biblical responsibility to rule with the view of the majority in mind—in other words, they were not to "lord" it over their flock.[72]

The court ruled in November 1937 that it was without jurisdiction in the case because no property rights were involved. The plaintiffs petitioned for a new trial, but without success.[73] In the meantime, apparently in late 1938, Strother published a thirty-one-page booklet titled *The Church and a Faction*, which included a copy of Nichol's testimony and an essay titled "Law and Order in the Church versus Majority Rule and Chaos" by Wallace. The latter included transcripts of the *Gospel Advocate* articles by Brightwell and D. W. Kelley. The point of the publication was to belittle the concerns and actions of the majority of the members of the McAlester Church of Christ. Describing the majority's action as "anarchy," it was widely circulated by church leaders who championed elder rather than pastor rule in the church. "It [was] really surprising how many people there [were] in the church who [thought] that the church should be run like the democratic party or a labor union," said Wallace elsewhere.[74]

Fortunately, the damage to the unity of the congregation was not permanent. In the fall of 1945, the parties to the conflict acknowledged their share of the responsibility for the confusion and discord and pledged to work together in harmony thereafter.[75]

Notable Ministers

Oklahoma Churches of Christ were served by notable ministers between the wars. Most but not all of these had grown up in other states and come to Oklahoma to find preaching positions, who then after establishing their credentials as excellent ministers resigned and took positions in more lucrative fields, generally in Texas. Among these was John H. Banister (1910–95), who had very successful ministries at Elk City and Oklahoma City (Culbertson Heights) between 1935 and 1948, and then moved to Dallas. There, at Skillman Avenue, he became one of the best-known located ministers in the Church of Christ fellowship.[76]

On the other hand, Byron Fullerton (1889–1978) was born in Texas but came to Oklahoma when he was fourteen and stayed. He grew up in Hobart, attended Southwestern State Teachers College in Weatherford, and took bachelor and master degrees from the University of Oklahoma. He held teaching positions at Hobart, Atoka, Rocky, and Gotebo, among other places, and for ten years he was superintendent of the Tipton Home. He also served on the original board of trustees for Central Christian College at Bartlesville. Fullerton generally combined preaching with teaching, but held full-time preaching appointments in Chickasha, Oklahoma City (Culbertson Heights), Norman (University), and Marlow. When he died in 1978 at Ada, he was the grand-old-man of Oklahoma's preaching fraternity.[77]

Irene Mattox

Like mainline Protestant and Catholic churches, women had limited roles in church worship services and leadership responsibilities in Churches of Christ in the 1920s and 1930s. Those were limited presumably because of the scriptural injunction for women to be silent in the church. That injunction was widely honored in Oklahoma Churches of Christ for most of the twentieth century, yet women still found ways to express their faith and participate in the work of the kingdom of God. Certainly that was the case of Meta Chestnutt Sager earlier in the century, but it was also the circumstance of Irene Mattox in the period between the wars. Both are representative of twentieth century women participating in the work of the church.

Irene Mattox (1881–1970) was a native of Texas, the daughter of a well-known preacher, an alumna of Jane Addams's famous Hull House in Chicago, the wife of J. P. Mattox, and the mother of seven children. She moved with her husband from Texas to Bristow in 1914 and then to Oklahoma City in 1920. An experienced teacher, she soon found employment as a substitute in the Oklahoma City Public Schools and just as quickly became active in the Parent Teacher Association (PTA), being selected as city president in 1924 and then again in 1930.[78]

Under Mattox's leadership, the PTA became a political force of significance in Oklahoma. It championed educational opportunities, of course, but also child health and welfare programs external to the classroom. In the midst of the Great

Depression, the PTA organized a clothing drive to assist the poor then living in shantytowns along the banks of and under the bridges crossing the North Canadian River in Oklahoma City. Mattox and her colleagues also worked with Governor William J. Holloway to secure legislative approval for a proposed children's commission. She was a confidant of U.S. senator Josh Lee as well[79]

Irene Mattox's compassion for children, human beings in distress, and political connections were well known. In 1931, she was selected by the Oklahoma County Commissioners to lead the Bureau of Social Services. Under her leadership, the agency dispensed government welfare to the indigent within the county at a time when counties did not do that kind of thing.[80] Her work was so much appreciated that in December she was nominated as Oklahoma City's "Most Useful Citizen," along with luminaries like Charles F. Colcord and Tom Braniff.[81] She was not selected for the honor, but her supporters, including General William S. Key, director of the WPA in Oklahoma and a candidate for governor in 1938, took some satisfaction in knowing that Mattox had been recognized for "aiding, materially and spiritually, the needy and unemployed in this community . . . [bringing] hope and comfort to all whom she contacted."[82] In other words, she was known for putting the gospel into action.

For unknown reasons, Mattox relinquished her position as director of the Social Services Bureau in December 1932.[83] Thereafter, she devoted herself to club and church work. To the surprise of some, she took a leading role in the Women's Bible Study Club in Oklahoma City, which prided itself on having "members of different denominations . . . [with a] diversity of gifts and visions" and of having "eliminated sectarian differences, giving broader views and higher ideals for service to God and humanity through the study of the Bible." So motivated, the club had "helped secure" child labor legislation, compulsory education for children, a reform school for juvenile courts, a pure foods commission, women's vote in school district elections, domestic science as part of the public school curriculum, and public libraries.[84]

Only once did Mattox try to leverage her network of PTA, women's clubs, and Woman's Christian Temperance Union (WCTU) friends in the interest of a political campaign. In 1938, her colleague in poor relief, William S. Key, ran for the nomination for governor in the Democratic primary. She agreed to help organize the women of Oklahoma's ten central counties. She won the lasting gratitude of Key, but not the campaign. Key lost to Leon Phillips by the small margin of only 3,300 votes. The loss did not diminish the fact, however, that Mattox was a woman of considerable influence throughout Oklahoma.

Despite the level of recognition, Irene Mattox's basic community interest was her church. She and her husband first attended the Tenth and Francis congregation and then became charter members of the Oklahoma City Twelfth and Drexel Church of Christ, which was organized in 1930. She taught the weekly women's Bible class there for thirty-five years. She was rightly called a "heroine, leader, and pioneer in the role of women in the church." She was one of the first to address women's groups at lectureships and meetings, despite objections from ministers who thought it was too much like preaching. In 1927, A. R. Holton, the minister at Norman, asked her to lecture to an all-day meeting of Christian women on "A Christian Woman's Responsibility." After in depth reviews of scripture, she concluded, "God has not commanded women to preach or oversee the congregation! This is plainly man's responsibility and for this we are glad, but a Christian woman must prepare herself for effective teaching lest she receive the judgment given to the disobedient and slothful one-talent servant."[85] Few could match her knowledge of scripture.

Evangelist K. C. Moser believed that salvation came to humankind by faith rather than works, a controversial position that challenged the presumption that salvation came from obeying certain commands. When he was the pulpit preacher at Twelfth and Drexel, he shaped much of his theology of grace in conversations around Irene Mattox's kitchen table. He found her to be a better student of scripture than most men, sensible in her application of the gospel, and faith filled. Said Moser at her memorial service in 1970, "Irene was a sinner, and she knew it. Irene had a Savior, and she knew it."[86] In other words, Irene Mattox knew who she was.

Mattox's brothers and sisters in the Churches of Christ in Oklahoma were learning who they were within the context of an economic boom and bust in the 1920s and 1930s and the trauma of World War II in the 1940s. As noted, this stronger sense of self emerged through radio programming, organized lectureships, international missions, educational opportunities via Bible Chairs and colleges, and the leadership of talented elders, laymen, ministers, and women. All of this, combined with a distinctive message of Christian unity and salvation, caused most Oklahoma Church of Christ members to believe that the Stone-Campbell plea was both valid and relevant.

9

CHALLENGING DISORDERS
1920–1945

Although the Churches of Christ in Oklahoma had clearly grown in number and stature in the post–World War I era, they also suffered doctrinal disputes and racial prejudices that, to their chagrin, debilitated them both internally and externally. They were not as united as they had proclaimed. Disputes, of course, were not unique to the fellowship, but they did suggest that the sense of self was less strong than members had believed and was influenced more by the past than the future.

Disappointment with the Digressives

Warfare with the digressives of the Stone-Campbell movement over the use of instrumental music in worship continued. The principal weapon, of course, was debate, which the Church of Christ leadership continued to seek. One of the more notable discussions occurred in 1924 at the Capitol Hill Church of Christ in Oklahoma City. F. B. Srygley, well-known for his essays in the *Gospel Advocate*, supported the proposition that mechanical instruments in worship were unscriptural, while J. B. Briney, noted minister and author among the

Disciples, defended their use. According to a reporter for the *Daily Oklahoman*, the debate focused on the true translation of the Greek word *psallo*, and the "[e]nthusiasm of the speakers gr[ew] as the argument progresse[d], although neither . . . gained any distinct advantage over the other."[1] Nor did either ever gain an advantage—it was just two elderly men (sixty-five and eighty-five) trying to recreate the unified fellowship of their youth. That sodality was not likely to happen, at least in Oklahoma.

But sometimes the fellowship of old was recreated. The Stone-Campbell church at Chandler in Lincoln County had embraced instrumental music in worship but had resisted other innovations like the Christian Endeavor and missionary society programs. The progressives withdrew and organized their own congregation. The original restoration church remained instrumental until 1935, when the elders of the Shawnee Church of Christ and their minister, Perry Cotham, persuaded the Chandler congregation to substitute a capella singing for instrumental music in worship.[2]

Similar attitudes prevailed at Rush Springs. There the Stone-Campbell church was established, or had constructed a building, in 1901. The congregation included both conservatives and progressives. In 1910, the conservatives organized a Church of Christ, but did not withdraw from the building. Thereafter, the progressives used the building in the morning on Sundays, while the conservatives, or Churches of Christ, used it in the evening. Every six months, the schedule would reverse. The arrangement continued in this fashion until 1923, when the Church of Christ folks bought out the progressives. They continued to occupy the building until 1930, when the congregation constructed a new one.[3]

Sunday Schools

The WPA surveyors were not far off with their observation that there dwelled in Oklahoma Churches of Christ a strong strain of sectarianism—that is, that salvation depended upon holding certain beliefs and executing certain actions without prioritization. But frequently members could not determine just what those beliefs and actions were. The adding of Sunday Bible classes, or schools, was a case in point. Many rural and most urban churches gathered an hour or so before the worship assembly for Bible study in graded classes and often with commercially prepared instructional materials. The Sunday school was not associated with an external institution or organized by individuals not reporting to the elders; it was a systematic, effective, and convenient way of studying the Bible. In 1930, the Tenth and Rockford congregation in Tulsa counted 410 in Sunday school; five years later the Tenth and Francis congregation in Oklahoma City built a large annex to accommodate its Bible school of some 500 or more. The robust programs clearly contributed to the growth of the congregations. In 1939, the Oklahoma City church replaced its adjacent auditorium with one that seated 1,100 for worship services, the largest in Oklahoma among Churches of Christ at the time.[4]

Some considered Sunday schools as additions to the faith and practice of the New Testament church; they were unauthorized, indeed not even mentioned, by scripture, just like instrumental music in worship services. Clearly, according to the critics, the church was relying on techniques and institutions rather than divine providence to carry out its mission. Not only did Bible schools divide the assembly, but they also incorporated women into the teaching function of the church. George W. Phillips from Ringling, Oklahoma, was especially concerned by this drift. He challenged Joe Warlick to defend the proposition that "the congregations of the Church of Christ that teach the word of God in what is known as the Sunday School, using the class system, are Scriptural in their teaching and practice."[5]

The debate began orally in Mannsville, Oklahoma, in July 1921, and continued as a written exchange, which was published as a book three years later. By then, however, the breach between the class and nonclass congregations was so distinct that separation could not be avoided. In 1925, the nonclass congregations published a directory of preachers who opposed the Sunday school. Most were located in Oklahoma, Texas, and Arkansas. A decade thereafter the nonclass folks divided again over the issue of multiple cups rather than a single communion cup. Seventy-five years later, 107 of these congregations (52 nonclass and 55 single cup) remained active in Oklahoma, but with only 8 having adherents of more than 100. The average attendance was forty-two. *Gospel Tidings*, which circulated as one of the faction's principal periodicals, was published in Bethany, Oklahoma.[6]

Premillennialism

The debate over premillennialism was far uglier than the one over Sunday schools. Millennialism is the notion that at his second coming Christ will usher in a final golden age on earth when he will literally rule with his saints for a thousand years (the millennium). God alone will inaugurate the new age after humankind has rejected the ministry of Christ and the promise of the church in the premillennial era. Championed by William Miller and Charles Russell, American religious leaders of the nineteenth century, the doctrine found only a few adherents within Churches of Christ, who generally embraced the postmillennial views of Alexander Campbell, the idea that Christ would return after one thousand years of progress ushered in by the kingdom of God, or the church. This was especially true after Russell and others added dispensationalism to the theory, which saw the church as a weak substitute for the ministry of Christ.[7]

The apocalyptic worldview of men like R. W. Officer, not to mention Barton Stone, David Lipscomb, and James Harding, who wished to live as if the final rule of the kingdom of God was here and now, seemed to flow from the same spiritual fountain as did premillennialism. At least that appeared to be the position of Robert H. Boll (1875–1956), a German immigrant, a front-page editor of the *Gospel Advocate*, and a graduate of Nashville Bible School, who introduced the subject to his readers as early as 1909. As elsewhere in American Christianity, Boll found a lot of interest among members of Churches of Christ insofar as the timing and nature of the last days were concerned.[8]

Still, into the 1930s most Church of Christ members in Oklahoma considered premillennial eschatology as speculation and conjecture that had little to do with salvation. By mid-decade that had changed, however, as Churches of Christ came to view premillennialism as a heresy that diminished the significance of the New Testament church as the kingdom of God on earth. This transformation was due largely to the influence of Foy E. Wallace Jr. (1896–1979). Born in Texas and a one-year alumnus of Thorp Springs Christian College, Wallace made his name initially as a very successful evangelist, holding meetings that resulted in thousands of baptisms. Churches in Oklahoma City hosted at least twenty of those, many in tents. After a controversial sojourn in Tennessee, Wallace moved his family to Oklahoma City in 1935, placing his church membership with the Tenth and Francis congregation, of which, he said, there was no "better, finer, truer body of people."[9] Wallace did not know of a city where the church was progressing "quite so satisfactorily." He would name one of his children after A. W. Lee, a respected elder of the congregation. From Oklahoma City, he published the *Gospel Guardian* and the *Bible Banner* between 1935 and 1947, where he attacked premillennialism in acerbic and confrontational language.[10]

During his Oklahoma residency, Wallace engaged in some of his more famous "fighting-style" debates. These too addressed what he considered to be the unscripturalness and dangers of premillennialism. Among his opponents were Charles M. Neal in 1933, J. Frank Norris in 1934, and E. F. Webber in 1937. The latter debate was staged in Oklahoma City.[11] Webber, a native of Oregon, was a nationally known evangelical preacher who also made Oklahoma City his home. He and Wallace agreed to debate three propositions, with Webber arguing the affirmative and Wallace the negative. In contention were the following: that "the Bible teaches that a . . . sinner is saved by grace through faith before baptism"; that "the Bible teaches that it is impossible for a child of God to so sin as to be finally lost"; and that "the Bible teaches that after the second coming of Christ, there will be an age or dispensation (known as the millennium) during which period Christ will occupy the literal throne of David in Jerusalem (Palestine) and reign on the earth one thousand years."[12]

Moderated by former Oklahoma lieutenant governor Robert Burns, the debate extended over five evenings in December 1937. It drew an estimated daily audience from seven states of eight thousand people to the Oklahoma City Coliseum. Most were preachers and members of Churches of Christ. According to one, "Wallace routed Webber on every argument made." The general audience tended to agree. Each evening it voted as to who had won the debate: a hundred or so voted for Webber, while several thousand voted for Wallace. One evening when calling for the vote, Governor Burns was heard to say, "I suppose the result is obvious."[13]

Given Wallace's large shadow in Oklahoma, premillennial eschatology found rocky soil in the state's Churches of Christ. Only a few would challenge him, one being the husband of Irene Mattox. J. P. Mattox actually edited and published the *Good Way* (1946–48), a monthly periodical championing premillennialism, which circulated modestly in the 1940s. He was convinced that "All things written point to the present and final exaltation and kingship of Christ and His Father" in a thousand-year reign.[14] Wallace, of course, could not have disagreed more. That was also his response to the new hymnal *Great Songs of the Church*, which he labeled as premillennialist in theology. Consequently, the songbook hardly circulated in Oklahoma, and those who approved of the hymnal were spurned.[15] This response was fairly remarkable given the lingering influence of J. N. Armstrong, the pre–WW I president of Cordell Christian College then serving as president of Harding College in Arkansas, whose apocalyptic worldview restrained him from rejecting premillennialism outright. But in Oklahoma the passage of two decades had changed the landscape, with church members captivated by the force of Wallace's personality and with none of them wanting to suffer his wrath. It remained that way for another thirty years.[16]

The Gospel of Grace

Another internecine conflict that reflected a sectarian spirit in Oklahoma Churches of Christ had to do with the doctrine of grace. K. C. Moser (1893–1976) raised the issue initially through his grace-oriented preaching and teaching.

Although Texas-born and -educated, Moser served Oklahoma churches for thirty-five years beginning first at Wewoka (1921–23), then Tenth and Francis at Oklahoma City (1923–26), Frederick (1926–33), Ardmore (1935–37), Twelfth and Drexel at Oklahoma City (1940–47, 1950–64), and Enid (1947–50). While in Frederick, he became convinced that God's grace was to be found not in his commands but in the cross of his son, a conclusion that he published in *The Way of Salvation* (1932).[17] Moser discovered, writes historian Richard Hughes, that "while baptism and good works were important, the proper response to the gospel was not so much a matter of believing facts and obeying commands as it was of trusting in 'Christ crucified, buried and raised for our justification.'"[18] In the apocalyptic tradition of Stone and Lipscomb, Moser's teaching was both welcomed and criticized. In Oklahoma City, his preaching was embraced and celebrated by the Twelfth and Drexel congregation, while just a mile away at Tenth and Francis it was considered unsound if not heretical.[19]

Although the two had been friends, Moser's chief critic in Oklahoma was Foy E. Wallace Jr. Influenced by the rationalism of Alexander Campbell, Wallace and most Church of Christ leaders traditionally thought of salvation as deriving from human initiative and obedience to a plan of action—hearing, believing, repenting, confessing, and being baptized—rather than from God's unmerited favor. Moser's book and subsequent articles evoked "a storm of controversy" over their celebration of unmerited grace, especially within Wallace's network. For the next forty years, Moser himself would be persona non grata in the Wallace household. During dinner-table conversations, remembered Foy's son, William, Moser was "one of the bad guys."[20]

In 1940 at the peak of the controversy, the Twelfth and Drexel Church of Christ in Oklahoma City engaged Moser as its full-time minister, where he remained for the next twenty-four years, save one three-year hiatus in Enid. Given Wallace's influence in Oklahoma City, it was a surprising appointment. But the Twelfth and Drexel church was cut from a different cloth. Organized in 1930 by a group that formerly worshipped at Tenth and Francis, the congregation from the beginning reflected a worldview championed earlier in Oklahoma's church history by J. N. Armstrong, whereby the believer lives/acts as if the final rule of the kingdom of God is in the here and now. Instrumental in this orientation was the J. P. Mattox family, which was one of the charter families of the congregation. Irene Mattox taught the women's Bible class while her son, F. W. Mattox, preached for the congregation between 1932 and 1940. The family's sense of Christ as the source of salvation rather than a set of commands was profound. To that extent, the

Mattox family resonated with K. C. Moser, whom they knew well because of his earlier service at Tenth and Francis, and they were delighted when he accepted the pulpit at Twelfth and Drexel.[21]

With Moser preaching, the Twelfth and Drexel congregation occupied somewhat different ground than most other Churches of Christ in Oklahoma. A Sunday morning visitor would not have noticed any difference when it came to the form of worship, but she would have noticed a difference in the substance of the lesson presented. The gospel would have been defined christologically rather than as the steps of salvation, with grace being the unmerited gift from God rather than the results of a plan of action accomplished by human beings. For most church leaders, and especially Wallace, the difference was dangerous if not heretical in that it seemed to relieve humans of any responsibility for their own salvation. Consequently, the Twelfth and Drexel congregation, like Moser himself, was suspect of being on the left of Church of Christ orthodoxy. That position did not bring large numbers of members, but it did nurture a theological perspective of the Stone-Campbell movement that had all but faded until it could be revived in the 1970s.[22]

Theological Modernism

If issues regarding end times and grace troubled Oklahoma Churches of Christ before World War II, so too did theological modernism. In the 1920s, modernists believed that Darwin's theory of evolution and the German principles of higher criticism should be adapted to modern culture. Such an adaptation, of course, would bring into question the inerrancy and inspiration of the Bible. Rather than from the hand of God, it suggested, scripture was pieced together by writers guilty of plagiarism, as revealed by the synoptic Gospels. Above all, modernism would challenge the creation account in the first chapter of Genesis, insisting that the universe evolved over millions of years rather than being created in six, literal twenty-four-hour days.[23]

Churches of Christ members in Oklahoma, as in the case of other Protestant fellowships, generally scoffed at the claims of evolution and higher criticism. They readily identified with so-called fundamentalists, who upheld the inerrancy of scripture and who tried to force perceived modernists out of the various Christian denominations. They were also eager to preserve American values and culture by outlawing the teaching of Darwinian evolution in the public schools. For U. G. Wilkinson at Comanche, the notion that "long periods of time" and "natural selection" were required for creation of the universe was ridiculous. Wilkinson agreed with seventeenth-century archbishop of Ireland James Usher's dating because he believed that all genealogies in scripture were literal history. Said Wilkinson: "The world is now 5,921 years old since God . . . said, 'Let there be light.'"[24] Moreover, right thinking on all of this was a matter of salvation, for, quoting Mark 6:16, he noted, "He that believeth not shall be damned." Most of Wilkinson's preaching brethren held similar views, although there had not been widespread interest among the Churches of Christ in the question of the Bible and science until the 1920s.[25] As D. S. Ligon complained, "It is hard to get our brethren to see the awful need of exposing the dogma of evolution."[26]

By the mid-1920s, that was beginning to change. Leroy Elkins organized his own lecture circuit through Oklahoma, eager "to reach each community with three or four lectures on 'evolution as it is taught in the textbooks of the schools of the country vs. the Bible.'"[27] J. L. Barnes believed that the evolutionists represented the Antichrist of the end times and would bring about an end to marriage and morals. "We Oklahomans," he wrote, "know that the Bible says that such degeneration and ungodliness will be taught, but we want them to use their own money to advance such rot and not the taxpayer's money that don't [sic] want it used anyway."[28] Perhaps that was one of the reasons why J. H. Lawson—preacher, educator, and an assistant attorney general—was so active in statewide political efforts to prevent teaching of evolution in public schools.[29]

Lawson and other Oklahomans of faith succeeded in their campaign. The state legislature passed the nation's first law restricting the teaching of Darwinian evolution in the public schools on March 23, 1923. The governor signed it into law three days later. Church leader and editor of the *Christian Worker*, D. T. Broadus, was thrilled: "I am more and more of the opinion that more of our state legislatures should do as the Oklahoma legislature and enact laws to prevent such teaching in our schools. Of what benefit is it to your boys and girls when they enter the business arena of life?"[30] U. G. Wilkinson thanked God "that . . . the great state of Oklahoma has again taken the initiative and by legislative act eliminated the infidelity of Darwinism from its educational system. May its example quickly be imitated by all the others."[31] Leroy Elkins was pleased by the passage of the bill but appalled that "the leading ministers in this state condemned the House and upheld Darwinism. What does that mean? Are the ministers infidels? I flatly charge that they are."[32]

Oklahoma church members continued their campaign opposing evolution. In July 1925, John D. Boren, subsequently a U.S. Army chaplain and minister of a Church of Christ in Oklahoma City, attended the Scopes trial in Dayton,

Tennessee, and wrote a popular song defending William Jennings Bryan.[33] Along with minister Will J. Cullum, the elders of the Central congregation in Shawnee were so concerned about the perceived connection between evolution and atheism that they addressed it in a traditional Church of Christ way: a debate between W. L. Oliphant, a native Oklahoman then preaching in Dallas, Texas, and Charles Smith, president of the American Association for the Advancement of Atheism in New York City, in August 1929. There were three propositions debated: that there was a supreme being, that atheism was more conducive to morality than "Any Theory Known to Man," and that "All Things Exist as the Result of Evolution, Directed by a Known Intelligence." A standing-room-only audience attended the debate, reflecting a deep skepticism of Churches of Christ to theories or facts that challenged the traditional interpretation of biblical truth and inspiration.[34]

But there were dissenting voices. Joe Warlick (1866–1941), considered one of the foremost Church of Christ debaters and editors, who spent much time in Oklahoma, argued that Genesis 1:1 could refer to a long period of time before the six-day creation. A Yale PhD, a former member of the faculty at Cordell Christian College and subsequently at Abilene Christian College, William Webb Freeman (1887–1954) held that the Bible served as a guide in religion but not "in political science, geology, astronomy, medicine, farming, cooking, journalism or other secular works."[35] In other words, not all scripture was infallible.[36] Initially, Freeman's views created only a few ripples, but by the early 1920s the measure of grace extended to him was withdrawn by traditionalists. He had to find employment beyond colleges affiliated with Churches of Christ, although he continued to preach in the church's pulpits.[37]

The overall effect of theological modernism among Oklahoma Churches of Christ, historian Mike Casey believed, was to push them more in the direction of fundamentalism. E. M. Borden, a writer for the *Firm Foundation* who had traveled extensively in Oklahoma, would declare in 1925, "A preacher who is not a fundamentalist is not a servant of God."[38] Price Billingsley echoed similar sentiments in the *Gospel Advocate*: if one did not embrace "inerrancy of the Bible," he wrote, one was "irretrievably" lost.[39] Put differently, if you were not a fundamentalist, your salvation was in question.

With the onset of the Great Depression in the 1930s, the fundamentalist movement lost steam in Oklahoma Churches of Christ and elsewhere. It was difficult to get too excited about modernism and evolution when the fellowship was united in opposition. Instead, preachers turned their attention to the premillennial question and the effort to force those with premillennialist views out of the Churches of Christ.[40] As we have seen, Foy Wallace, then living in Oklahoma City, led that movement. Since many fundamentalist leaders were premillennial in belief, their influence among Churches of Christ weakened.

Pacifism

A weakened influence within the church was true too of pacifism. A strong commitment to that position had characterized Cordell Christian College faculty and students and had fueled the socialism of O. E. Enfield and others. It remained strong in Oklahoma and elsewhere despite the fact that leading periodicals within the faith community (the *Gospel Advocate* and *Firm Foundation*, for example) had dropped opposition to World War I and urged physical and moral support of the military efforts of the United States.[41]

The attacks of Nazi Germany on Europe in the 1930s and on Asia by Japan in the early 1940s, especially at Pearl Harbor, took the United States into World War II. Pacifism was again an issue of consequence in Churches of Christ. The *Advocate*, for example, resumed its openly pacifist position, one that it held through the duration of the conflict. In contrast, the *Bible Banner*, edited and published by Foy Wallace out of Oklahoma City, took a strident pro-war position. Those who did not support the war effort, he argued, were too much influenced by premillennialism, a charge that no one wanted directed at themselves.[42]

As it turned out, most Church of Christ members in Oklahoma came to agree with Wallace. L. R. Wilson (1896–1968), the minister of the Tenth and Rockford congregation in Tulsa, even questioned the integrity of pacifists in the church, who "enjoy[ed] the peace and security . . . purchased by the blood of others" but refused "to hold up the hands that gave [them] these blessings."[43] Because of such a perspective, eligible young men and women in significant numbers accepted military service during World War II without much thought as to pacifism or premillennialism. In 1942, the Twelfth and Drexel congregation in Oklahoma City had twenty-six young men in the armed services, while Capitol Hill had thirty-one in 1944. During the course of the war, fifty-eight men served from the Central church in Shawnee.[44] As historian Robert Hooper has noted, this kind of response to the call to serve illustrated that pacifism in the church effectively ended with World War II.[45]

But there were pockets of resistance. Hugo McCord, a respected church scholar, continued to recommend that young men choose noncombatant service.[46] And some of them did, while others claimed conscientious objection status. The latter spent much of the war in one of sixty-seven government-authorized but privately supported Civilian Public Service camps. Only 199 members of Churches of Christ were assigned to these camps, of which probably no more than a dozen or so were from Oklahoma. After some delay, when the historic peace churches picked up the tab for the cost of the camps, sympathetic church members paid the incarceration expenses of the Church of Christ COs (conscientious objectors).[47] Besides doing fieldwork for the U.S. Soil Conservation Service, the men themselves paid highly for their faithfulness to conscience. One group from a camp at Magnolia, Arkansas, was denied communion by the local Church of Christ because leaders of the congregation considered the COs to be slackers.[48]

Race Matters

In 1920, the African American population in Oklahoma was 149,408, some 7.4 percent of the total population.[49] How members of Churches of Christ responded to race issues was more individual than corporate. As already noted, the Klan was so influential in Oklahoma that some churchgoers of all denominations were doubtlessly active members in the 1920s. Surreptitiously, they supported community-wide efforts to "keep the black man in his place." There were major exceptions, of course, but even the Christians who were appalled by social racism were noticeably quiet in the pulpit.[50]

Among the latter were some members of Churches of Christ. In 1922, evangelist Foy Wallace had dramatically rejected an unsolicited contribution from the Ku Klux Klan, representatives of which, dressed in their iconic white robes and hoods, had showed up at his gospel meeting in Oklahoma City.[51] As praiseworthy as this appeared, probably more reflective of his actual view was the very public scolding he gave Marshall Keeble, the preeminent black evangelist from Tennessee, for not preaching about the illegality and evils of social equality.[52] Equally indicative was his censure of Oklahoman Ira Rice Jr. for having shared a bed during a snowstorm with R. N. Hogan, an equally preeminent African American preacher, which to Wallace was "an infringement on the Jim Crow law [and] a violation of Christianity."[53] Given Wallace's standing within the Churches of Christ community in Oklahoma, it is fair to conclude that the scourge of racism was not a topic of discussion in the worship assemblies of the church.[54]

Marshall Keeble

The experiences of Marshall Keeble (1878–1968) in the Sooner State confirmed as much. On September 15, 1931, Keeble arrived in the train depot at Muskogee. Immaculately dressed, short in stature, and straight in posture, Keeble stepped from the third-class car to the station platform with a smile on his face, a twinkle in his eye, and an extended hand. He was met by an angry, red-faced J. W. Brents, the white minister of the Spaulding Street Church of Christ, who had invited Keeble to Muskogee to evangelize the community's black residents. Brents shouted, "Keeble, you lied to me! You were supposed to be here earlier in the week." He did not even take time to say "hiddy," Keeble remembered later. Brents probably regretted his greeting: in the course of the three-week meeting that followed, Keeble baptized 204 individuals, not including whites or one Cherokee Indian, and organized what is now the Eighteenth Street congregation. Also, Brents would subsequently teach at the Nashville Christian Institute, a school for African Americans of which Keeble served as president. Yet the exchange rightly reflected the predominant racial attitudes of many Oklahomans, including Church of Christ members.[55]

Although Keeble generally focused his meeting work east of the Mississippi River, he returned to Oklahoma from time to time. In 1933, he preached at both Clinton and Oklahoma City. At Clinton, his evening audiences ranged from five hundred to three thousand, and during the course of the meeting he baptized thirty-five, including a Methodist and a Baptist preacher.[56] At Oklahoma City, he preached for two weeks, baptized nine, and organized a group that five years later would begin to meet on Northeast Seventh Street and would become the mother church of black congregations in the city. The Capitol Hill Church of Christ, a white congregation, sponsored Keeble's meeting in Oklahoma City and deployed one of its elders and his wife (C. A. and Helen Ward) to work with the congregation until it could be self-sustaining.[57] By 1940, Northeast Seventh Street had 480 in worship services. A similar sequence of events involving the Tenth and Rockford congregation in Tulsa facilitated the establishment of the North Peoria church in 1934. After assuming the presidency of Nashville Christian Institute, Keeble often took some of his "preacher boy" students with him on his tours. Four of those, Arthur Fulsom Jr. (Hugo), Hassan Reed (Atoka), Alvin Simmons (Guthrie), and Dwayne Winrow (Shawnee) were from Oklahoma.[58]

Rather than as one of his "boys," Luke Miller (1904–62) often traveled with Keeble as a song leader. Miller was also an exceptional preacher. In the excitement of Keeble's 1933 tour of Oklahoma, Miller responded to the call of the white church in Holdenville to evangelize the community's large population of African Americans. In a three-week meeting, Miller baptized forty and set a church in order. Over the next decade he returned to Holdenville at least twice more, with additional stops at Wewoka, Ada, Pauls Valley, and Oklahoma City.[59]

R. N. Hogan

While Keeble's influence was significant in Oklahoma, it was not as great as R. N. Hogan's. Although a native of Arkansas, Hogan had been raised by the noted black educator, publisher, and churchman G. P. Bowser. Bowser was the spiritual and intellectual mentor of scores of young men who would occupy the pulpits of black Churches of Christ in Oklahoma and elsewhere, one of whom was Hogan.[60]

The church that Marshall Keeble reconstituted in Muskogee in 1931 called Hogan to serve as its evangelist the following year with a stipend of ten dollars per week. Hogan accepted the invitation, with the Muskogee congregation serving as a launching pad for major evangelistic efforts in other parts of the state. In 1934, for example, he organized African American congregations at Wetumka, Shawnee, Haskell, and Okmulgee, baptizing 323 persons. In those same congregations, he baptized 215 more the following year. In 1936, Hogan's meeting in Guthrie resulted in seventy-six black and twenty-seven white baptisms, and in Langston it produced forty-one, including the mayor, city treasurer, and postmaster, as well as the Methodist preacher and steward, a Baptist deacon, a school principal, and an administrator at Langston University. In 1938, a year or so after he had left Muskogee, Hogan baptized 148 in Oklahoma City, including five denominational preachers. The next year, eighty-six more were baptized. Thereafter, the Oklahoma City congregation especially was strong and stable. Walter Weathers, a Muskogee native, was its first evangelist.[61] Of Oklahoma's current black Churches of Christ, 60 percent were organized between 1931 and 1945.[62]

Given the hundreds he was baptizing and the number of congregations he was establishing, Hogan was eager to create an informed and trained leadership for the churches. For that reason, he strongly supported the efforts of his mentor G. P. Bowser in organizing Bowser Christian Institute at Fort Smith and in editing the *Christian Echo*. Additionally, he established a school for prospective preachers in Muskogee. Among his students were Russell H. More, H. H. Gray, and J. S. Winston.[63]

From the late 1930s on, Hogan made Los Angeles his permanent residence. There, he organized the Figueroa Street Church of Christ, which in time became one of the largest Churches of Christ in the United States, either black or white. He often returned to Oklahoma as an evangelist, however. Among the churches he served in that capacity were Oklahoma City (1940); Tulsa, in a debate with a representative from the Church of the Living God (1941); and Oklahoma City again with a series of sermons (1945).

Hogan's time in Oklahoma City followed what was the first meeting of an annual national lectureship of black Churches of Christ. Hogan, along with J. S. Winston, Levi Kennedy, and G. E. Steward, the preacher at the Northeast Seventh Street church in Oklahoma City, was one of the conveners of that gathering, which was designed to provide for black church members and evangelists what lectureships elsewhere provided for white ministers and members but excluded people of color. Held during the first week of April 1945, the initial lectureship attracted thirty-six participants, including G. P. Bowser.[64]

The National Lectureship

The National Lectureship met annually after 1945, held in Oklahoma twice, once in Tulsa in 1976 and again in Oklahoma City in 1994. Over that time, the purposes of the lectureship remained constant: (1) to unify the speech of preachers, teachers, and church leaders; (2) to enhance spiritual fellowship by joint participation in study and worship; (3) to offer doctrinal teaching against liberalism, digression, and apostasy; and (4) to encourage and strengthen the work of the congregations in whose area the lectureship was held. In contrast with the three dozen evangelists who attended in 1945, the National Lectureship now attracts well over a thousand ministers and church leaders.[65]

In 1931 when Marshall Keeble had his successful meeting in Muskogee, J. S. Winston (1906–2001) was in his audience. Born in Arkansas but reared in Muskogee, Winston was impressed with Keeble's energy and simplicity of message. Consequently, he decided to identify with Churches of Christ rather than the Christian Church, for which he had served as minister. Thereafter, R. N. Hogan mentored him in his training school at Muskogee and utilized his singing and speaking skills in his evangelistic work in Oklahoma. From 1934 until his relocation to Texas four years later, Winston assumed leadership of the infant congregations at Okmulgee, Ardmore, Langston, and Guthrie. At the latter, his wife and other women of the congregation hauled stone from the riverbed to erect a new church building. Winston would develop into one of the four major leaders of African American Churches of Christ during the post–World War II era, along with Hogan, Levi Kennedy, and G. E. Steward. Especially interested in higher education, he was one of the principles in arranging for the opening of Southwest Christian College in Terrell, Texas, in 1949.[66]

Oklahoma was a difficult field for evangelists like Keeble. It suffered from the same racial prejudice that plagued other southern states, if not all states. African Americans could not vote, send their children to proficient schools, or drink from "whites only" water fountains, among other things. The prejudices from which such Jim Crow laws emerged also produced the horrific Tulsa Race Riot in 1921, which left thirty-six dead, hundreds injured, and hundreds of thousands of dollars in property lost. In the reactionary 1920s and the depressed 1930s, there was a lot of mistrust between the races in Oklahoma.[67]

The situation was not much different in Churches of Christ. There is no evidence that members in Tulsa reacted any differently to the riot in 1921 than other whites in the city. Nor is there evidence that journal editors raised their voices in dismay. It is true, of course, that Churches of Christ considered social-action issues beyond the purview of the restored first-century church and of less consequences than the saving of souls via preaching the simple gospel. The spiritual burden did take white Churches of Christ into black communities, accounting for invitations to men like Marshall Keeble to come and preach there at the expense of their white brethren. This was the approach of the Tenth and Rockford church in Tulsa, the Spaulding Avenue church in Muskogee, and the Capitol Hill church in Oklahoma City.[68] It was also a fact that organizing a black church in a black community forestalled any need to let black members worship with white members. The latter could create problems in the use of a baptistery, among other things, which the congregation at Wewoka solved by baptizing the black maid of T. E. Burch in Burch's cow pond.[69]

Social Action at Tipton

As a rule, Churches of Christ were skeptical of social action, an expression of Christianity that sought social justice for the urban poor by bringing about God's kingdom in the context of temporal human relationships. The church was to be a transformational institution that would speak for those who had no voice and provide for those who had no resources. In terms of programming, the Central Church of Christ in Nashville, Tennessee, was one of very few that took the concerns of the social gospel seriously. In the 1920s and 1930s, it became a role model among Churches of Christ in the matter of serving the needs of the urban poor.[70] In Oklahoma, no congregation attempted to replicate the Nashville model of services. The work of Irene Mattox was state rather than church organized. The level of need was not any different in Tulsa or Oklahoma City, but the level of resources was. Moreover, Churches of Christ feared that the social gospel would pervert "Christ's simple gospel," which emphasized soul salvation and confined the church to proclaiming the kingdom of God. The closest that Oklahoma Churches of Christ got to the social gospel institutionally in the pre–World War II era was their strong support of the Tipton Home for orphans and by individual acts of charity.[71]

The Tipton Home had its genesis in Canadian, Texas in 1921. The Church of Christ there, however, lacked the resources to provide the services needed. Within a year, the leadership let it be known that other congregations were welcome to assume responsibility for the work. The church at Tipton, Oklahoma, was quick to seize the opportunity. Organized in 1903, the congregation was stable and mature in its understanding of the gospel. S. J. Tipton, one of the elders, had a deep passion for helping the fatherless. Accordingly, he offered to give his eighty-acre farm and orchard to the church as the site of a home for the orphaned children. The church leadership agreed to construct a main building at a cost of some $64,000 that would house the orphanage itself. The Canadian church elders accepted the terms; fund-raising and construction followed; seventy-three boys and girls occupied the campus by June 27, 1924.[72]

Robert Chitwood provided the initial leadership that made the home for the homeless a functioning reality. Beginning in 1925, he, along with his self-sacrificing wife, served as superintendent for two decades. One of his biggest challenges as superintendent was finding adequate financial resources to operate the home. He publicized the needs of the institution through the pages of the *Tipton Messenger*, via performances of a female a capella ensemble, and by means of field representatives like J. H. Lawson. Once congregations and friends knew of the necessities required, Chitwood had absolute faith that those necessities would be met. Ends generally were met, but it happened with the special assistance of both church and state. The churches contributed food staples, clothes, pigs, and baby chickens that were gathered by scheduled runs of the Tipton Home truck. State aid came when local legislators appealed to Governor William Murray for emergency assistance. Murray found some unbudgeted dollars to help the institution, and subsequently signed legislation that provided state money for private agencies that cared for orphan children. Despite state aid, Chitwood had only five dollars per month per child to sustain the home during the Great Depression.[73]

Chitwood stepped aside as superintendent at the end of World War II, during the course of which some one hundred of the Tipton residents and almost 1,300 alumni served.[74] E. A. Sanders, an experienced public school educator from Quanah, Texas, succeeded Chitwood. Sanders's hope for significant upgrading of the plant and curriculum, however, were stymied by a fire that destroyed much of the main building in November 1946. Fortunately, he was able to rebuild with government surplus materials taken from the abandoned airbase at Frederick. Reconstruction also provided the opportunity to create a complex of cottages that housed the 220 residents in units of only 40 children rather than dormitories that housed 100 or more.[75]

At the end of the twentieth century, Tipton Home was a far different institution than it had been for most of its seventy-nine years. Most notably, it was no longer only an orphans home in that it accepted children into its care who were at risk even with living parents. Also, children were housed in one of five cottages, or residential groups, that replicated a normal home environment with parents and siblings. Only fifty children were in residence. The home's principal funding sources were congregations of Churches of Christ and generous friends. The board of directors for the home continued to be the elders of the Tipton church.[76]

The Gospel in Lawton

What happened at the Sixth and Arlington congregation in Lawton in the midst of the Depression also evidenced a social consciousness among Oklahoma Churches of Christ. When federal legislation authorized designated individuals or agencies to purchase surplus materials from a government warehouse in New York at the rate of four pounds for a penny, the Lawton church requested certification for its minister, Burton Coffman, as an agent. Governor Murray agreed with the request. The congregation then raised some $2,000 and purchased forty tons of woolen blankets, boots, shoes, underwear, overcoats, shirts, and trousers, among other things. The church then distributed the surplus items to hundreds of destitute people in the Lawton area. This good work raised the profile of the congregation in Lawton. In his three years in the community (1931–34), Coffman baptized 409 people, on average 3 people per week.[77]

So, then, the sense of self that emerged among Churches of Christ in Oklahoma following World War I took root despite enervating quarrels and changing conditions. Evidently, the majority of church members were not all that interested in the importance of *psallo*, or whether Sunday schools were biblical, premillennialism was relevant, or grace was more important than works in the salvation equation. Doubtlessly, members had a modest understanding of Darwinian evolution, but little to none of higher criticism. Pacifism, as a philosophy of life, had dissipated. And African American civil rights were not even acknowledged.

But the needs of the homeless children gathered at Tipton were. The recipients of clothes, blankets, and food at Lawton were. And judging from the WPA survey of the 1930s, Church of Christ congregations in Oklahoma took some pride in that acknowledgment. They were not premillennialist, pacifist, modernist, or nonclass folk. They probably did not understand the full meaning of salvation through grace rather than works. But they did believe that as persons of "the Book," they could achieve personal salvation and religious unity.

10

"THE CHURCH IS GROWING"
1945–1970

The *Christian Chronicle*, publishing positive news about Churches of Christ since 1942, printed on its masthead in the 1950s, "The Church Is Growing." The editors had every reason to be optimistic, for standard sources widely reported that the Church of Christ nationally was by percentage one of the fastest growing religious communities in the United States. According to one count, there were 1,650,000 members nationwide.[1] The Shawnee Church of Christ illustrated the rapid growth locally. Its Sunday school attracted 275 in 1952, 365 in 1958, and 411 in 1966. By 1962–63 there were 604 in worship services. Led by minister J. T. Marlin, the congregation baptized forty-one persons in 1959, and its weekly contributions exceeded its budget.[2] This was all in keeping with the spirit of the age. The United States had triumphed in its war with Germany and Japan; through the Marshall Plan, Europe was rebuilding; the U.S. economy was producing more jobs at a higher rate of pay; Americans were moving to the suburbs, where television entertained, credit cards paid bills, and science promised an extended life and space travel; Congress adopted "In God We Trust" as the national motto; and on Broadway, *Oklahoma!* celebrated the "bright golden haze on the meadow." It was an "Affluent Society" on the cusp of a "New Frontier," or so said President John F. Kennedy.

Several developments in the post–World War II era reflected the growth and advancement of Churches of Christ in Oklahoma. One of the more significant of these was the establishment of Christian education, from collegiate to kindergarten.

Oklahoma Christian College

Since the closing of the college in Cordell in 1931, church leaders across Oklahoma were eager to replace it. For a growing church seeking identity, or respectability in the larger Christian community, they all agreed, such an institution was required. In 1946, when the old ammunition plant and prisoner-of-war facilities (320 acres) at Pryor were offered to them as the location of a new college, most church leaders responded favorably, choosing a name (Mid-States Christian College), selecting a board, and writing a charter and by-laws. But not all were positive, including Frank Winters of the Culbertson Heights church in Oklahoma City. For him, the property was too far outside of Pryor; the buildings were of wood construction; the land was not suitable for agriculture; and it was not a place parents would want to send their children. Consequently, the proposal was rejected in February 1947.[3]

But the idea of a Christian college lingered. A series of regional meetings fanned the flame. A steering committee resolved that the envisioned school would carry the name of Central Christian College (CCC), that it would be organized as a business, that only Church of Christ members would serve on the governing board, and "that no funds shall be solicited or accepted from any congregation of the Lord's church, but that contributions be confined to individual Christians and those interested in Christian education." This stipulation was unlike any applied to sister colleges across the United States with the exception of Pepperdine University in Los Angeles. The provision reflected the strong feelings of some Church of Christ members in Oklahoma and elsewhere that supporting Christian colleges from the church treasury violated scriptural principles. There was no example in the New Testament, it was argued, of that kind of use of the "Lord's money."

By 1948, the trustees had chosen Bartlesville, Oklahoma, as a site for CCC. The architecturally impressive Foster Mansion and associated grounds, purchased for only $150,000, constituted the campus. It was fully functional following the construction of a gym/cafeteria and two dormitories. As the school's first president, the trustees selected L. R. Wilson, who assumed office on September 1, 1949. Wilson had been the founding president of Florida Christian College and a local minister in Tulsa and Ada. His immediate task was to raise $250,000.

School opened in September 1950. The dean of the college was James O. Baird (unrelated to the author of this study). Baird was a Tennessee native, having done his graduate work at Peabody College and Princeton Theological Seminary. He had served on the faculty at David Lipscomb College in Nashville, Tennessee, and had benefited from traveling around the world, literally, with his cousin, Norvel Young. He had also done work as a local preacher in Tennessee, Kansas, and Oklahoma.

Roy H. Lanier Sr. chaired the Bible department. A native Oklahoman, he held a master's degree from Hardin Simmons University and a reputation as an ardent debater and evangelist, holding an average of twenty-four meetings per year. Harold Fletcher, who would become an icon for the college, chaired the music department. All faculty were members of Churches of Christ. The chair of the board of trustees was L. B. Clayton, one of the elders of the Tenth and Francis congregation in Oklahoma City.

Initially, CCC was a two-year college that offered only an AA degree. The curriculum emphasized general education and required students to take a course in the Bible each term. With the first year began the musical tradition of one-act operas. The cocurriculum included attending daily chapel, having evening devotionals, and participating in the chorus, writing for the newspaper, publishing the yearbook, engaging in intramural sports, and joining a preachers club. The annual lectures began in March 1951. Personal conduct rules were strict. There were ninety-four students enrolled the first year; six graduated.

Financially, CCC was always on the borderline of bankruptcy in its early years. The Bartlesville elite, especially the leadership of Phillips 66, did not support the college's expansion plans. For scriptural reasons, as already noted, board chair L. B. Clayton had strong reservations about the college appealing to congregations of Churches of Christ for financial support. Frustrated over this and other money-raising issues, President Wilson resigned as of September 1, 1954, to become the full-time minister at the Central church in Amarillo, Texas. Two years later he accepted the position as editor of the *Voice of Freedom*, a journal best known for its anti-Catholic diatribes.

James Baird (1920–98) succeeded Wilson as president. Financial solvency of the college was of primary importance to Baird and his colleagues. For leadership in that realm, they turned to George S. Benson, then president of Harding College in Searcy, Arkansas, an Oklahoma native, a decade-long missionary to China, and a highly successful fund-raiser. He had sold Harding College as a bastion of Americanism, anti-communism, free enterprise, and personal responsibility to the scions of Wall Street, resulting in substantial gifts that transformed the campus. Desperate for money, Central Christian, like other colleges, wanted to duplicate the system. Benson was appointed chancellor as of 1956, serving in that post until 1966.

Almost simultaneously, Baird had told the board that if the college was not moved to Oklahoma City he would resign. He had become weary of the apathy, frustration, and "vague feeling of being in a hostile environment" that he experienced in Bartlesville. He understood that such a move would be costly: the new plant in Oklahoma City was estimated to cost $1,250,000. Where would that money come from? As it turned out, $255,000 came from church members in Oklahoma City and across the state. Oklahoma City leaders themselves raised $200,000. Corporate interests, influenced by the Benson sales pitch, provided a substantial portion of the rest. At the campus site on Memorial Road and Eastern Avenue, ground was broken for the new campus in May 1957. Classes began in fall 1958.[4]

Notable changes took place almost immediately. In 1959, Central Christian College became Oklahoma Christian College (OCC). The next year, junior and senior classes were added, and in 1962 the first senior class of nineteen graduated. Meanwhile, Baird and Benson organized a three-day "Freedom Forum" at the Skirvin Hotel for Oklahoma City's power brokers, featuring U.S. senator John McClellan of Arkansas, and established the American Citizenship Training Center to provide appropriate materials for high school teachers, publish a monthly newsletter for the business community, and bring speakers for public events. The center was unapologetically anti-communist, anti-socialist, and anti-liberal. The center championed the free-enterprise system, constitutional government, and faith in God as the three foundations of American life.[5] The purpose of all this was to fill a gap in the economic and political educations of Oklahoma's young people and to present OCC in a role many prospective donors saw as positive. For this reason, Baird permitted himself to serve as chair of Oklahomans for Right to Work, an anti-labor movement of the 1960s, and the college to host such groups as the John Birch Society and anti-ERA groups in the 1970s.[6]

The work of the American Citizenship Training Center (ACTC) and the role of George Benson, however, presented some problems. When the college came to request accreditation as a senior institution from the North Central Association of Colleges and Schools in 1966, President Baird discovered that the accreditors had reservations about college sponsorship of a training center that was so politically charged and a chancellor who had created similar programs at two other institutions (Harding College and Pepperdine University). To preempt the criticism, Baird and Benson moved quickly to separate the ACTC from the college. They determined not to move it off campus, but to reorganize the center so that it reported to its own board of trustees with no organic connection to the college. As for Chancellor Benson, he promised to retire from the college in the near future, although he would do so immediately if his presence threatened accreditation. These proved to be wise decisions, and in April 1966, the North Central Association granted the school full accreditation.[7]

The blessing of the association brought not only legitimacy but growth. The number of full-time students increased from 730 in 1965 to 1,835 in 2005. Between 1950 and 2008, more than 25,000 students attended Oklahoma Christian. Every state in the Union and seventy-five foreign countries had been represented, although Oklahoma provided about 45 percent of the students. There was about an equal number of men and women. The number of students who were from Churches of Christ ranged from as many as 90 percent early on to 73 percent in more recent times.[8]

But that population was not particularly diverse. This became evident in March 1969 when an off-campus celebration, following a basketball victory, according to administrators, and the birth of a child, according to students, extended deep into the night, so deep that the revelers did not get back to campus until the next morning. Subsequently, fourteen students were dismissed, the majority of whom were African American. Student Ron Wright and other African Americans considered the decision racially biased. Wright was not involved in the incident, but he took leadership in the subsequent protest. The next day he and nineteen other students marched on the administration building, declaring that they would continue to occupy the building until their grievances were addressed. Baird considered this a violation of board policy—on the books for less than a year—that prohibited "sit-in" demonstrations and promised dismissal from the college. He asked the students to leave; only two did. Sixteen of the eighteen who stayed were African Americans. Baird called the police and had them arrested and taken to jail. Students, faculty, and friends paid their bail. Two weeks later they pled guilty to the no trespassing charges and were released without further prosecution, but they were not allowed to return to school that term.[9] Wright transferred to Pepperdine University, where he led similar protests that were resolved with less trauma. He went on to a successful career in higher education, and early in the twenty-first century was honored by both Pepperdine and Oklahoma Christian. Oklahoma Christian latter expressed regret for what had happened on its campus.[10]

According to historian Stafford North, the fundamental purpose of Oklahoma Christian was to encourage spiritual growth. It was achieved by choosing faculty and administrators who shared in its spiritual goals; by insisting on high standards of student conduct; by requiring courses in the Bible, daily chapel attendance, and evening devotionals; by organizing student religious clubs, offering personal contact between faculty and students, and connecting students with a local congregation; and by involving students in Christian service opportunities locally, nationally, and internationally.[11] Presumably, spiritual development stirred the missionary spirit, and students participated in door-knocking campaigns and Let's Start Talking tours, and served in established missions.

Surely one of the consequences of such spiritual growth by Oklahoma Christian students was to help shape the character of Churches of Christ in Oklahoma. The faculty contributed as well in that it taught both the Bible courses students took as part of the general education program and the classes taken by majors and graduate students who hoped to preach as a profession. One of the faculty was Raymond Kelcy (1916–86), who held a doctorate of theology from Southwestern Baptist Theological Seminary in Fort Worth, had preached at Tenth and Rockford in Tulsa and Wilshire in Oklahoma City, as well as three Texas congregations, and had printed a tract entitled "Christianity is Undenominational." He chaired the Bible department, was considered erudite but traditional in matters of doctrine, and related well with preachers in the area. During his tenure at Oklahoma Christian College, leaders of the church had great confidence in the ability of the school to produce a "sound" preacher.[12]

Hugo McCord (1911–2004) and William E. Jones (1918–2007) assisted Kelcy in training ministers and other workers in the church. A Mississippi native with a worldview typical of that state, McCord took his ThD at New Orleans Baptist Seminary. He ministered to Churches of Christ in Indianapolis, Indiana; Washington, D.C.; Alexandria, Virginia; Gretna, Louisiana; Dallas, Texas; and Bartlesville, and Midwest City, Oklahoma. Beginning in 1954, he served Baird as vice president. In 1960, he joined the Oklahoma Christian College Bible faculty.

William (Bill) Jones was a native of Missouri who also received his doctorate at Southwest Baptist Theological Seminary in Fort Worth. He had extensive service as a minister at congregations in Texas and at Britton in Oklahoma City. Oklahoma Christian College added him to its Bible faculty in 1964. Like Kelcy, both McCord and Jones in their teaching and preaching moved away from the fighting preacher style of Foy Wallace, and embraced instead the style, sensitivity, and conservatism modeled by their seminary teachers. They gave more attention to grace than some of their peers, but essentially they embraced traditional Church of Christ views on inspiration, apologetics, church organization, plan of salvation, and worship. They opposed liberal views on evolution, Biblical criticism, the social gospel, experiential conversion (a conversion that "feels" Christ), and a congregational governance system dominated by the pastor. As good teachers are supposed to do, they conveyed their views to their students and shaped a generation of Oklahoma preachers.[13]

In 1972, Lynn McMillon, an Oklahoma Christian College alumnus who held a PhD from Baylor, joined the Oklahoma Christian faculty teaching both Bible and history. After four years, he taught in the Bible department only. He was joined the next year by Howard Norton, a Texas native who held his doctorate from the University of Sao Paulo, Brazil. Between 1961 and 1977, he served as a missionary in Brazil, which brought him on different occasions to Oklahoma Christian as a missionary in residence. In 1977, he joined the Bible faculty, and he would become chair of the department in 1986. Missions were his priority as a leader. Both McMillon and Norton would help produce the *Christian Chronicle*; both had the confidence of church leaders and college administrators.[14]

In addition to the work of the Bible department, Oklahoma Christian reached out to the churches through its annual lectureship. The concept was not new inasmuch as J. N. Armstrong had employed it at Cordell Christian College before World War I and individual congregations such as Culbertson Heights in Oklahoma City in 1949. Oklahoma Christian's lectureship had its origins at Bartlesville in 1950.

In 1974, James O. Baird resigned as president of the college. J. Terry Johnson succeeded him, serving until 1995. Johnson was an Oklahoma Christian alumnus who took his juris doctor from the SMU law school. He was thirty-one when he became president. On his watch, Enterprise Square opened, the institution offered its first graduate program in Bible, and the college came to define itself as a "University," taking the name of Oklahoma Christian University of Science and Arts (OCUSA), and then just Oklahoma Christian (OC), so as not to be confused with Oklahoma City University (OCU), a Methodist institution.

Kevin Jacobs succeeded Terry Johnson as president of Oklahoma Christian in 1996. Jacobs was also an alumnus of the college but held his juris doctor from Vanderbilt. He was President Baird's son-in-law. Jacobs's tenure as president was controversial, and when he chose to resign five years later only a few were disappointed. In the academic year of 2001–2, Alfred Branch served as acting president. Mike E. O'Neal succeeded him. O'Neal grew up in Oklahoma, attended Oklahoma Christian but took his bachelor degree from Harding College, served with the U.S. military in Vietnam, earned his juris doctor from Stanford, and was part of the administrative team at Pepperdine University for nearly three decades. His major contributions were fiscal soundness, expansion of the board of trustees, revision of the mission statement, creation of a written covenant between faculty and the university, an organization for donors who gave $1,000 a year, development of a faculty association, and improvement of student housing.[15]

In Oklahoma in the post–World War II era, little was of more importance in the history of Churches of Christ than Oklahoma Christian University. The institution set the tone of the church's faith and practice, trained many of its preachers, instilled in students traditional family values, and commended a particular political, economic, and social worldview to faculty, students, and supporters. Without pressing the point too hard, the Church of Christ in Oklahoma today is what it is in large part because of Oklahoma Christian.

Invisible Christian Colleges

As Oklahoma Christian College appealed for support from the Church of Christ faithful across the state, it left the impression that it was the only place where students could combine faith with their learning. In reality, that was not the case. As has been noted, the Bible Chair at Oklahoma A&M College sponsored by the Stillwater Church of Christ had offered basic Bible courses on the college campus since 1929, which were accepted by A&M for full academic credit. These courses were taught by the minister of the Stillwater congregation, who had creditable academic credentials, and Church of Christ students made up the largest number of enrollees. By 1960, the Stillwater Bible Chair could count six former students who taught at OCC and more than forty ex-students who were full-time preachers.[16] The situation at Norman was somewhat different in that the biblical courses taught were through the Oklahoma School of Religion, but it no doubt remained true that most of the students taking the courses taught by A. R. Holton and John P. Lewis had grown up in Churches of Christ.

Although the data is skimpy, in the 1950s and 1960s there were far more students with a Church of Christ heritage in Oklahoma state colleges and universities than at Oklahoma Christian College. Concern about the spiritual training of this group was strong. Initially, congregations in the college towns utilized the Bible Chair model as a remedy. Church-state issues, however, soon required the program to use a separate facility, and it limited courses taught to those that were transferrable through Oklahoma Christian College. By the mid-1960s, such complications required most would-be Bible Chairs to retool and become campus ministries, with emphasis upon spiritual development and evangelism rather than academic credits. Ensuing cost considerations required some programs to dispose of their off-campus centers.[17]

There were not many state colleges in Oklahoma during the post–World War II era that did not have an invisible Christian college nearby. Offering accredited Bible courses as of 1960 were Cameron (Lawton); East Central (Ada); Oklahoma State (Stillwater); and Panhandle A&M (Goodwell). Chairs with student programs only included University of Oklahoma (Norman); Northwestern State College (Alva); Southwestern State College (Weatherford); Western State College (Altus); University of Arts and Sciences (Chickasha); Southeastern State College (Durant); Central State College (Edmond); University of Tulsa (Tulsa); Northeastern State College (Tahlequah); and Eastern State College (Wilburton). The Bible Chair–campus ministry epoch reached its zenith in the 1970s, when it was replaced by Campus Advance, a program almost wholly concerned with collegiate evangelism.[18]

K-12 Education

Oklahoma Churches of Christ had considerable enthusiasm for faith and learning at the collegiate level in the three decades after World War II. Some of that actually filtered down to impact education between kindergarten and high school. To realize the full benefit of that excitement, however, was a challenge. To illustrate, consider the Oklahoma Christian Academy (OCA) in Edmond. OCA had its origins when its founders organized the Living Word Academy (LWA), which offered a K-12 graded curriculum in the mid-1970s. Leaders of the academy purchased the buildings and property of the Tenth and Francis church as a campus for the school. LWA was dogged by financial challenges from its beginning, however, and was forced to close its doors and sell its assets in the mid-1980s. Starting afresh in 1987, the supporters of Christian education at the K-12 level reorganized as OCA, moved its central office to the Edmond Church of Christ, and entered into a working relationship negotiated between the church's elders and the academy's board of trustees. For some fourteen years, the school used the classroom facilities of the Memorial Road and the Edmond Churches of Christ. In 2001, it opened its present campus on the grounds of the Edmond church.[19]

The other accredited K-12 Christian school in Oklahoma is Hope Harbor Children's Home and Christian Academy near Claremore, the educational arm of the old Turley Children's Home, with the elders of the Claremore congregation serving as a board of trustees. A K-5 school is offered at McAlester. The two accredited K-12 schools and the one K-5 school in Oklahoma pales in comparison to the number in Texas, which has thirty.

An initiative to establish a K-12 academy associated with Churches of Christ in Tulsa failed. Launched in 1979 as Green Country Christian Academy, the school utilized the classrooms of the Garnett Road and Memorial Drive Churches of Christ until it acquired property on Admiral Place from Tulsa Public Schools. Early on, Green Country was closely connected with Churches of Christ, with 80 percent of students, faculty, and trustees members. That preponderance, however, did not make the school particularly spiritual or financially successful. A heavy indebtedness caused the academy to shut its doors in May 1989. Bondholders, a large percentage of whom were Church of Christ members, lost thousands of dollars. A bank in Amarillo, Texas, went bankrupt.[20]

Nonetheless, a group of Church of Christ men were able to reconstitute the school in August 1989, but with a nondenominational Christian commitment. It quickly reopened as Wright Christian Academy, named for the venerable J. E. Wright, and then in 1993 as Greater Tulsa Christian Academy. Today, the remnants of the Southern Hills Church of Christ and the Garnett Road Church of Christ meet for worship services in the academy's new gymnasium. The academy retains a strong Christian commitment, but a relationship with Churches of Christ is hardly apparent.

Preacher Training Schools

Concern about whether young people would retain their faith or preachers know how to "rightly divide the word of truth" caused a significant number of conservative Churches of Christ members to seek "safe" training in what were known as schools of preaching. Unaccredited, the schools were not designed to give students broad training in biblical studies and theology, but primarily to nail down doctrinal points of view. One of the earliest in the state was the tuition-free Oklahoma College of the Bible and School of Preaching established by the McCloud congregation in 1965. Others were at Elk City (1971–75), Mangum, Owasso (1982–present), Duncan Westside (1988), and Elmore City (1989–91).[21] The Oklahoma City School of Biblical Studies on Gardner Drive opened in 1989 with Marion R. Fox as director under the supervision of the Barnes Church of Christ in Oklahoma City. Fox was an Oklahoma native, holding bachelor, master, and doctorate degrees, primarily in the sciences. He had preached for well over four decades and in addition had taught in schools of preaching sponsored by five different Oklahoma congregations.[22] If the prospective preachers did not find the Oklahoma schools satisfactory, more than likely they entered Brown Trail School of Preaching in Bedford, Texas, "Where Old Paths [were] Still New."[23]

A Passion for Building

A building boom among Churches of Christ in Oklahoma in the postwar era also demonstrated that the faith community was growing. According to Olan Hicks, editor of the *Christian Chronicle*, there were 653 congregations in Oklahoma in 1946, only 14 of which African Americans dominated.[24] Because of the growth and prosperity of the 1950s, many of the congregations, black and white, undertook the construction of new buildings or major renovations of the old one, at the same time hoping to incorporate some architectural distinction into the final structure.[25] The Culbertson Heights congregation in Oklahoma City demonstrates how that worked out. Located just east of the state capitol, the congregation found its building inadequate in terms of size and its neighborhood transitioning from white to black. In 1957, it chose to construct a new building on Northwest Fiftieth Street in the Federalist style with red brick walls topped by an elegant spire. Architecturally, it was unmatched by any other Church of Christ in Oklahoma—indeed, by only a few of any denomination. The members at Culbertson named their new congregation "Mayfair Church of Christ." Within a dozen years, it had an average of 560 in worship services and 450 in Bible school.[26]

As in the case of Mayfair, most Churches of Christ in Oklahoma did building of some kind in the 1950s and 1960s. In Oklahoma City, that included Capitol Hill, Memorial Road, Midwest City, Del City, Northwest, and Wilshire. In Tulsa were Memorial Drive, Brookside, Twenty-Ninth and Yale, Park Plaza, and Garnett Road. Other cities with new buildings included Altus, Ardmore, Catoosa, Duncan, Bartlesville, Edmond, Enid, Elk City, Jenks, Lawton (Northwest), Muskogee, Mustang, Norman (University and Westside), Owasso, Poteau, Shawnee, Skiatook, Stillwater, and Yukon, to name some of the larger ones.

A unique aspect of some of the new structures, but also of some older, was the inclusion or addition of pastoral scenes to the church baptistery. Some of the best of these paintings were done by Blanche Garrett Perry of Denver, Colorado. Born in Alabama in 1890, Perry moved to Colorado as an antidote for tuberculosis in 1925. To fill her time as she recuperated, she learned to paint, a vocation she followed the rest of her life. Her paintings were highly symbolic pastoral scenes. "'The Church,' [is] symbolized by snowcapped mountain enshrouded in a cloud of mystery," she wrote on the back of a canvas sent to the Church of Christ at

Prague. Between 1940 and 1950, she completed thirteen paintings for Oklahoma churches. Those who saw them were impressed. "The painting in the baptistery is grand, the best I have ever seen. I stand and look and study and admire; it is wonderful. A great work you are doing, preaching The [sic] gospel in picture," wrote Gray Carter of Lawton. Preston Cotham, minister at Pauls Valley, declared, "While holding meetings this summer, I saw many beautiful baptistery scenes you have painted. You will never know how much good you are doing for the work of the Lord in this respect."[27] Church house aesthetics apparently added some stature to Churches of Christ in their local communities.

Domestic Evangelism

Many of the leaders and members of Oklahoma Churches of Christ attributed their postwar growth to domestic evangelism. Of the techniques employed, most notable was the *Herald of Truth*, a sophisticated radio and television production produced by the Highland Church of Christ in Abilene, Texas, beginning 1953. With the cooperation of hundreds of congregations and individuals, it explained effectively the church's faith and distinctive practices (baptism for the remission of sins and a capella music, for example), but it also emphasized the basic doctrines, interests, and objectives (the trinity, for example) the church shared with other Christian communities. George Bailey, formerly the minister of Culbertson Heights in Oklahoma City, narrated the program on the radio, and Batsell Barrett Baxter, from Nashville, Tennessee, on television. In the two mediums, the program reached an audience of millions. Churches of Christ in Oklahoma were strong supporters of and took pride in the productions, which made them part of the mainstream of religious practice in the United States. Many congregations took pleasure in identifying themselves as "supporters of the *Herald of Truth*." A growing number, however, took exception to the way the programs were produced, that is by a "sponsoring congregation," whose leadership solicited and accepted funds from "cooperating" congregations. This practice was considered antithetical to that recorded in scripture.[28]

Seeking National Stature

With an improving national standing, Church of Christ leadership saw value in constructing church buildings of architectural substance in the political and economic capitals of the United States, namely Washington, D.C., and Manhattan. Of course, to build the kind of structure desired was beyond the resources of any single congregation. For that reason, church leaders launched two fellowship-wide campaigns to raise the necessary money. The result was a beautiful, federalist style building at Sixteenth and Decatur Streets in the national capital in 1948.[29] The four-story building in Manhattan was not completed until 1968, although it actually opened in 1957.[30]

Church leaders also saw value in creating an exhibit at the World's Fair at New York City in 1965. The exhibit would feature the plea of Churches of Christ for Christian unity and publicize the church's growth as a religious organization. The Queens congregation constructed the exhibit, but it was financially supported by almost 1,500 individuals and congregations across the United States. The exhibit declared that the Churches of Christ were "On the March" with "An Old Message, a New Spirit," and a "dynamic future."[31]

A distinct program that exemplified the claims of the World's Fair exhibit was Exodus Bay Shore. The objective of Exodus, sponsored by the Richland Hills congregation in Fort Worth, was to plant a Church of Christ at Bay Shore, Long Island, with as many as sixty young professional families who would immigrate as a group from the American Southwest in 1963. Some 210 did go; the West Islip congregation was established; twelve years later, some thirty southwesters still worshipped with it.[32]

In all of this, Churches of Christ in Oklahoma participated. To achieve impressive buildings and a church plant on the East Coast, they cooperated with each other and accepted the leadership of a sponsoring congregation. They contributed to the cost; they were involved in the project itself. For example, Burton Coffman, the former minister at Lawton, organized and executed the Manhattan campaign. The Mayfair and Memorial Road congregations in Oklahoma City each contributed one hundred dollars a month into the mid-1960s.[33] Bob Goodrich and his family from Edmond moved to Bay Shore to be part of that church plant. And C. E. McGaughey, formerly the minister at Tenth and Francis at Oklahoma City and then preaching in Washington, D.C., launched the drive to construct the building in the national capital that, he believed, would be worthy of the fastest growing church organization in the United States. The Tenth and Francis congregation was an early contributor to that project, a practice that some of their leading men would soon come to question.

Local Evangelization

Most members of Churches of Christ considered the initiatives on the East Coast and the programming of the *Herald of Truth* as evangelistic endeavors. At least that was the way they were categorized in church budgets. Other activities were also considered valuable as ways of introducing individuals to the faith and practices of Churches of Christ—that is, the New Testament Church. One of these was the Campaign.

Campaigns

With only modest exaggeration, the Campaign was an Oklahoma contribution to the evangelistic techniques of Churches of Christ nationally. It was heavily promoted by Ivan Stewart at the Twenty-Fifth and Geraldine Streets congregation in Oklahoma City.[34] Stewart was born in Texas; held a diploma from Shawnee High School (in Oklahoma); had witnessed Pearl Harbor as a U.S. sailor; and had attended Pepperdine College in Los Angeles. The idea undergirding his technique was to take a group of people from local congregations to a distant community, flood that community with door knockers and handbills, sign people up for correspondence classes on the Bible, and attract residents to a gathering of praise and instruction. The ultimate objective was to baptize as many as possible and to organize a new or strengthen an existing congregation. Stewart led at least forty-nine groups and over four thousand workers to urban areas where Churches of Christ were not strong, especially in Canada, Australia, Hawaii, the northeastern United States, and got satisfying results. Few urban congregations in Oklahoma did not follow suit.[35]

But there were critics of Stewart's practices. Not only were they expensive, but workers were inexperienced and could do little more than knock on doors, hand out tracts, and sign people up for correspondence courses or Bible study classes taught by someone else. Moreover, campaigners were often spreading the word about Jesus in the target community when they were not apt to do something similar in their home community. Organizers like Stewart, however, ignored the critics and continued to promote summer campaigns.[36]

Gospel Meetings

More traditional evangelistic practices were still in practice during the 1950s and 1960s. One of these was the gospel meeting hosted by a local congregation. They were different from those of the prewar era in that they seldom extended beyond a week and were area wide in reach—that is, hosted by several congregations. In 1948, for example, five Oklahoma City churches held five days of lectures that featured twenty-eight speakers. In March 1962, Marshall Keeble conducted a six-stop tour of Oklahoma in the interest of Oklahoma Christian College. Eight thousand heard him speak at the Municipal Auditorium in Oklahoma City.

There were lesser but still robust crowds at Ponca City, Tulsa, Altus, Lawton, and Muskogee. In 1964, a similar meeting in Tulsa attracted 8,500 hearers and in Oklahoma City 10,000.[37] Singing schools also persisted. In 1960, L. O. Sanderson directed one attended by 529 singers.[38]

Debates

Less ubiquitous than a generation earlier, the debate was another evangelistic technique that found currency in the postwar era. One of the more notable debates occurred in Stillwater in May 1952. Dr. Eric Beevers, priest of the St. Francis Xavier Catholic Church, challenged Eldred Stevens, minister of the local Church of Christ, to discuss the propositions "The New Testament Is the Supreme Authority in the Christian Religion" and "The Roman Catholic Church Is the Original Apostolic Church of Christ." Interest was so great that the four-night debate attracted an estimated audience of five thousand persons from fourteen states. Attendees spilled out of the church building on to the courthouse lawn. The event was widely covered by the press (United Press, Associated Press). Not surprisingly, partisan Church of Christ witnesses judged Stevens the victor, but Beevers did not help his cause when he declined to participate in the last session. The status of the Church of Christ in Stillwater and around the state rose as a consequence of the debate. One reporter declared, "Harmony, peace, zeal, faith and love . . . permeates every function and activity of this congregation." After distinguishing himself on the debate platform, four months later Stevens moved to Nashville, Tennessee, to teach at David Lipscomb College.[39]

Youth Programs

Oklahoma Churches of Christ sponsored a variety of new youth programs with evangelistic intentions. Among these were youth rallies, bus ministries, and summer camps. In Oklahoma, the greatest advocate of youth rallies was "Big" Don Williams of the Twenty-Fifth and Geraldine church in Oklahoma City. He was one of the earliest ministers with a commission solely to youth in Oklahoma as well as the nation. His rallies early on occurred on Saturdays with a menu of speakers that appealed to teenagers and song leaders who led up-tempo hymns. The idea was to convince attendees of the blessings of the cross and their obligation to share those blessings with those who knew nothing of them. Other individuals and congregations sponsored their own youth rallies, often following different formats. Eventually, Williams called his youth program the "Under-20 Church," in the interest of which he traveled one million miles during the course of his career.[40]

Bus Ministries

New too was the bus ministry, whereby a congregation sent buses through its neighborhood to gather up children to attend Sunday school and worship services. To get participation often required inducements that might include everything from providing food (breakfast) to giving away kites and Bibles. It also required tolerance for disruptions of one kind or another in classes or worship services. The so-called Joy Bus Ministry was particularly effective in urban areas like Tulsa (as at Eastside, Garnett Road, and Memorial Drive) and Oklahoma City (as at Del City, Edmond, and the Village.) But it was also useful at places like Ponca City and Seminole, among others.[41]

Summer Camps

Another evangelistic tool adopted by Oklahoma Churches of Christ in the postwar era was the summer camp, already in widespread use by Baptist churches, most notably at Turner Falls. These camps were designed to provide intensive Bible instruction, wholesome recreation, and social interaction. Above all, the camps were a place where youngsters could be encouraged to examine their spiritual condition and consider baptism. Some of the better-known Church of Christ camps were WA-KI-CU-BE Christian Camp (Washita, Kiowa, Custer, and Beckham Counties), near Cordell (1947); Camp Jack Little, near Lake Murray (1947); Camp Rock Creek, near Norman (1956); Burnt Cabin Christian Camp, on Lake Tenkiller, near Muskogee (1958); Camp Lu-Jo-KISMIF (after benefactor *Lu*cille *Jo*nes, with advice to *K*eep *It* *S*piritual, *M*ake *It* *F*un), near Faxon (1962); Quartz Mountain Christian Camp, near Lone Wolf (1961); Pettijohn Springs Christian Camp, near Madill (1971); Lariat Creek Christian Camp, near Geary (1973); Frog Road Christian Camp, near Mannford (1970s); Black Mesa Christian Camp, near Boise City; Mountain Fork Christian Camp, near Beavers Bend; and West of Heaven Christian Camp, near Stillwater. Most if not all of these camps met the standards of the National Christian Camping Association, a Church of Christ organization. They also provided spiritual experiences that impressed campers for the rest of their lives.[42]

International Missions

After World War II, congregations of Churches of Christ across the United States were enthusiastic about spreading the gospel in foreign lands, especially in Europe, Asia, and Africa. In Oklahoma, however, such enthusiasm was limited.

Of the 160 missionary families sent by Churches of Christ to foreign fields in 1959, only 10 were supported by Oklahoma congregations.[43] Whether that was due to limited financial resources or some theological issue is unclear, but to a mission enthusiast like Wendell Broom, who grew up in the Tenth and Francis congregation in Oklahoma City and was supported by it in a mission field in New England, it was an embarrassment.

The mission families supported by Oklahoma churches identified by Broom as being in the field in 1959 included those of the following men: Eugene Peden in Nigeria (sponsored by the Altus congregation); James Hobby in Northern Rhodesia (sponsored by the Canton church); Duane Hindsley in France (sponsored by Thirty-First and Pennsylvania congregation in Oklahoma City); Loyd Collier in Germany (sponsored by Twelfth and Drexel church in Oklahoma City); Elmer Shackelford in Hawaii (sponsored by the Miami church); Don Shackelford in Italy (supported by the Broken Arrow church); Bert Perry in the Philippines (sponsored by the Wilson church); Mitchell Greer in Sweden (sponsored by the Midwest City church); Joe McKissick Jr. in South Africa (supported by the Twenty-Ninth and Yale church in Tulsa); and Wendell Broom in Nigeria (supported by Tenth and Francis congregation in Oklahoma City).[44]

At least three families supported by Oklahoma churches had served their time in the mission field and were back to the United States by 1959. This included the H. E. Pierce family, who, with the support of the Frederick church, had served in Capetown, South Africa, beginning in 1949.[45] The Culbertson Heights church in Oklahoma City had sent Roy Palmer and family to Frankfurt, Germany, in 1954. Edward Brown, an Okemah native, served with his family in Japan between 1949 and 1954.[46] In 1947, the Eighth and Lee church in Lawton sent Army Airforce veteran Thomas Ward Jr. and family to Southern Rhodesia; sadly, Ward contracted polio there and died in the field.[47]

In the 1960s, the track record of sending missionaries abroad improved for Oklahoma churches. More individually or cooperatively sent missionaries abroad. Under the auspices of the Garden Oaks congregation in Oklahoma City, for example, African American Robert James went to Kingston, Jamaica, where in 1963 he successfully utilized radio programming in his evangelistic work. Three other nonblack Oklahomans joined James in a campaign.[48] The Sixth and Arlington congregation in Lawton sent their pulpit minister, Robert Douglas, an Oklahoma City native, and family to the Muslim countries of Libya (Benghazi), Egypt (Cairo), and Lebanon (Beirut) between 1962 and 1969.[49] As might be expected, Douglas learned that Christian missionaries were not welcomed in Muslim nations.

In the late 1960s, Howard Norton helped establish a vital outpost in Sao Paulo, Brazil. Early in 1971, he came to Oklahoma to serve as missionary in residence at Oklahoma Christian College and at the Memorial Road Church of Christ. In the course of the subsequent decade, he made several trips back and forth to Brazil. During the last one, he helped prepare Teston Gilpatrick for service in Brazil under the sponsorship of the Memorial Road church.[50]

Supported by Stillwater and other Oklahoma congregations, Joe Watson, campus minister at Oklahoma A&M College, went to South Africa in 1966, where he was well received.[51] So too was David Roper, a Muskogee native who had preached at the Village in Oklahoma City and the Westside congregation in Muskogee, who went as a missionary to Australia in 1968 and served until 1977.[52]

Meanwhile, Oklahoma congregations were deeply concerned by the challenges facing Church of Christ missionaries in Italy in the 1950s. There, Italian officials, all influenced by the Catholic Church, were troubled by the number of converts facilitated by Church of Christ missionaries after World War II. Consequently, the authorities expelled them from the country and demanded that they close the twenty-two churches that had been established in Italy. The missionaries, including Don Shackelford from Broken Arrow, Oklahoma, appealed to Church of Christ members across the United States to bring pressure on Italian officials to change their policy. Among many others in Oklahoma, the McLish Avenue congregation in Ardmore took ads in the *Daily Ardmorite* telling of the difficulties in Italy and enlisting Oklahoma's U.S. senators Robert S. Kerr and Elmer Thomas and U.S. representative Carl Albert to do something to alleviate the situation. The Italians did reverse their policies and admit Church of Christ missionaries, although it is unclear how much of that was due to the influence of the Oklahoma congressional delegation.[53]

In the 1960s, Oklahoma Churches of Christ also participated in notable mission work in Vietnam. Of course, Vietnam had long been at war, although U.S. troops did not arrive until March 1965. Well before the nation was so deeply divided by the war, the Memorial Road church next to the Oklahoma Christian College campus as well as the Village church at Britton had a strong desire to minister to U.S. servicemen and women in Vietnam as well as share the gospel message with Vietnamese nationals. Those and other congregations sponsored the OCC faculty family of Ralph and Gladys Burcham as missionaries in Saigon beginning in 1966 to the Tet Offensive in 1968, and again in 1969 and in 1973. While there, they ministered to the Saigon church made up of Vietnamese and Americans, encouraged conversion to Christianity, helped organize an orphanage, and established an international school. The Burchams' congregation in Saigon became a refugee center and helped scores of Vietnamese resettle in the United States, most notably Oklahoma. The Memorial Road church provided temporary housing for the immigrants at the Lion's Club Camp adjacent to the Oklahoma Christian University campus.[54]

Although he technically was not a missionary, Claud Fly, an Oklahoma A&M alumnus who held a doctorate in agronomy and soil science, was a committed Christian and Church of Christ member. After a career with the U.S. Department of Agriculture, he traveled internationally as an agriculture consultant. In August 1970 when he was on assignment to Uruguay, five Tupamaro rebels burst into his Montevideo office and at gunpoint took him prisoner. For the next 208 days, he lived in wire cages, dank basements, and dungeon-like hideouts. Of his captors, he pleaded for and was finally given a New Testament. They asked for a $1 million ransom, which the U.S. State Department refused to pay. The rebels finally released Fly after he suffered a devastating heart attack and nearly died. His survival he attributed to his Christian faith.[55]

Caring for the Orphans and Elderly

Although fully committed to evangelization, Oklahoma Churches of Christ continued to consider themselves obligated to care for homeless children and needy elderly. They would not have defined that interest as "social justice," a term used primarily by Catholics, but they certainly would have identified it as a New Testament charge and as one of the things that Christian denominations in the United States did.

Children's Home at Turley

As we have seen, Oklahoma Churches of Christ had long supported a home for homeless children at Tipton. In the postwar era, two more such facilities were organized. Opening in 1947 under the care of the North Main Church of Christ in Tulsa, the oldest of these was the Turley Children's Home, situated on Cincinnati Street just north of Tulsa. J. E. Wright, one of the elders of the North Main church and subsequently of Brookside, provided much of the leadership and money in the initial years; he was even the first superintendent of the home. Oscar Slagle donated twenty-six acres of land west of Turley for the facility.[56]

The home had sacrificial leadership. J. C. Florence served as superintendent between 1947 and 1951. He added to the campus a new twenty-bedroom dormitory and a large community dining hall for the residents. Food was donated to the home, much in the same manner as it was at Tipton, but the children also raised rabbits and poultry to supplement food from other sources. Claud Green followed Florence as superintendent, serving between 1951 and 1956. He published a monthly tract entitled *Our Children*, and he organized the Home Singers group that promoted the institution among the Tulsa churches.[57]

Thomas Lloyd Connel assumed leadership in 1956. Well-known for his preaching in the Tulsa area and later for his service as editor of the esteemed *Christian Worker* soon to be relocated to Tulsa, he was "loved and respected for his interest in young people." Connel also proved to be an effective fund-raiser, securing support not only from Churches of Christ in Oklahoma but from philanthropic sources in Tulsa, particularly the Mabee Foundation. He also started tree-planting and pig-feeding programs; he succeeded in getting individuals or congregations to donate one beef per month for meals; and he managed for a friend of the home to gift it a working ranch and group home just north of Porter. He was also a builder, finding the money to construct the home's first cottage. By 1964, Turley cared for some ninety-one children in five separate units; twenty-three children lived in foster homes. Ten years later, sixteen house parents and eight staff members, including the superintendent, served the institution. Connel retired as superintendent in 1977, although he was wooed back to handle some financial mismanagement for a year in 1981. Bill Hamrick replaced him as superintendent. In 1983, the home had an operating budget of $50,000 per month, 80 percent of which came from Churches of Christ and individual Christians.[58]

In December 1980, to complete the story, Robert O. Tucker gifted the home with 240 acres of land north of Claremore. The home was required to build a cottage on twenty-five acres and to let Tucker live on the remainder until he died. He had no connection with Churches of Christ, only an interest in helping disabled, mistreated, and homeless boys and girls. In the years to come, three family-style homes were built on the property as well as a classroom building and gym. The program housed at Turley moved to the new campus at Claremore and was renamed Hope Harbor Children's Home and Academy in 1999. The elders of the Claremore church served as the board of trustees.[59]

Westview Boys Home

In 1956, a group of caring Christian men was eager to provide a refuge for needy boys in western Oklahoma. The opportunity to do so materialized when Billie Sol Estes, a Pecos, Texas, businessman and a member of the Church of Christ, donated his one-half interest in seven large apartment houses in Frederick, Oklahoma, together with $1,500 in cash, to start the project. Simultaneously,

Lillie Mae Armstrong Burton of Nashville, Tennessee, paid $10,000 for the half-interest belonging to Estes's partner and donated it.[60] With the leadership of Clarence Overstreet, the group purchased the thirteen-acre campus of the Westview school system near Hollis and organized the Westview Boys' Home.

At first, the boys slept dormitory-style in the old school building and used the gymnasium for recreation. Five years later, Superintendent Jack Sikes, formerly of the Tipton Home, introduced family-style living with the construction of Molloy Cottage, a 3,500-square-foot home. At the time, the concept of family living was an innovative approach to child care. The campus, more accurately considered a ranch, covered 1,600 acres and featured six individual brick cottages. Each individual home offered six to eight youngsters a comfortable, warm, family-type atmosphere with parent models of the Christian lifestyle. Altogether in 1961, Westview served twenty-eight boys.[61]

Unlike Tipton and Hope Harbor, the Westview Boys' Home was independent from the elders of the Hollis Church of Christ. Board members were church members, but they did not constitute the eldership of a particular congregation. As such, the home had more flexibility. All residents and staff members, however, attended every meeting of the Hollis church. The boys were encouraged to attend youth group activities, including devotionals, parties, and youth rallies. Each also attended at least one session of church camp every summer. They participated as well in home devotionals, where they learned to lead a devotional and present a believer's message.[62]

Retirement Centers

In addition to homes for the homeless, Churches of Christ members in Oklahoma also opened assisted-living retirement centers for the elderly. One of the earliest and most successful was Cordell Christian Home. Opened as a retirement home in 1962, the $400,000 cost of the facility was financed though the provisions of the federal Housing Act of 1959. Initially, it housed eighty-two retirees. In time, however, it converted to a 110-bed nursing home. It was considered a ministry of the Cordell Church of Christ, under the leadership of the church's elders.[63]

The same was true of the complex of retirement homes of the Highland Church of Christ in Tecumseh. Completed in 1990, the church owned but did not operate the Tecumseh facility, which rented twenty-two one- and two-bedroom units to retirees. The units were clustered in a circle not far from the church building.[64]

Tealridge Manor retirement facility, next to the campus of Oklahoma Christian College (now University) in Edmond, opened in 1989. It was owned and operated by the college's investment corporation and offered both independent and assisted living for as many as seventy-five residents. It valued its close relationship with Oklahoma Christian and the Memorial Road Church of Christ. Because of the housing needs of the university, however, the facility slowly transitioned into a student-living community beginning 2018.[65]

The Tulsa Christian Home on East Thirty-Sixth Street was a skilled nursing facility that provided for as many as fifty persons. Under the authority of a board of trustees made up of Church of Christ members, it opened in the 1960s. It always struggled financially, however. In the 1980s, the board closed the facility and sold the property. The profits of the sale were turned over to the Tulsa Foundation, managed by many of the men who had served the home, who in time allocated most of the foundation's assets to Wright Christian Academy, the K-12 facility in Tulsa.[66]

Rather than a retirement facility, the Central Oklahoma Christian Home at Sixty-Third and Portland in Oklahoma City was an assisted-living facility. It cared for some fifty patients. The leadership, including the board and staff, were all members of Churches of Christ, as well as many of the residents. It too encountered serious financial problems, found it necessary to shut down operations, sold its physical plant, and merged its assets and governing board with Tealridge Retirement Center early in the twenty-first century. The promised improvement of Tealridge as an assisted living facility, however, was slow in coming.

Despite an occasional setback, Churches of Christ in Oklahoma experienced dynamic change in the post–World War II era. Evidence of this ranged from the founding of Oklahoma Christian University, to the construction of architecturally impressive church houses, to utilization of different means of evangelization both domestic and international, to special attention bestowed on the youth of the church. All of this seemed to have had positive effects, as the growth of the Seminole congregation suggested. From this vantage point, the future of the Oklahoma church seemed bright.

11

POLITICAL AND
THEOLOGICAL CHALLENGES
1950–1970

The good times that brought church growth and prestige in the post–World War II era could not last. The United States engaged in a cold war with Russia that brought stress domestically in the form of McCarthyism and internationally in the form of the Korean and Vietnam Wars. The election of John F. Kennedy as president raised fears about Catholicism's expansiveness. The persistence of racial prejudices and the disappointing results of President Lyndon Johnson's "War on Poverty" stimulated the Civil Rights revolution and radicalization of many of America's best and brightest. Feminists pushed for an Equal Rights Amendment to the U.S. constitution that seemed to some to strike "at the very foundation of American life," the home.[1] To that volatile mix, conservative members of Churches of Christ added their fear that the church had lost its way, having forsaken the premise that all religious practices required New Testament examples. To them, suburban America seemed unsettled and uncertain. The consequences were apparent in the church. By 1980, only 193 attended Sunday school at the Shawnee Church of Christ, and only 241 attended its worship services.[2] Nationally, according to a fairly accurate count, total membership of Churches of Christ had declined to 1,239,612.[3]

Manifestations of Religious Nationalism

In response to the perceived threat of postwar communism, church members virtually abandoned the historic apocalypticism of Barton Stone and David Lipscomb, or whatever was remaining, following World War II. George S. Benson advocated religious nationalism as an alternative. From his perspective, "the America way of life" was threatened by a complex of oppressors. Of those, most significant were the prospects of communist and Catholic domination. At Harding, Benson centered his concerns about communism in the National Education Program (NEP), which he adroitly sold to East Coast elites as a way to restore the American way of life, to pay off Harding's accumulated debt, and to improve and extend the school's facilities. The NEP became a model for Oklahoma Christian College, as we have noted, as well as for George Pepperdine College in Los Angeles. But there was a downside to the model: abroad, Harding came to be known as the "academic seat of the Ultra Right." Nonetheless, Benson and his causes were widely respected and endorsed in Oklahoma Churches of Christ.[4]

The *Voice of Freedom* was another expression of religious nationalism. While the NEP defended Americans from communism, the *Voice of Freedom* defended them from Catholicism. The periodical began as an anti-communist publication in 1953, but, with the editorship of L. R. Wilson in 1956, assumed the mantle of anti-Catholicism. Although self-defined as "non-denominational," the organizers, editors, and writers were primarily Church of Christ men. Their prejudices had been shaped by the recent experiences of the church's missionaries in Italy, where they had been expelled from the country because of the objections of the Catholic Church. Probably of more immediate concern to these men was the prospect of John F. Kennedy, a committed Catholic, being elected as president of the United States in 1960.

Like other conservative Protestants, most Church of Christ members did not believe that Kennedy could be a good president and a good Catholic, or be loyal to the United States and to the State of the Vatican City at the same time. "Therefore," concluded the Muskogee Church of Christ *Reflector,* "let it not be said we are opposing Kennedy's nomination on the basis of his religion. It is his allegiance to a foreign power that prevents his complete loyalty to the Constitution and freedoms of the United States." In addition, it disturbed church members that Catholics presumably were free to tell "falsehoods" under certain circumstances.[5] These conditions partially explained why *Voice of Freedom* had a circulation of 100,000 nationwide in 1960 and anti-Catholic sentiments made their way into church bulletins and Sunday sermons in Oklahoma Churches of Christ. After Kennedy won the election, however, circulation of the *Voice of Freedom* decreased rapidly, as did anti-Catholicism within the church.[6]

As Conservative Republicans

As in the case of the state itself, the political orientation of Oklahoma Church of Christ members was never the same after the election of 1960. Prior to it, the state voted for the Democrat candidate all but once in presidential elections and almost always in state and federal office elections. After 1960, however, Republicans won the presidential elections all but once and slowly but surely came to control most state and federal offices. Church of Christ members doubtlessly voted as did the state, as suggested by a 1975 survey by Royce Money, subsequently president of Abilene Christian University. He found that 76 percent of all Church of Christ members considered themselves politically conservative.[7] Given that orientation, it is safe to assume that Oklahoma Republicans can count on the support of the Church of Christ faithful in political as well as cultural matters.

Opposing the ERA

That certainly was the case in the debate over the Equal Rights Amendment (ERA), although with a difference. Heretofore, men generally took the leadership roles in the life of the church in matters of worship but also in how the church related to the community at large. As we have noted, most men and women in the church, even Irene Mattox, accepted the biblical admonition that women should not serve in leadership roles in the community of faith. That is not what happened in the ERA debate. For the first time, women in Churches of Christ overshadowed men in leadership positions.[8]

The proposed amendment to the constitution was only a sentence long: "Equality of rights under of the law shall not be abridged by the United States or any State on account of sex." Approved by the U.S. Congress and submitted to the states for ratification on March 22, 1972, the Oklahoma state senate approved it by voice vote the following day. Passage by the state seemed assured. But there was unexpected opposition. The *Phyllis Schlafly Report* took issue, insisting that the ERA would destroy family life as it was known. Oklahoman Ann Patterson—Republican, Episcopalian, and former member of the John Birch Society—had the same concern and would become the leader of the anti-ERA forces in Oklahoma. Baptist and Mormon women joined the effort, but the majority came from Churches of Christ, drawn in by Beverly Findley of Oklahoma City. She too was a former member of the John Birch Society and had met Patterson at a seminar of the society hosted by Oklahoma Christian College. Drawing on her network of Church of Christ women, Findley attracted five hundred of them to another conference at the college during which she educated them about her fears as to the consequences of the ERA. "God's plan" for the family was in danger, she said, and moral decline a virtual reality. During that meeting, conferees formally organized Women Who Want to be Women, or the Four Ws, and selected Findley as Oklahoma coordinator. In the fight that followed in Oklahoma whereby the state House of Representatives refused to affirm the amendment, 43 percent of the anti-ERA women were members of Churches of Christ. Seventeen percent were Baptist; 9 percent, Mormon; and 5 percent, Methodist.[9]

The Oklahoma churchwomen cooperated in the national campaign to defeat the ERA with their sisters in other states. The Four Ws organization actually had its beginning in Texas under the leadership of Lottie Beth Hobbs. Tottie Ellis organized the women in Tennessee. Hobbs and Ellis were both Church of Christ women. Their decade-long effort did not go unrewarded. Thirty-five states ratified the amendment, three states short of the necessary three-fourths. Oklahoma never ratified it, and five states sought to rescind their adoption. After 1982, the anti-ERA movement morphed into such groups as Eagle Forum, Moral Majority, Focus on the Family, Traditional Values Coalition, and Concerned Women for America. The common concern was a fear of moral decline. Participation of Church of Christ women in these groups was negligible, however. Following the defeat of the ERA campaign, they seem to have rediscovered the church's traditional teaching about politics: Christians should not become involved.[10]

Racism

The great concern about moral decline that motivated opposition to the ERA barely extended to social issues like racism. In 1969, Franklin Florence, the African American minister of the Rochester, New York, Church of Christ and close friend of Malcom X, told a black church audience in Oklahoma City that "brethren in the Church of Christ" were "doing absolutely nothing about the problems of our day." The white church, he said, was "reactionary and racist" and was unconcerned about the "dilapidated" churches and "worn out song books" relegated to their "black brothers." Hugo McCord, member of the Bible faculty at Oklahoma Christian College, penned a response. The chief problem of our day, he said, "as it was in Jesus' day, is sin." McCord believed that white Churches of Christ were actually doing a great deal to alleviate racial tensions, although they were not preaching that "love requires artificial integration." Insofar as dilapidated churches and worn-out songbooks were concerned, McCord thanked God that there were many black brethren "who have appreciated getting something rather than nothing."[11]

McCord was not defending racism among Oklahoma Churches of Christ, but it appeared that he was denying that it was a major problem. And the churches and Oklahoma Christian College seemed to act that way. The Civil Rights movement, which nationwide was something more intense and disturbing than previously experienced, was largely ignored. Indeed, there were few sermons from white pulpits or commentary in church bulletins encouraging repentance for racial sins. As we saw earlier, there was also no groundswell of support for the black student protestors at Oklahoma Christian College who had been arrested, jailed, and expelled for demonstrating in the president's office. Since the demonstration and Florence's comments occurred essentially at the same time, it perhaps does explain the testiness of McCord's response to the Rochester preacher.

Those who actually addressed racial issues were generally black. Franklin Florence was clearly one of those. But so too was Clyde Muse, minister of the Northeast congregation in Oklahoma City, an alumnus of Prairie View University and a Korean War veteran. In 1968, he spoke poignantly at a race relations workshop in Los Angeles on "The Christian and Racial Conflict" and "The Sin of Racism." His context may have been the Watts riots that had occurred three years earlier, but surely it also included the environment in Oklahoma that the next year would justify arresting students for demonstrating at Oklahoma Christian College.[12]

Religious nationalism embraced anti-communism, anti-Catholicism, anti-equal rights, and the reality of racism. It also championed mores traditional to conservative Protestantism. Among other things, that meant support of prohibition of alcoholic beverages in Oklahoma. This was an issue often discussed in congregational bulletins, like the one published by the Culbertson Heights church urging that liquor ads be made illegal in 1954.[13] And, of course, in the pages of the church bulletin, writers railed against dancing and how it was damaging the rising generation.[14]

The Noninstitutional Challenge

During the post–World War II era, as noted in the previous chapter, Oklahoma Churches of Christ built a college, constructed substantial church buildings, engaged in evangelization domestically and internationally, and developed facilities for homeless children and the elderly. They also saw themselves as national guardians against the dangers of communism and Catholicism. All of this meant, in some quarters, that the pessimism of pre-millennialism had given way to the optimism of post-millennialism.

But there were those who were suspicious. For them, being respectable was not necessarily a good thing. It implied that the church had institutionalized, that it had conformed to the twentieth century's expectation of an upstanding religious denomination rather than to biblical models of the "true" church. Current Church of Christ members, the critics believed, had forgotten that the quest for "innovations" like missionary societies, mechanical instruments in worship, and Endeavor organizations had fractured the unity of the Stone-Campbell movement earlier in the century and was likely to do so again.

At the national level, spokesmen for this perspective were Foy Wallace Jr., Yater Tant (1908–1997), and Roy Cogdill (1907–1985), all three of whom had spent considerable time living and preaching in Oklahoma. Their clarion call to guard the gates was issued through the columns of the *Bible Banner* and the *Gospel Guardian*. Their primary concerns were the means by which a local Church of Christ accomplished its benevolence and evangelistic work. Specifically, those tasks, they believed, had to be under the direct supervision of the elders of a single congregation. It was unbiblical, the argument ran, to take money from the church treasury and apply it toward a good work controlled by leaders elsewhere. "The [New Testament] churches were not tied together in any inter-congregational organization, neither was there any organization over them," declared one critic. That had been the problem with the missionary society that the "digressives" had championed fifty years earlier; it was now the problem with international missions supported by sponsoring churches, with the *Herald of Truth* radio and television programs, and with homes for the homeless, to name only three.[15]

The Tenth and Francis Streets Congregation

Nowhere did this tension play out more than with the Tenth and Francis Streets Church of Christ in Oklahoma City. As already noted, it was central Oklahoma's mother church, and the largest of all congregations in the state by 1950. In an auditorium that would comfortably seat 1,000 persons (1,300 if the balcony was included), some 700 attended Sunday morning services, and in a commodious annex, 540 attended Bible school. The annual budget in 1951 totaled $40,040, with more than one-third of it dedicated to evangelism. The congregation always supported at least six mission points annually and occasionally as many as thirteen. It also had an active radio ministry.[16]

Into the 1950s, the Tenth and Francis congregation was led by a core of talented elders and deacons. As we have noted, A. W. Lee and L. L. Estes were particularly able. Lee was a successful oil-products distributor who helped put the congregation upon a strong financial basis. Simultaneously, he chaired the board of directors of Western Oklahoma Christian College and served on the board of the Oklahoma School of Religion.[17] Estes was a successful banker and life insurance underwriter before he took an administrative position as a civil servant at Tinker Air Force Base. At church, he was a superb song leader and Bible class teacher. For reasons that can only be surmised, Lee and Estes had a falling out over the qualification and selection of additional elders and deacons in early 1952.[18] The rift was so deep that Lee and an associate elder, Caleb R. Todd, refused to meet with the newly named elders; Estes and his supporters thereafter publicly refused to recognize Lee and Todd as elders. It was a turning point in the life of the congregation.[19]

After Lee and Todd stepped aside, Estes's influence in the leadership of the congregation increased. According to one observer, "Much of the credit for the historic soundness of th[e] congregation [was] due to his righteous influence."[20] Despite the Tenth and Francis church's status as the mother church in central Oklahoma (spawning as it did so many plants) and as one of the most affluent in the state, it had remained faithful to its sectarian roots. Those, of course, had been nurtured by some of the most conservative full-time ministers in the fellowship, specifically Foy Wallace and Yater Tant. Others subsequently burnished that proclivity, including ministers Jack Meyer Sr. (1948–52),[21] James W. Adams (1956–64),[22] Dudley R. Spears (1964–71),[23] and Cleo Blue (1971–74). Adding to the polish were visiting revivalists like Roy Cogdill (1945), Delmar Owens (1954), Homer Hailey (1959), Hoyt Houchen (1959), and Harry Pickup (1960). It followed then that, as early as 1958, the elders, particularly influenced by James Adams, published a proclamation as to their position on the institutionalization of the church in Oklahoma and beyond. Not biblically authorized, they said, was support of (1) Christian colleges and schools, (2) some foreign mission programs, (3) a nationwide radio and television program, (4) youth programs and rallies, and (5) orphan homes and retirement centers. In such activities, they believed, God had directed his people to function through congregations, each with its own overseers or elders. They insisted that "Each church was, and is, separate, apart, and independent of each other. . . . Therefore, any effort on the part of an individual, or group of individuals, church or group of churches, to establish control over other churches [was] contrary to God's divine plan."[24]

Thus, it was believed, mission programs like those under way in postwar Germany, sponsored by elders of the Broadway congregation at Lubbock, Texas, and supported financially by individuals and "cooperating" congregations, were operating in error. Direct support of the missionary was being bypassed and the autonomy of the cooperating congregation compromised. Besides, there was no scriptural pattern for the practice. They had identical concerns about the *Herald of Truth* radio and television programs.[25]

The Tenth and Francis elders also considered area and statewide youth rallies a dangerous trend. They anticipated the emergence of a youth organization with a general president, secretary, treasurer, etc., an innovation that had been so divisive earlier in the century. In their view, youth social affairs, regionally and locally, should be directed by parents rather than the church.[26]

The elders also opposed congregational support of educational institutions. They took pride in the fact that individual members of the congregation had liberally supported the relocation of Central Christian College from Bartlesville to Oklahoma City, and that one member, L. B. Clayton, even served as chair of the college's board of trustees. But beyond that support, there had been no allocation from the church treasury. Doubtless, they also took some satisfaction in that Central Christian had adopted by-laws that bound the college not to solicit or accept funding from any Church of Christ congregation. The elders were ever watchful that the college would make no effort to exert any control over the churches.[27]

The leadership also had reservations about supporting orphan and homes for the elderly, although they had done it for years. They had concluded that in doing so they had corrupted the New Testament plan whereby churches contributed to needy congregation, evangelists, and their coworkers only. In other words, they contributed to organizations that were identical to their own. The good works of orphan homes should be supported individually, just like colleges.[28] So the objection was not to missions, televangelism, youth programs, colleges, or orphan homes per se, but to how those activities were managed and funded. If there was no New Testament example for the activity, it was argued, the church's treasury must be closed to it.

The budget of the Tenth and Francis congregation soon reflected the commitment to bring the Churches of Christ back to first principals. Monthly contributions to the Tipton Home and to Turley Children's Home ceased. The church, however, was willing to collect independent contributions to the homes and then pass them on.[29] Rather than join in support of the *Herald of Truth*, even greater emphasis was placed on evangelism in county-seat towns like Altus, Alva, Chandler, Duncan, El Reno, Kingfisher, Lawton, Medford, Muskogee, and Stillwater. The congregation also supported mission work in Cyril, Oklahoma City (Village and Green Pastures), and Wellston as well as in Alaska, Hawaii, Illinois, Mississippi, Montana, Nebraska, North Carolina, and Nigeria. The basic idea was to plant a "faithful" congregation, or one that undertook the "Lord's work" according to the New Testament as they understood it, in each of Oklahoma's seventy-seven counties, even if a "mainstream" congregation already existed.

That was the case in Stillwater. The congregation there dated back to 1920. Membership had grown to the extent that the church built a new building with an auditorium that would seat one thousand. With the help of others, it also constructed a new facility for its widely acclaimed Bible Chair. That the Stillwater congregation was mainstream, however, was a problem for the Tenth and Francis church leadership, which saw itself as anything but mainstream, preferably noninstitutional. Consequently, as a part of its mission work it opened a church plant on South Husband Street in Stillwater in 1968, supporting Howard E. Miller as minister. Miller had trouble getting any traction in the community. He seldom had more than thirty people in worship services and fifty dollars in the collection plate. In 1971, he moved to Iowa. His brother, Herman, succeed him, and John E. Hurn served as minister between 1973 and 1975.[30]

A similar situation existed in Altus. Despite the health of the local Church of Christ (at Elm and Hudson Streets), a mainstream church, the Oklahoma City congregation planted a noninstitutional church, or a "true" church, on Altus's east side in 1965. This concerned the leadership of the Elm and Hudson church, who wrote to their members that "some . . . preachers have decided to make war on Southwestern Oklahoma, and in cooperation with a church in Oklahoma City . . . have decided to divide as many congregations as possible." They did not intend to let that happen. A preacher selected by Tenth and Francis filled the pulpit of the new congregation, much of the support of whom came from Lindy McDaniel, a southwestern Oklahoma young man who pitched for the Saint Louis Cardinals for two decades and attended (and preached at) Churches of Christ. Prior to opening the East Side church, McDaniel had given his weekly contribution to Tenth and Francis. The Oklahoma City congregation, however, did not protest McDaniel redirecting his financial support. Actually the church considered it a blessing. The Tenth and Francis congregation's leadership saw itself as supporter and encourager of noninstitutional churches in Oklahoma and elsewhere.[31]

The new modus operandi meant that the Tenth and Francis church would not participate in activities that involved multiple congregations. Among other things, such programs involved regional lectureships. "The very putting on of such a program by a large number of churches, the very framing of a program for the churches, which has to be at least partially engineered by some sort of a central steering group raises grave dangers," said elder L. E. Diamond.[32] The same was true of colleges and Bible Chairs.[33] Not only would congregational autonomy be imperiled, but the church would find itself supporting social and recreational activities.[34] So concerned was one Tenth and Francis minister about the Lord's money going for recreation that he locked up the kitchen and other common space to prevent its use for social occasions, excepting wedding receptions.[35]

For some members of the congregation, the direction taken by the Tenth and Francis elders was inadequate. Indeed, two of the elders (Orman Henderson and George Willis) were quite convinced that the majority of their colleagues were too reasonable and flexible, too interested in unity, when it came to applying the principles of noninstitutional thought. In 1969, they withdrew from the congregation as a whole and began meeting first in the YWCA building and subsequently on Southwest Eighty-Fourth Street in Oklahoma City. Genuine efforts to retrieve the secessionists were unsuccessful. In due time, however, the two factions were reconciled though never rejoined.[36]

Simultaneously, the leadership of the Tenth and Francis congregation found that the progressive element among them was not dramatically seceding so much as it was quietly leaving, especially with the ministry of James W. Adams (1958–63). Between 1950 and 1970, Sunday morning worship attendance declined by two-thirds, from 471 to 149, most of this in the period after 1958. To disguise this loss, the leadership removed five rows or eighteen pews from the central auditorium and covered the empty space by spreading out the remaining pews.[37] Bible school attendance decreased from an average of 437 in 1950 to 238 in 1966; the annual budget dropped from $70,000 to $44,200 between 1958 and 1961. Given the strain on the budget and the changing demographic of the church's neighborhood, the Tenth and Francis leadership concluded that it was time to make a change in location. But it was clear that the congregation had paid heavily for objecting to the institutionalization of Churches of Christ.

In 1977, the elders sold the historic complex of buildings of Tenth and Francis to the Living Word Academy, a K-12 education organization associated with Churches of Christ, for $200,000. On property on Thirty-Eighth Street that the congregation had purchased eight years earlier, the elders constructed a new building known as the "Broadview Heights Church of Christ." In time, the building grew inadequate, and early in the twenty-first century the congregation constructed a new facility on north May Avenue west of Edmond named the "Seminole Pointe Church of Christ." It was one of thirty-three noninstitutional churches that met regularly in Oklahoma. At least one-half of those had been either planted or sustained by the state's mother church, notably at Altus, Duncan, El Reno, Lawton, Muskogee, Mustang, and Stillwater.[38]

Journalistic Support for Noninstitutional and Conservative Critics

Those in Oklahoma who worried about the unscripturalness of institutionaliza-tion found support in books like *Axe on the Root* (1966; 1967; and 1970) and periodicals like *Spiritual Sword* (1969), *Contending for the Faith* (1970), and the *Gospel Guardian* (1935). Roy Cogdill and Yater Tant, both of whom had close ties with the Tenth and Francis congregation, had purchased the *Guardian* and made it the mouthpiece of the noninstitutional movement.

Ira Y. Rice Jr. (1917–2001), who grew up in Oklahoma and attended the univer-sity at Norman, published the three volumes of *Axe on the Root* as well as monthly issues of *Contending for the Faith*. Often he expressed his disdain for Christian colleges and liberal theology, positions fully embraced by noninstitutionalists. But he himself was not of that movement and is best seen as a conservative critic of the mainstream church.[39] The same could be said of Thomas B. Warren, of Memphis, Tennessee, who in the *Spiritual Sword* opposed skepticism, liberalism, and relativism and affirmed the infallibility of the "inspired word of God and that men *can* learn and obey the truth."[40] For both Rice and Warren, the "truth" was to be discerned by the commands, examples, and necessary inferences of scripture, a hermeneutic in play since Alexander Campbell. That was the approach of most Oklahoma congregations whether they were noninstitutional or mainstream. It was not uncommon for the leaders of a congregation, for example, to send copies of the *Spiritual Sword* to every member, as did the elders of the Eastside church in Midwest City in 1991.[41]

Foy Wallace was certainly a critic of mainstream Churches of Christ, but to the surprise of many, he did not identify with the noninstitutionalists. Wallace had objected to premillennialism, to pacifism, and to Christian colleges, among other things, before World War II, issues he continued to discuss and write about after the war, in addition to his objections to the Revised Standard Version translation of the Bible. But he considered the noninstitutional movement divisive and after 1964 separated himself from it entirely. That decision disappointed many, even his son, William, who attributed his father's rejection to fear of jeopardizing financial support. The traditional congregation at Altus, Oklahoma, for example, kept the elder Wallace in its budget for more than a decade.[42]

Traditional Churches of Christ Respond

By 1970, it was clear that some of Oklahoma's Churches of Christ had divided into two different camps when it came to institutional developments: those who opposed them and those who did not. It was the institutionalists versus the noninstitutionalists; the digressives versus the anti-cooperationists; and the progressives versus the legalists. It was the language of division that the Stone-Campbell movement in Oklahoma had heard before in the late nineteenth and early twentieth centuries. It was disruptive then; it was just as disruptive toward the end of the twentieth century.

To respond to the criticisms of noninstitutionalists as well as some mainstream traditionalists, Church of Christ scholars like J. D. Thomas at Abilene Christian College used the same interpretive paradigm of scripture the noninstitutionalists used but more rigorously. In *We Be Brethren* (1958), he insisted that the traditional hermeneutic—command, example, and necessary inference—fully supported the practices of the institutionalized church.[43] Lewis Hale, a native of Cowlington, Oklahoma; an alumnus of Freed-Hardeman College, Abilene Christian College, the University of Oklahoma, and Texas Tech; and minister of the Southwest Church of Christ in Oklahoma City, embraced that line of reasoning. He argued in sermons, bulletin articles, and debates that there was nothing unscriptural about congregations combining resources to "preach the word" via missionaries or television and to shelter widows and orphans.[44] So too did most other preachers in Oklahoma. Consequently, the response in Lawton was not dissimilar to that across the state: "6th & Arlington and the other congregations were never burdened by the theological controversy of the 1950s or the non-institutional issue," insisted one observer.[45]

Some Church of Christ members who were put off by the claims of the noninstitutionalists and by the lack of social engagement by traditionalists expressed their discontent through the pages of *Mission Magazine*, a periodical that was published between 1967 and 1987. The magazine's goal was to explore the scriptures and their meaning; to understand fully the world in which the church lived; and to communicate the meaning of God's word to the contemporary world. All of this would lead to a fuller understanding of grace, it was said. To the surprise of many, these goals were unsettling to both the mainstream and the noninstitutional churches. In 1967, few of them were willing to admit that Churches of Christ were open to substantive criticism. For that reason, *Mission Magazine* in its twenty-year history circulated to no more than three thousand subscribers, generally far fewer. But those who were on the list found in its pages reasons to affirm their faith and the Stone-Campbell tradition. The geographical location of the subscribers has been lost, but it is reasonably certain that not many of them were located in Oklahoma. No Oklahomans, for example, were ever on the board of trustees, excepting Robert Douglas. Thus the progressive influence of the magazine, so much feared by traditionalist and noninstitutionalists alike, surely was limited in the state.[46]

In the three decades following World War II, the institutionalization of church work that extended beyond the local congregation troubled some of the leaders and congregants in Oklahoma. Foremost among these were the ministers and elders of the Tenth and Francis congregation in Oklahoma City. Concerned about preserving the "true" church, they ceased to support cooperative missions, television programs, Christian colleges, and homes for the orphans and elderly. The traditional Churches of Christ countered with new publications and changed hermeneutics. But division could not be avoided. The institutional controversy had furthered morality, William Wallace later reflected, but not spirituality.[47]

12

THE CHURCH IN DECLINE
1970–2000

In the 1950s and 1960s, the reports that the Church of Christ was the fastest-growing denomination in the United States put a smile on the face of members. Oklahomans saw no reason to doubt the report. They knew that in Tulsa the Eastside church enrolled 1,200 in Sunday school and that the Garnett Road congregation baptized 300 persons a year. In 1970, the Central Church of Christ in Ada hosted a campaign that attracted 1,200 persons per night and resulted in twenty-nine baptisms. In Oklahoma City, the Quail Springs congregation attracted 1,000 to 1,200 to worship services on most Sunday mornings. But numbers can be deceiving. Church growth scholar Flavil Yeakley has demonstrated that Church of Christ membership nationwide peaked in 1973 and thereafter declined at the rate of one-third of 1 percent per year until it reached zero in 1980. In the decades that followed, membership waned even further. In Oklahoma, there were 71,942 baptized members of the church (a number that did not include children) in 1980, but only 66,234 in 1990 and 62,322 in 2006, a decrease of 13.4 percent. All of this occurred even as the population of the state of Oklahoma was increasing by 18.3 percent. Church members found the trend line most concerning and even difficult to believe.[1]

Yeakley attributed the decline in Oklahoma to the failure of evangelism by church members rather than to economic factors. In the mid-1960s, there had been one baptism for every twelve members. By the mid-1970s, the ratio had increased to one in twenty. If the work of the ministers and evangelists were subtracted, the baptism-to-membership ratio would have been one to forty, according to Yeakley. Put differently, only 2 or 3 percent of the church's membership was "involved in the work of leading the lost to Christ," said Yeakley. Until that changed, total membership would continue to decline.[2]

Other Explanations

In Oklahoma, some of the faithful also attributed the decline in membership to unexpected confrontation with legal and cultural brokers. Especially challenging was the state's assertion of constitutional rights in the arena of church-state relations. Certainly that was the case of the invisible Christian colleges that functioned on the campuses of state colleges and universities. As already mentioned, the earliest Bible Chairs offered courses on the campuses of the adjacent state college that were accepted for academic credit. There was pushback on this arrangement from parties, academics as well as politicians, who believed that the practice was a violation of the constitutional provision separating church and state. In response, the Bible Chairs first moved their programs to off-campus locations, offering the courses there that they had been teaching on campus. Since the lines of the church-state division remained opaque, in the 1960s Bible Chairs offered their courses through Oklahoma Christian College, which then as a service transferred them for full credit to the state school.

The process of granting academic credit became so convoluted, however, that most of the Bible Chairs dropped the OCC option from their program and focused only on the broader aspects of ministry. At Edmond, the building constructed for the Bible Chair in 1965 was sold in 1976. Thereafter, campus ministry operated out of the Edmond church building. At Norman, the Alameda congregation supported campus ministry at the Bible Chair building just off campus, while the Westside congregation provided such a ministry at its building. The University Drive congregation at Lawton closed the Bible Chair at Cameron College in 1985. Thus in the 1970s the teaching programs of the invisible Christian colleges across Oklahoma changed dramatically because of external concerns that the Chairs were violating the constitutional provisions regarding separation of church and state.[3]

Two Legal Cases

Oklahoma church leaders also attributed the membership stasis to some bad publicity. No doubt they had in mind the pushback from two legal cases, one involving the North Pennsylvania Avenue Church of Christ in Oklahoma City and the other the Church of Christ in Collinsville, Oklahoma.

In the case of the North Penn congregation, its elders formally "disfellowshipped," or withdrew fellowship from, eleven of its members for irregular attendance in November 1968. They announced their action in the church bulletin, *Your Friendly Visitor,* which they then mailed unsealed to two hundred members and some four hundred nonmembers. When "sin enters the church," they wrote, "it must be purged out." Those who are "unclean," they asserted, will in the hereafter have their place "in the lake which burneth with fire and brimstone." The eleven members had "absented themselves from the assembly of the saints of the Lord on the Lord's day in violation of Hebrews 10:25." In doing so, they had "failed to let their lights shine for a good influence for God and ha[d] become an occasion of stumbling to others." If the eleven did not repent and return to their first love by November 17, 1968, the elders threatened, they would recommend that the church withdraw from the eleven. None of the eleven members did, and withdrawal followed.[4]

The eleven former church members were highly offended. They urged the elders to withdraw their statement and to readmit them to fellowship. The elders declined to do so. With that decision, the humiliated members sought a summary judgment in civil court against the elders. In their petition, they insisted that the elders "'maliciously' prepared and published this defamatory creation [notice of withdrawal] knowing it falsely imputed to them both directly and by innuendo or insinuation that they were impure, spotted, unclean, disorderly, untruthful, and sinful with 'appetites of the flesh.'" The elders responded that their announcement was made in "good faith" and "without malice toward" the plaintiffs "in the honest belief that they had merely exercised their duty."[5]

The district court of Oklahoma County tried the case. Judge Fenton R. Ramsey concluded that the statement of withdrawal was "libelous per se," but "nevertheless the church leaders had a qualified privilege to publish it so long as they believed they were doing their religious duty and did so in good faith and without malice." He concluded that was what had happened, and, therefore, the elders were entitled to an exonerating summary judgment."[6]

Of course, the eleven plaintiffs disagreed and appealed the decision. The appellant court proved more receptive. As it saw the facts, the withdrawal statement of the elders had diminished public esteem, respect, and goodwill and was designed to excite adverse, derogatory, or unpleasant feelings against or opinions of the eleven petitioners. Clearly, as the trial court had ruled, the document was libelous. Moreover, the elders "went beyond the necessities of performing their churchly duties and for an unwarranted purpose heaped unnecessary and false ridicule upon appellants." As evidence, the court turned to the Bible. Citing passages in the New Testament, it noted that writers John and Paul had urged withdrawal from cowards, traitors to the faith, the depraved and murderers, the fornicators and sorcerers, the idol worshippers and deceivers of every sort, as well as those who caused dissension and scandal. The court noted that the elders themselves admitted that none of these sins were at play. Then why not, it asked, follow the words of Jesus: "If your brother should commit some wrong against you, go and point out his fault, but keep it between the two of you. If he listens to you, you have won your brother over." From the court's point of view, there was no justification for the disparaging notice of withdrawal either by civil or biblical law. In February 1973, therefore, it ordered reversal of the summary judgment and remanded the case for further proceedings. The elders appealed the decision to the Supreme Court of Oklahoma, which the following year denied the motion.[7]

The North Pennsylvania Avenue church's legal challenges had hardly been resolved before the elders of the Collinsville, Oklahoma, Church of Christ encountered a similar problem involving one of its members, Marian Guinn. In March 1974, Guinn had been baptized at the 110–25-member congregation. Not long before her baptism, she had moved to Collinsville, a small agricultural and oil town northeast of Tulsa, to live with her sister and brother-in-law, both members of the local church. At the time, she was a twenty-seven-year-old mother of four children, living on welfare and going through a difficult divorce. After her baptism, she attended services of the church faithfully and from its members received numerous gifts of food, clothing, and money. With the church's assistance, she was able to earn her high school diploma and license as a registered nurse.[8]

In 1980, Guinn's relationship with the congregation turned sour. It was rumored in the community that she was responsible for the breakup of the marriage of the former town mayor. Based on that gossip, the three elders of the congregation felt compelled to meet with Guinn and advise her not to get involved with the man. When she downplayed the relationship, nothing further was done. But the rumors did not cease to circulate, and it became apparent that Guinn's relationship with the ex-mayor was more intimate than the elders had been led to believe. They asked her to meet with them again at the church building.

At this meeting, Guinn admitted to being intimate with the former mayor. The elders asked her to stop that relationship—which, using biblical language, they labeled as "fornication"—and return to the congregation, repent of the relationship, and seek the prayers of her Christian brothers and sisters. Guinn, however, declared that she intended to continue the liaison and left the meeting. At that point, acting in the role of shepherds, the elders determined to "disfellowship," or separate out from the flock, Marian Guinn in an ultimate effort to bring her back into the fold. In their judgment, the process was biblically based and with considerable precedent among Christian groups. The elders informed Guinn of the steps they were taking, that she would be disfellowshipped from the congregation if she did not "come forward," or step out, confess her sin, and respond to the prayers of the congregation.

Within a few days, Guinn delivered a letter of resignation from the church to one of the elders. "You have no right to judge me," she wrote. "Only God can judge me." Simultaneously, she asked that if they had to disfellowship her they do so on the basis of nonattendance rather than fornication. The elder replied that it had to be done on the basis of her relationship with the ex-mayor. With no further action on the part of Guinn, on October 4, 1981, the elders read a letter to the congregation withdrawing fellowship from her on the basis of fornication. There were no specific details identified. That letter of withdrawal was sent to four small Churches of Christ in nearby communities.[9]

In late October, Guinn filed a complaint alleging libel and slander, amended the next month to assert intentional infliction of emotional harm and intentional invasion of the right of privacy. The amended complaint asked for $1.3 million in compensatory and punitive damages. The case was tried in Tulsa County court before two hundred plus spectators in a standing-room-only courtroom in March of 1984, likely the most highly publicized and closely watched civil trial in Tulsa County District Court history. After four days of litigation, the jury in a shocking judgment found in favor of Guinn and awarded her $205,000 in compensatory and $185,000 in punitive damages, the total a figure five times the annual contribution of the Collinsville Church of Christ.[10] Clearly, said attorney Truman Rucker, "The judge and jury had an obvious inability to understand the motives of the church in its actions. They disregarded the spiritual aspects of the case and viewed it in a purely secular manner, much as if the church had simply been a fraternity or social club." Emerson L. Flannery of the *Guardian of Truth* insisted that it was "a blatant crossing by the state into church affairs." The Collinsville church appealed the case to the Supreme Court of Oklahoma.[11]

While litigation before the state high court was sorting itself out, the case attracted national attention. The *New York Times* covered it, *Sixty Minutes* had a segment on it, as did *Donahue* (August 1984). Stories appeared in most major newspapers. These accounts generally trivialized the issues and caricaturized Churches of Christ. Guinn's attorney set the tone. He found it difficult to grasp that a church and its elders might withdraw fellowship in an effort to bring Guinn back into the fold because of their love for her. "They loved her so much," said the attorney, "that they loved her plumb out of Collinsville." Accounts of the litigation also inspired an assortment of copycat suits throughout the country. In addition to other Churches of Christ in Garden Grove, California, and Memphis, Tennessee, similar suits were filed against Christian Community Church in San Jose, California, and the Central Baptist Church in Philadelphia, Pennsylvania.[12]

At least one-half of the religious community was appalled by the litigation. "It is hard to imagine a more intrusive involvement in private affairs of church than the tort actions in the *Collinsville* case," said Professor of Law James M. McGoldrick Jr. at Pepperdine University. Allowing the verdict to stand, he opined, "will lead to perpetual conflict between church and state . . . and the emasculation and destruction of the personally involved church and church leader. No state interest in the *Collinsville* case begins to outweigh that catastrophic impact on religion in this country."[13]

The appeal to and perhaps from the state supreme court was costly. In this case, the defendants, or the church, had to put up $740,000 in bonds to cover the judgment and accumulated interest for the period until the court made a decision. Far beyond the means of the Collinsville church, the Church of Christ community throughout Oklahoma and the nation launched a fund-raising campaign among its own, some four thousand individuals and congregations, to raise in excess of $1 million. Much of that was raised in one emotional appeal by Marvin Phillips, the minister of the Garnett Road church, at the Tulsa Workshop in April 1984.[14]

The state supreme court finally ruled on the appeal in January 1989. It threw out the $390,000 judgment. It said Guinn could have a new trial, through which she could seek damages for injuries she said she suffered after she withdrew membership from the church. No damages were allowable, however, for alleged injuries sustained while a member. With regard to damages, no distinction was made at the trial between the two time frames. That would have to be done by the court to which the case was remanded. Further litigation never occurred, however, for the parties settled out of court. The resolution required the settlement to be kept confidential, but it is on record that no judgment or award was paid by the Collinsville church from the fund established by donations given by Churches of Christ. Some of the balance of that account was refunded to donating churches. The county clerk released the $740,000 in bonds in August 1989.[15]

Judging from the literature, Churches of Christ in Oklahoma and elsewhere, as well as churches in other religious communities, struggled with the implications of the Collinsville case, and even the North Pennsylvania Avenue legal case, well into the twenty-first century. How was the church to discipline its members and not make its leadership liable for damages? The biblical model seemed dangerous. To attorney Rucker, that was an unfortunate consequence because "all that the Collinsville church and elders did with regard to Marian Guinn was consistent with their rights under the U.S. Constitution," not to mention scripture. Nevertheless, the better-known Collinsville case had a chilling effect upon the practice of withdrawing fellowship among Churches of Christ, to the extent that instances of it seldom if ever occurred thereafter.[16] For members who had serious reservations about the necessity of disfellowshipping, this was no great loss. Indeed, it was considered a positive development. But all understood that the litigation had changed the standing of the church in the church-state arena and put it on the defensive within the community at large.[17]

The Response to Negative Growth

Given the reality of membership decline after 1973, Churches of Christ in Oklahoma doubled down on evangelism, as Flavil Yeakley had suggested. To illustrate, they reaffirmed their commitment to the *Herald of Truth*, and they generously sponsored *SEARCH for the Lord's Way*, which featured both radio and television programming. Organized initially by Oklahoman Mack Lyon (1921–2015), then minister at Wewoka, *SEARCH* began broadcasting in September 1980 from an Ada station. The programs were well-received by local-market stations. Relative to the *Herald of Truth*, production and broadcasting costs were modest, making it unnecessary to appeal to multiple congregations for financial support, something that had left the church divided in the 1950s and 1960s. But Lyon did need support that was beyond the means of a small congregation. Accordingly, after two years he moved the operation to Edmond, and the elders of the congregation there assumed oversite for the program, which continued radio and television broadcasts into the twenty-first century. The Edmond church also provided the congregational singing associated with the program. By 2018, *SEARCH* appeared in all 210 television markets in the United States, on 150 cable stations, and on 50 radio stations. Lyon died in 2015; Phil Sanders succeeded him as the program's spokesperson.[18]

The International Soul Winning Workshop, better known as the "Tulsa Workshop," reflected the new energy. Begun in 1976, the Memorial Drive and Garnett Road Churches of Christ sponsored the workshop, and ministers Terry Rush and Marvin Phillips directed it on alternate years. During the first year, 9,000 attended. In 1981, 15,000 were present, attending 100 classes, listening to 36 speakers, and interacting with 250 exhibitors. It was the largest gathering of Church of Christ members in the world. Noninstitutional spokespersons initially criticized the two congregations because they were working together and grace was often the theme of the sessions. For forty years, the workshop stimulated the evangelistic ambitions of its participants, but in later years both participants and financial support declined. By 2017, it required a change. "Sometimes," observed Terry Rush, "we need to let ministries die so God can allow new ministries to sprout." Surely, the Tulsa Workshop was one of the most influential gatherings of Church of Christ members in the history of the Sooner State.[19]

Campaigns

As in previous decades, Oklahoma Churches of Christ continued to employ campaigns (door knocking, sermonizing, baptizing, and providing correspondence courses) as an evangelistic method. Most of those were in communities in other states and nations, but some were staged in the congregation's hometown. Since 1976, the Northwest church in Lawton, for example, took at least one group of twenty to forty members almost every year to conduct an evangelistic promotion, called "Back to the Bible," in Texas, Colorado, Kansas, Nebraska, or Missouri. The Central church in Ada focused on its own town. In 1970, its Campaign for Christ featuring Jimmy Allen attracted an average of 1,200 attendees per night. Twenty-nine were baptized.[20] A goodly number of Oklahoma congregations sponsored Allen crusades that more often than not drew one thousand attendees.[21]

Special Interest Seminars

As did the Tulsa Workshop, multiple lectureships and frequent campaigns reflected that the ubiquitous gospel meeting and religious debate had mostly run their course as effective evangelistic techniques by 1980. Special-interest seminars helped replace them. Among the earliest of these was the Brecheen-Faulkner Marriage Enrichment Seminar, first offered in 1974. Carl Brecheen was a native of Hollis, Oklahoma, and a professor of Bible at Abilene Christian University, while Paul Faulkner taught Bible and marriage and family courses at ACU too. They presented their ten-hour seminar hundreds of times over the course of thirty-two years, many of those in Oklahoma, often in repeat performances, as at the Twenty-Ninth and Yale church in Tulsa, where they presented three times. Other special interest seminars circulated in Oklahoma as well. These included the Life Coping Seminar (presented by Joy and Lynn McMillon of Oklahoma Christian University); Helping Hurting People (by Randy Becton at ACU); Christian Evidences (John Clayton); How We Got the Bible (Don Owen); and No Debt No Sweat (Steve Diggs). Sometimes the special interest seminars merely presented films such as James Dobson's *Dare to Discipline*. How effective the seminars were as evangelistic tools was unclear, however.

Let's Start Talking

Oklahoma-inspired Let's Start Talking was another notable evangelistic effort but with international objectives. The program had its genesis at the Day Springs congregation in Edmond in 1980. Mark Woodward, a professor at Oklahoma Christian University, and his wife, Sherrylee, conceived of the program, although it was not dissimilar from an outreach effort crafted at the Stillwater church begun by Aaron and Sylvia Duncan. The Duncans offered lessons in English via reading biblical texts to Oklahoma State University's international student population. Let's Start Talking, however, recruited teams of college-age students to go to international locations, where they offered one-on-one instruction in English with the Gospel of Luke as the text. Over a six-week period, readers usually became interested in spiritual concepts and some even embraced Christianity. A Let's Start Talking team was the first to introduce Churches of Christ to Moscow, Russia, in 1991. The program outgrew Dayspring's resources, and it moved to the congregation at Richland Hills in Fort Worth, Texas, in 1999.[22]

Social Services

To be more contemporary in its outreach to the local community, Oklahoma Churches of Christ provided a number of social services. Early on, a substantial majority made available to needy locals or transients used clothing and canned goods stored at the church house. On call, they furnished similar items to Tipton and Turley children's homes. Occasionally, congregations situated in working-class neighborhoods turned this traditional ministry into a major outreach. The Christian Service Center in Capitol Hill in Oklahoma City illustrated the approach. It was a function of the Oakcrest Church of Christ although also supported by several other congregations. In one month in 1996, volunteers gave out to 1,446 people some 6,735 clothing items and 491 pairs of shoes and enrolled 34 people in Bible correspondence courses. The Christian Service Center at Luther, Oklahoma, did comparable work but in a smaller setting.[23]

In the late 1980s and early 1990s, urban congregations broadened their menu of social services. Beginning 1998, the Memorial Road congregation in Oklahoma City offered free of charge almost daily counseling services and medical care through its Light House Medical Clinic in Capitol Hill. Directed by Beverly North, the mission distributed donated prescription drugs valued at more than $1.2 million to 1,700 clients in 2017.[24] The Cross and Crown Ministries, offered by the Quail Springs congregation in Oklahoma City, also sponsored a medical clinic but was more modest in size. At Edmond, the congregation provided help for grieving families through Kid's Place. At Duncan, the Chisholm Trail Church of Christ supported a Compassion Care Center, which, in addition to clothes and food, offered legal aid and free medical, dental, and vision services weekly. Congregations at Ada, Weatherford, and Ardmore implemented a similar package of services.[25] The Duncan center also housed the Christian Homes Adoption Agency, a field office for a program situated in Abilene, Texas.[26] Contact in West Tulsa, a mission point of the Park Plaza church, provided a monthly medical clinic, housing, and twelve-step meetings for men struggling with chemical addictions.[27]

Nonprofit agencies organized by Church of Christ members but not under the authority of a particular congregation carried out other social services. Most notably, Christian Services of Oklahoma, first (1990) at the Memorial Road congregation in Oklahoma City and then in Edmond, offered maternity home care as an alternative to abortion for young women with crisis pregnancies, as well as adoption services and foster families.[28] The Christian Service Center in Capitol Hill established a Literacy Resource office at the Oklahoma Department of Libraries that tutored Vietnamese immigrants in English at the South Central and Drexel Boulevard Churches of Christ.[29] The Northeast Church of Christ, one of Oklahoma City's predominately African American congregations, used a government grant to form the Central Urban Development, Inc., a 501(c)3 agency managed by members of the congregation, to construct at the sight of the old fairgrounds in Oklahoma City just off Martin Luther King Jr. Boulevard at Northeast Seventh Street thirty-two new brick homes of 1,200 to 1,500 square feet. The project was named after John F. Kennedy, but it would have been more appropriate to have named it after Arnelious Crenshaw, the minister of the

Northeast church and promoter of the housing project. Crenshaw said of the venture, "We need to be salt and light in this area where we are . . . [and] minister [to residents both] emotionally and physically." Those reasons also accounted for the Northeast church introducing a film to the larger community on the 1921 Tulsa Race Riot and how to deal with the scourge of racism and violence.[30]

A successful social service ministry required planning, preparation, numerous volunteers, and careful execution. Sometimes, however, the need was completely unexpected and immediate, as in the case of natural disasters like the tornados that struck Morris (1984) and Moore (1999), and Hurricane Katrina (2006), which hit the Gulf Coast. On those occasions, many Churches of Christ in Oklahoma filled trucks with food and clothing and quickly delivered them, as well as cash contributions, to the congregation nearest the disaster. The response was essentially the same as that to the Oklahoma City bombing in 1995, which claimed the lives of four church members and fourteen relatives, and injured six more. Given the nature of the tragedy, there was a greater need for cash and prayers than household goods. Accordingly, area churches contributed more than $200,000 to help relieve the suffering among its own. Fifteen congregations accepted the funds; six established grief support groups.[31]

More sensitive socially than earlier in their history, Churches of Christ within the state reached out to two populations in the last decades of the twentieth century that heretofore had been largely ignored. These were Spanish speakers and prison inmates. The Southeast congregation on Grand Boulevard in Oklahoma City offered Spanish-language services in addition to English (ESL), beginning 1982. Congregations at Ponca City, Poteau, Heavener, Durant, and Clinton offered similar services. Spanish speakers organized independent Iglesia de Cristo Tulsa in 1988 and Iglesia de Cristo Capitol Hill in 2003.[32] At least eighteen congregations maintained prison ministries, including two that operated independently within the correctional facilities at Antlers and El Reno.[33] The ministry at Owasso so inspired inmate Jerry Frazier that he was baptized, completed AA and BA degrees, and wrote a 153-page book entitled *Vital Fundamentals: Simply Discussed* (2005). Frazier's approach to the fundamentals of Christ and his church was traditional, but given the seat from which he wrote no reader, whether progressive or conservative, could be critical.[34]

Christian Chronicle

Moving the *Christian Chronicle* to Oklahoma was still another effort to reenergize evangelism. Founded in Texas in 1943 when the nation was consumed by World War II, the *Chronicle* was dedicated by the publishers to furthering international missions and reporting on the positive accomplishments of Churches of Christ.[35] In the 1970s, the monthly publication experienced hard times economically and even managerially. To have a larger role in evangelism but also to keep the school's name before the Churches of Christ nationally, Oklahoma Christian College purchased the *Chronicle* in 1981. The school's leadership retained the publication's historic objectives: "to tell good news about Churches of Christ around the world and to support the evangelization of the entire world." Howard Norton, chair of the Bible department, was named editor, and James O. Baird, then chancellor of the school, was designated publisher. The tabloid had 60,000 subscribers by 1986; it circulated to 105,000 by 2007, with readership two and a half times that number. Raymond Kelcy was probably correct, writes historian Stafford North, when he said that taking ownership of the *Chronicle* was one of the most significant decisions the college ever made. It brought Oklahoma Christian College's name to the attention of 250,000 individuals monthly, and, because of its own editorial policies and journalists, conveyed the impression that church members in Oklahoma were sober minded, level headed, and positively oriented.[36]

Changing the Hermeneutic

When it came to recommitting Churches of Christ to evangelism in the 1970s, a younger generation of church members, *Mission Magazine* readers for example, thought that the outreach should have less to do with evangelistic techniques (radio and television programs, International Soul Winning Workshops, special interest seminars, campaigns, social service ministries) than with the depth of one's faith. The new generation, historian Richard Hughes suggests, had come to question or reject outright the rational and legalistic premises associated with the Stone-Campbell heritage. Younger scholars sought "a more subjective, relational understanding of the Christian faith" that they believed was embedded "in the biblical documents that had been their focus [of study] for so many years," says Hughes. In the rereading of those texts, they de-emphasized the traditional hermeneutic that the Bible was the blueprint, pattern, or explicit rule book for determining the faith and practice of the contemporary church—that is, that Christians were to speak where the Bible spoke and be silent where the Bible was silent; and that truth was discerned via biblical command, example, and necessary inference. Instead, they emphasized reading scripture in subjective and relational ways that revealed more wondrously "the love and grace of God and the power of an indwelling Holy Spirit."[37] Or as Tom Olbricht put it, in the new approach, "First ask who God is and what he has done, then base what we are to do on God's prior action."[38]

That approach also surfaced new opinions about long-held beliefs and practices. Younger members of Churches of Christ had concluded that there were saved souls in other Christian communities, that women could participate fully in worship services, and that the use of mechanical instruments in worship was merely a matter of taste. Moreover, they held that there was no set New Testament pattern for public worship, and that praise teams were acceptable. They held that the church had social justice responsibilities in the community at large, that divorce was not the ultimate sin, and that family life facilities supported the mission of the church. The latter provided recreational space for basketball, physical fitness, dramatic performances, and the like. Such centers in Oklahoma existed at Norman (Alameda), Lawton (Western Hills), Enid (Garriott Road), Ada (Central), Tulsa (Park Plaza and Crosstown), Broken Arrow, Bixby, Duncan (Chisholm Trail), Oklahoma City (Memorial Road), Edmond, and Del City, among others.

Braced by a modified hermeneutic, the members of the new generation revisited some of the issues that had divided the restoration movement in previous years. Encouraged by Karl Ketcherside and Leroy Garrett, formerly ultraconservative Stone-Campbell adherents, the younger cohort launched discussions with Disciples of Christ, Independent Christians, non–Sunday school, noninstitutional, and noninstrumental Churches of Christ. In 1970, the Putnam City congregation hosted a daylong unity meeting organized by Roy B. Young, then minister of the Cherokee Hills congregation. It was essentially a gathering of Oklahoma folks representing the different branches of the tradition. A much larger gathering occurred at the University of Tulsa in 1973. It, however, was one of ten so-called Freedom Forums organized by Ketcherside and Garrett. All major branches of the restoration tradition participated. The opening session saw 250 registrants attend; 340 were present for the closing session. Stan Paregien, the associate minister of the Mayfair Church in Oklahoma City, was the only Oklahoman who participated on the program, but certainly not the only one to attend. Still, unity within the Stone-Campbell tradition was not high on the wish list of Church of Christ members in Oklahoma.[39]

Among Churches of Christ, the prominent advocates of the "new" hermeneutic, like Tom Olbricht, then on the faculty of Pepperdine University, were not in Oklahoma.[40] One of the more vocal opponents was, however, specifically Howard Norton. At the invitation of the president of Freed-Hardeman College,

Norton and Olbricht, and their seconds, met in a debate moderated by Stafford North of Oklahoma Christian on the subject at Henderson, Tennessee, in 1998. The tone of the discussion was civil, but Olbricht found it strange that Norton spoke as if he did not know him although Olbricht had been one of Norton's teachers at Abilene Christian.[41]

Norton did not speak for all Oklahoma preachers. There were ministers and congregations in the Sooner State who had long since discovered grace and the power of the Holy Spirit. K. C. Moser, of course, had been preaching as much in the 1930s at the Twelfth and Drexel congregation in Oklahoma City. Later in the twentieth century, so too were Marvin Phillips at the Garnett Road church, Terry Rush at the Memorial Drive church, and Dan McCaghren at the Southern Hills church, all in Tulsa; Ronnie White at the Village (Quail Springs) church in Oklahoma City; Bud Ross at the Central church in Ada; and the founding group at the Day Springs church in Edmond.

Notable layman found voice also because of the changing hermeneutic. Outstanding among these was Oliver Howard, a native of Holdenville who held degrees from Oklahoma Christian, Abilene Christian, and University of Cincinnati, the latter a PhD in Jewish Hellenistic literature and a juris doctor in law. Howard began preaching when he was twelve, and continued to do so during the course of his education and practice as an attorney. His presentations at Pepperdine University lectureships in Malibu, California, between 1983 and 1993 demonstrated how much he had been shaped by the new approach to biblical understanding. For example, he suggested that there were different ways of looking at marriage and divorce, the nature of Christian worship, the life of the Holy Spirit in the early church, the elements of unity, God's presence in the midst of crisis, and the roles of men and women in Christ Jesus. Howard's lectures captured the attention of the church at large, and demonstrated to many that legalism was limited as an interpretative paradigm of scripture.[42]

Oklahoma Christian Lectureship, 2004

But not all agreed. There were traditionalists who strongly objected to the new hermeneutic. That became apparent when Oklahoma Christian University hosted its annual lectureship in January 2004, if not before. The theme for the three-day event was "The Kingdom of Inclusion," with the panel of speakers from outside of Oklahoma. A substantial number of ministers attending the lectures concluded that the kingdom envisioned by the speakers included far too many as eligible members.[43] Clearly, they concluded, the speakers did not have their theology right, did not understand the essentials, and had disconnected the Holy Spirit from scripture. Even the venerable Mack Lyon, producer of *SEARCH for the Lord's Way*, was disturbed. He was quoted as saying that the 2004 lectureship was the most divisive event he had ever witnessed. If the program reflected the direction the new administration and trustees wanted to take the school, Lyon, as a matter of conscience, would not be back. Oklahoma Christian had been a good influence over time, he said, but "The school as it has now become is no longer associated with the church."[44] President Mike O'Neal and his colleagues worked hard to convince Lyon and like believers that the university merited their support. They invested hours into listening to the preacher fraternity, responding to its concerns, and revising the format of the annual event, even changing its name to Quest. Many of the state's older church leaders would not be pacified by the changes, however, and continued to grumble.[45]

The reservations of church traditionalists generally stemmed from new premises of interpretation, or hermeneutic. Churches of Christ had generally held that all scripture was inspired by God and that Bible silence on an issue prohibited action. Judging from what went on at the 2004 lectureship, traditionalists feared that those premises were now in question. Some even suggested that the source of the heresy was the faculty of biblical studies at Oklahoma Christian. As evidence, they pointed to statements of a faculty member teaching a graduate class captured on a digital recording that seemed to suggest acceptance of a different hermeneutic. In a March 2004 letter, Lynn McMillon, dean of the College of Biblical Studies, denied that charge. "I cannot think," he said, "of a school that holds a higher view of Scripture as the Word of God than does OC and particularly the Bible faculty."[46]

The minister at the Elk City Church of Christ and like-minded preachers elsewhere in the state did not really believe McMillon, however. Having mulled over the matter for four years, they prepared a series of full-page ads published in the *Daily Oklahoman* in January, August, and September of 2008. The purpose of the ads was to reaffirm the traditional doctrinal views that the mainstream church seemed to have abandoned. All scripture, proclaimed the ads, was inspired of God and not just the words in red letters, not only Jesus's words but also those of the biblical writers. The inerrant words about worship practices, marriage, family, and salvation had as much force as those about the resurrection, they insisted. Thus when one heard the gospel message, one must respond to it. Specifically, the sinner must believe, repent, confess, and be baptized. The implication of the ads was that the mainstream Church of Christ had forgotten what the church taught about inerrancy and had embraced the theology and practices of worldly Christianity. It was no longer silent where scripture was silent.[47]

The minister of the McLish Church of Christ at Ardmore published multiple tracts with the same message. The church, he wrote, is confronting a liberal "wind of change" that is "blowing down many of the 'old paths' the Lord's church has held to." Women were embracing men's roles in the church; men and women were more accepting of denominations; some members were actually using instrumental music and resorting to hand clapping in worship; and divorce and remarriage was no longer considered a sin. These changes had nothing to do with a quest for a deeper relationship with God, the minister insisted, but were caused by "rebellion, emotionalism, and Biblical ignorance." Liberalism, the child of the new hermeneutic, was not bringing Christians closer to God but actually dragging the church into sin.[48]

The majority of the church membership and its leaders did not agree. Perhaps Roy Young, the minister then of the Apache Church of Christ, spoke for them. Said Young, "For far too long conservative preachers and congregations have held sway in Oklahoma." In the matter of the lectureship, he urged organizers at OC not to "give them another inch of influence in matters that affect . . . the Bible lectureship." Instead, he said, "Please continue to bring in men and women of faith who will challenge the status quo, test our thinking, and provoke our study."[49]

The 2004 lectureship at Oklahoma Christian reflected a church community uncertain about itself and its future. It had lost some confidence in the wake of the North Pennsylvania Avenue Church and Marian Guinn cases, the acceptance of a new hermeneutic, and the loss of membership. No longer could the church discipline its members or rely upon the "old paths" to frame its theology. The "new paths" broadened the role of the Holy Spirit, of grace, of women, of mechanical instruments in public worship, and of the church's provision of social services. To most traditionalists, and that included the majority of Church of Christ members in Oklahoma, the new paths were most problematic.

13

THE QUEST FOR UNITY CONTINUES

Excepting perhaps the ministry of James J. Trott among the Cherokees, the Stone-Campbell movement reached what is now Oklahoma in the 1880s. As we have seen, the movement's plea was for Christian unity by the use of scripture only as the guide to faith and practice. Scripture, it was held, revealed a pattern for the kingdom of God that was to be replicated in the here and now. If done, the result would be the salvation of souls, the unity of believers, and the arrival of the millennium.

Two decades into the twenty-first century, the quest for religious unity had not turned out that way, in Oklahoma or elsewhere. Unity, or harmony, proved ephemeral over the years. This was the experience of R. W. Officer in his Indian Mission at Atoka and of Meta Chestnutt Sager in her school at Minco. J. N. Armstrong closed Cordell Christian College because of the lack of unity within the church regarding pacifism. When O. E. Enfield remarked in a sermon that Christians should be socialists, the elders of the church where he spoke told him not to come back. Little harmony was in evidence when S. R. Cassius proposed to build a mission school for African Americans near Meridian. His white brethren virtually ignored him. And the dozens of evangelists who debated their way through Indian and Oklahoma Territories belittling their opponents left a legacy of discord in the Christian community.

The WPA survey in the mid-1930s judged members of Churches of Christ in Oklahoma as rural and poorly educated, or backward, who believed that of all God's people only they had the assurance of salvation. This was true, they believed, because they had followed the steps revealed in scripture. Such a conclusion, of course, limited the effectiveness of any plea for unity, internally or even externally. But peculiarly it did not seem to limit membership growth. Churches of Christ in Oklahoma were increasing in number even as the WPA was completing its survey. In the 1950s, the fellowship at large was considered the fastest-growing denomination percentage-wise in the United States.

The crown that Churches of Christ wore, however, was dulled by internecine controversies that would not go away. There were congregations in Oklahoma where the majority still objected to Sunday schools, to located preachers, to the use of multiple cups during communion, and to supporting institutions like Tipton, Westview, and Hope Harbor from the church's treasury. Other congregations objected to premillennialism, the extent of God's grace, modernism, pacifism, and matters of race. In the 1970s and beyond, controversy continued in the form of a different hermeneutic, how to address social justice issues, the role of women in the church, and the use of instrumental music in worship.

Given these circumstances, unity was a challenge for Oklahoma Churches of Christ. More recently there were also Church of Christ congregations who were experimenting with instrumental as well as gender-inclusive worship styles. If instruments had been introduced, it was usually into one of two services, with the other remaining a capella. In services that were gender-inclusive, women served communion, sang in praise teams, delivered prayers, offered homilies, and even acted as elders. Despite criticism, other congregations provided their communities with everything from medical clinics to recreational facilities, convinced that the church had a responsibility beyond merely preaching the gospel on Sunday morning. In faith and practice, then, Oklahoma Churches of Christ were reminiscent of Joseph's coat of many colors. There was a lot of variation among them, so much so that the quest for unity seemed problematic.

In 2006, the number of Church of Christ congregations in Oklahoma totaled 593, and adherents, including children, numbered 80,595, or almost one-fifth of Church of Christ members nationwide. Oklahoma was also the home of the second-largest congregation in the nation, Memorial Road in Oklahoma

City, with 2,700 adherents. But to the disappointment of many, the number of adherents in 2006 was less than it had been in 1970. In that interval, thriving congregations that had embraced new paths (instrumental music, new hermeneutics, gender neutral services, etc.) had largely disappeared—namely Quail Springs in Oklahoma City, now called "Springs"; and Garnett Road, now "Journey"; and Southern Hills, both in Tulsa.

When it came to faith and practice, then, Churches of Christ in Oklahoma tended to be more conservative than in other states like Tennessee, Texas, and California. In part, this was due to the influence of Foy E. Wallace Jr., who in the 1930s and 1940s was resident in Oklahoma City and showered Oklahomans with reactionary tirades on premillennialism, institutionalism, church hymnals, and the Revised Standard Version of the Bible. Doubtless, the Bible faculty at Oklahoma Christian University, given its training and experience, contributed to the conservative posture too. That only a few Oklahoma church members read *Mission Magazine* and only one served on its board of directors was strong evidence of conservativism. So too was the willingness of the North Penn and Collinsville church elders to exercise discipline as described in the Bible. As did their forefathers in the Stone-Campbell tradition, they had high regard for scripture. It alone, they believed, would bring unity to the religious world and direction to one's life in Christ.

But, as a message of unity and growth, would the conservative approach to faith and practice attract new members? Since 1970, the fellowship had tried to stem the tide of decreasing membership. The Oklahoma Christian University lectures, the SEARCH program, the International Soul Winning Workshops, Let's Start Talking teams, multiple campaigns, social service outreaches, a *Christian Chronicle* filled with encouragement, and a revised hermeneutic had not met expectations. Membership numbers continued to decline.

To fill the pews again would be the challenge of the Churches of Christ in Oklahoma in the twenty-first century.

NOTES

Abbreviations

BB   *Bible Banner*
CC   *Christian Chronicle*
CE   *Christian Evangelist*
CL   *Christian Leader and Way*
CS   *Christian Standard*
DO   *Daily Oklahoman*
FF   *Firm Foundation*
GA   *Gospel Advocate*
GH   *Gospel Herald*
OR   *Octographic Review*
PC   *Primitive Christian*
RWO   R. W. Officer

Chapter 1

1. The best standard studies of the Stone-Campbell Movement are David Edwin Harrell Jr., *A Social History of the Disciples of Christ*, vol. 1, *Quest for a Christian America: The Disciples of Christ and American Society to 1866* (Nashville: Disciples of Christ Historical Society, 1966); and vol. 2, *The Social Sources of Division of the Disciples of Christ, 1865–1900* (Atlanta: Publishing Systems, 1973); Richard T. Hughes, *Reviving the Ancient Faith: The Story of Churches of Christ in America* (Grand Rapids, Mich.: William B. Eerdmans, 1996); James DeForest Murch, *Christians Only* (Cincinnati: Standard, 1962); William E. Tucker and Lester G. McAllister, *Journey in Faith: A History of the Christian Church (Disciples of Christ)* (St. Louis: Bethany Press, 1975; and Earl Irvin West, *The Search for the Ancient Order*, vol. 1, *1848–65* (Nashville: Gospel Advocate, 1964); vol. 2, *1866–1906* (Indianapolis: Religious Book Service, 1950); vol. 3, *1900–1918* (Indianapolis: Religious Book Services, 1979); vol. 4, *1919–1950* (Germantown, Tenn.: Religious Book Service, 1987). The quotation is from Anthony Ward Kennedy, *They Came from Everywhere and Settled Here* (Conway, Ark.: Rapid Rabbit, 1995), 3:699.

2. William Garrett West, *Barton Warren Stone: Early American Advocate of Christian Unity* (Nashville, Tenn.: Disciples of Christ Historical Society, 1954), chap. 1.

3. Hughes, *Reviving the Ancient Faith*, 96.

4. West, *Barton Warren Stone*, 78–80. See also D. Newell Williams, "Last Will and Testament of the Springfield Presbytery," in *The Encyclopedia of the Stone-Campbell Movement*, ed. Douglas A. Foster et al. (Grand Rapids, Mich.: William B. Eerdmans, 2004), 453–55.

5. Hughes, *Reviving the Ancient Faith*, 97.

6. Ibid., xii, 11. Some forty years earlier, William Garret West in *Barton Warren Stone*, p. 206, reached essentially the same conclusion. He spoke of Stone's "left-wing Protestant" worldview rather than his "apocalyptic" worldview, comparing his view to that of such sixteenth-century groups as the Muentzerites, Swiss Anabaptists, Melchiorites, Mennonites, Hutterites, and Socinians.

7. West, *Barton Warren Stone*, chap. 7.

8. Robert Richardson, *Memoirs of Alexander Campbell* (1897; repr., Germantown, Tenn.: Religious Book Service, n.d.), 1:130–31.

9. Winfred Ernest Garrison and Alfred T. DeGroot, *The Disciples of Christ: A History* (St. Louis: Christian Board of Publication, 1948), chaps. 6 and 7.

10. Hughes, *Reviving the Ancient Faith*, 11.

11. Nathan O. Hatch, *The Democratization of American Christianity* (New Haven, Conn.: Yale University Press, 1989), 168.

12. Hughes, *Reviving the Ancient Faith*, 11; see also Leroy Garrett, "Campbell, Alexander," in Foster et al., *Encyclopedia of the Stone-Campbell Movement*, 121.

13. C. Leonard Allen and Richard T. Hughes, *Discovering Our Roots: The Ancestry of Churches of Christ* (Abilene, Tex.: Abilene Christian University Press, 1983), 103–5; see also Hatch, *Democratization of American Christianity*, 163.

14. Hughes, *Reviving the Ancient Faith*, 12.

15. Gary Holloway and Douglas A. Foster, *Renewing God's People: A Concise History of Churches of Christ* (Abilene, Tex.: Abilene Christian University Press, 2001), 61.

16. Richard T. Hughes and R. L. Roberts, *The Churches of Christ* (Westport, Conn.: Greenwood Press, 2001), 4.

17. Stephen J. England, *Oklahoma Christians: A History of Christian Churches and of the Start of the Christian Church (Disciples of Christ) in Oklahoma* (Oklahoma City: Christian Church in Oklahoma, 1975), chap. 4.

18. Richard T. Hughes and R. L. Roberts, *The Churches of Christ* (Westport, Conn.: Greenwood Press, 2001), 4–5. Hughes and Roberts note that, at their best, Churches of Christ think of "nondenominational" as a biblical ideal to which they aspire—the one church, or Body of Christ, that is unfragmented by denominational claims. As often as not, however, church members identified the one true church as themselves.

19. Holloway and Foster, *Renewing God's People*, 76–77.

20. Ibid., 79–82.

21. C. Leonard Allen, *Things Unseen, Churches of Christ in (and after) the Modern Age* (Siloam Springs, Ark.: Leafwood Publishers, 2004), 28.

22. Ibid., 29.
23. Ibid.
24. Ibid., 60.
25. Ibid., 77.
26. West, *Barton Warren Stone*, 206–9.
27. Allen, *Things Unseen*, 108.

Chapter 2

1. William G. McLoughlin, *The Cherokee Ghost Dance: Essays on the Southeastern Indians, 1789–1861* (Macon, Ga.: Mercer University Press, 1984), 397–422. Most accounts of this chapter of Cherokee history focus on the experiences of Samuel Worcester, probably because he was the principal in the famous U.S. Supreme Court case *Worcester v. State of Georgia (1832)*. See also England, *Oklahoma Christians*, 36–37.

2. "News from the Churches," J. J. Trott to Brother Fanning, *Christian Review* (1844), 237, in "J. J. Trott"; and "The Tennessee Evangelizing Association" *Christian Record* (July 1852), 9, both in James J. Trott, Biographical Files, Disciples of Christ Historical Society, Nashville, Tenn.; T[olbert] F[anning], "James J. Trott, Messenger of the Church of Christ at Franklin College, Tenn., to the Cherokee Nation," *Gospel Advocate* (hereinafter *GA*) 12 (Mar. 25, 1869), 271–72.

3. England, *Oklahoma Christians*, 38–39; J. J. Trott to Brethren, "The Indian Mission," Apr. 4, 1856, *GA* 2 (Apr. 1856), 110–12.

4. T[olbert] F[anning], "James J. Trott," *GA* 11 (Mar. 25, 1869), 271–72; England, *Oklahoma Christians*, 38–39. Trott located his mission as twenty-six miles west of Fayetteville, Arkansas, which placed it almost exactly at Westville, and some three miles distant from a "Christian Church," actually a Baptist church organized by the renowned missionary and abolitionist Evan Jones. The church is still active.

5. Joseph R. Bennett II, "The Biography of James Jenkins Trott, 1800–1868," History of the Restoration Movement, http://www.therestorationmovement.com/_states /tennessee/trott.htm (accessed Mar. 20, 2009).

6. Ibid.; T[olbert] F[anning], "James J. Trott," *GA* 11 (Mar. 25, 1869), 271–72.

7. England, *Oklahoma Christians*, 40; R. W. Officer (hereinafter RWO), "Indian Territory," *Octographic Review* (hereinafter *OR*) 33 (Dec. 25, 1890), 2; R. Moffett, "Indian Mission," *Christian Evangelist* (hereinafter *CE*) 21 (Nov. 13, 1884), 733; and RWO, "Indian Mission," *CE* 27 (June 13, 1889), 375, and (July 25, 1889), 477. See especially Mrs. R. A. Hawkins, "Indian Territory," *CE* 27 (Aug. 15, 1889), 519.

8. RWO, "Indian Territory," *OR* 33 (Dec. 18, 1890), 6.

9. RWO, "Indian Territory," *OR* 34 (Sept. 10, 1891), 2; RWO, "Indian Territory," *GA* 34 (Feb. 18, 1892), 108.

10. *Christian Standard* (hereinafter *CS*) 9 (May 23, 1874), 162ff., quoted in England, *Oklahoma Christians*, 41.

11. For the part of Officer's ministry prior to 1886, I have drawn upon one of my essays, "R. W. Officer and the Indian Mission: The Foundational Years (1880–1886)," which appeared in a festschrift edited by Thomas H. Olbricht and David Fleer, *And the*

Word Became Flesh: Studies in History, Communication, and Scripture in Memory of Michael W. Casey (Eugene, Ore.: Pickwick Publications, 2009). This usage is with the permission of Wipf and Stock, http://www.wipfandstock.com.

12. RWO, "Work Among the Indians," *GA* 29 (Jan. 26, 1887), 55; RWO, "Correspondence," *GA* 26 (July 16, 1884), 453.

13. RWO to Bro Poe, "Correspondence," *GA* 26 (Mar. 12, 1884), 164, 1–2; and James D. Elliott, "Our Indian Mission," *GA* 26 (Mar. 26, 1884), 194; see also Wayne Kilpatrick, "Murrell Askew: The Reluctant Baptist," History of the Restoration Movement, http://www.therestorationmovement.com/_states/oklahoma/askew.htm (accessed Dec. 2, 2008); and D. C. Gideon, *Indian Territory, Descriptive, Biographical and Genealogical.* (New York: Lewis, 1901), 541.

14. RWO to Brethren, "Correspondence," *GA*, 23 (June 23, 1881), 392; Gideon, *Indian Territory*, 558.

15. E. L. Dohoney and W. H. Sluder to Brethren, "Our Indian Mission," *GA* 25 (Nov. 7, 1883), 708.

16. "Letter from Bro. Officer," *GA* 26 (Aug. 27, 1884), 546; RWO, "Defense of Bro. R. W. Officer," *GA* 24 (Apr. 13, 1882), 229. Because of Officer's strong objection to the parachurch missionary society, historians have generally placed him in the conservative tradition of Churches of Christ. England is an exception, however.

17. RWO to Bro. Poe, "Our Indian Mission," *GA* 25 (Nov. 7, 1883), 708; RWO, "Letter from Bro. Officer," *GA* 25 (Dec. 12, 1883), 788.

18. RWO to Father in the Gospel, "Letter to N. B. Wallace," *GA* 26 (Jan. 23, 1884), 55; RWO to Bro. Poe, "Correspondence," *GA* 26 (Mar. 12, 1884), 164; and *GA* 26 (July 16, 1884), 453.

19. RWO to Bro. Poe, "A Mistake," *GA* 26 (May 28, 1884), 346; Jacob Creath to Bros. Lipscomb and Sewell, "Books for the Indian Mission," *GA* 26 (Aug. 20, 1884), 530.

20. There is little evidence beyond his ownership of a Choctaw-English dictionary that Officer tried to master the Choctaw-Chickasaw language. Nat Purkins assisted him as a translator on appropriate occasions.

21. O'Beirn, *Leaders and Leading Men of the Indian Territory*, vol. 1, *Choctaws and Chickasaws* (Chicago: American Publishers Association, 1891), 92; Atoka County Historical Society, *Tales of Atoka County Heritage* (Atoka, Okla.: Atoka County Historical Society, ca. 1983), 379.

22. RWO, "Correspondence," *GA* 28 (Nov. 10, 1886), 713; Chas. H. Lord to Bro. Officer, "Correspondence," *GA* 28 (Nov. 10, 1886), 707; A. Askew, "Mission Work," *OR* 30 (Jan. 6, 1887), 3.

23. "Letter from Bro. Officer," *GA* 26 (Aug. 27, 1884), 546; RWO to Bro. Poe, "Correspondence," *GA* 26 (Aug. 6, 1884), 500.

24. RWO "Texas," *CS* 21 (Mar. 27, 1886), 102; RWO to Advocate, "Correspondence," *GA* 27 (Nov. 18, 1885), 726; L. W. Oakes to RWO, Paris, Tex., Nov. 26, 1885, *GA* 27 (Dec. 16, 1885), 792; RWO, "Notes from Indian Territory," *GA* 27 (July 22, 1885), 455. See also RWO to Advocate, "Correspondence," *GA* 27 (Nov. 18, 1885), 726; RWO to

Advocate, "Correspondence," *GA* 28 (Feb. 17, 1886), 107; and RWO to Bro. L[ipscomb], "Correspondence," *GA* 28 (Apr. 14, 1886), 236.

25. RWO, "Indian Territory," *OR* 33 (Dec. 18, 1890), 6.

26. "Letter from Bro. Officer," *GA* 26 (Aug. 27, 1884), 546; RWO to Bros. Lipscomb and Sewell, *GA* 26 (Oct. 29, 1884), 691. See also "To the Choctaw Council Assembled," Texas, Sept. 1, 1884, book A, June 1890–1894, Professional Credentials, Central District, Ind. Ter., in Records of the Clerk of the Court, Pittsburg County, McAlester, Okla. (hereinafter Pittsburg County Clerk Records).

27. RWO to Bros. Lipscomb and Sewell, "Correspondence," *GA* 26 (Oct. 29, 1884), 691. The divisive issue was less about Officer's credentials than the proposal to charter a Christian Women's Board of Missions. See Stephen Daniel Eckstein, *History of the Churches of Christ in Texas, 1824–1950* (Austin: Firm Foundation, 1963), 237.

28. RWO to Bros. Lipscomb and Sewell, "Correspondence," *GA* 26 (Oct. 29, 1884), 691.

29. "Editorial Comment," *GA* 26 (Nov. 26, 1884), 756.

30. "Editorial Comment," *OR* 30 (Dec. 29, 1887), 8.

31. For example, the *Christian Leader and Way, Christian Standard, Firm Foundation*, and *Primitive Christian*, among others.

32. RWO, "Texas," *CS* 20 (May 16, 1885), 158; RWO, "Indian Territory," *GA* 20 (Nov. 11, 1885), 336; RWO, "Texas," *GA*, 21 (Mar. 27, 1886), 102; RWO, "Indian Mission," *GA* 28 (Apr. 21, 1886), 252; RWO, "Indian Mission," *GA*, 27 (Nov. 4, 1885), 696.

33. The Church of Christ at Paris, Texas, to the Christian Brotherhood, "Correspondence," *GA* 27 (Nov. 4, 1885), 699; RWO, "Correspondence," *GA* 26 (Dec. 23, 1885), 811.

34. RWO, "Correspondence," *GA* 27 (May 13, 1885), 292.

35. RWO, "Correspondence," *GA* 27 (Nov. 4, 1885), 699.

36. RWO to Advocate, "Correspondence," *GA* 27 (Oct. 28, 1885), 674. The official records of the Choctaw Council, now in the custody of the Oklahoma History Center in Oklahoma City, make no mention of Officer or his mission.

37. RWO to Bro. Lipscomb, "Correspondence," *GA* 34 (Mar. 21, 1892), 204.

38. RWO to Dear Advocate, "Correspondence," *GA* 27 (Dec. 23, 1885), 803.

39. [David Lipscomb], Editorial comment, *GA* 27 (Dec. 23, 1885), 803.

40. D[avid] L[ipscomb], "The Indian Mission," *GA* 28 (Mar. 31, 1886), 198.

41. RWO, "Notes from Indian Territory," *GA* 28 (Aug. 11, 1886), 497.

42. A. Askew, "Mission Work," *OR* 30 (Jan. 6, 1887); RWO, "Indian Territory," *OR* 33 (Nov. 27, 1890), 2; RWO, "Indian Territory," *OR* 40 (Apr. 20, 1897), 3. The lot was located just northwest of the county courthouse in Atoka. In 1908, the house was removed to East Atoka and divided into two homes.

43. Atoka County Historical Society, *Tales of Atoka County Heritage*, 67–68. See also RWO, "Indian Territory," *GA* 31 (Jan. 2, 1889), 14; RWO, "Indian Territory," *OR* 32 (Nov. 28, 1889), 6; RWO, "Reports from Indian Territory," *OR* 36 (Oct. 10, 1893), 6; and RWO, "Indian Territory," *OR* 36 (Oct. 31, 1893), 6.

44. As an example of Officer's column, see "Religious," *Indian Citizen*, Oct. 26, 1889, 2. In many ways, the *Indian Citizen* was a direct response to the *Indian Missionary*, another

weekly newspaper centered in Atoka that devoted itself primarily to Baptist news. Published between 1886 and 1891, the *Missionary* was edited by the distinguished Baptist divine and Masonic Order official, J. S. Murrow, and its pages were probably even less inclusive than the *Indian Citizen* when it came to religious topics.

45. "Religious," *Indian Citizen*, May 3, 1890, 5, and May 10, 1890, 2.

46. RWO, "Indian Territory," *GA* 33 (Aug. 26, 1891), 540; D. L., "Personal," *GA* 32 (Feb. 19, 1890), 122; "Letter from RWO," *Indian Citizen*, May 10, 1890, 2.

47. RWO, "Our Work in the Indian Territory," *GA* 28 (Sept. 29, 1886), 610; Editors, "Correspondence," *GA* 28 (Sept. 15, 1886), 586.

48. Rennard Strickland, *The Indians in Oklahoma* (Norman: University of Oklahoma Press, 1980), 44.

49. RWO, "Report from the Christian Mission, Indian Territory," *Firm Foundation* (hereinafter *FF*) (Dec. 18, 1890), 2; RWO, "Indian Territory," *OR* 33 (Dec. 18, 1890), 6.

50. RWO, "A Request," *GA* 31 (Nov. 27, 1889), 764; D. B. Cargile, "Indian Territory," *Primitive Christian* (hereinafter *PC*) 3 (Aug. 23, 1894), 4.

51. RWO, "The Saints Scatter Abroad," *GA* 36 (Nov. 1, 1894), 698; RWO, "A Common Mistake," *GA* 38 (Sept. 24, 1896), 623.

52. RWO, "Report from the Christian Mission, Indian Territory," *FF* (Dec. 18, 1890), 2, 3.

53. RWO, "Indian Territory," *GA* 31 (May 1, 1889), 288.

54. RWO, "Indian Territory," *GA* 31 (Jan. 2, 1889), 14.

55. *Indian Citizen*, Nov. 1, 1889, 6.

56. Atoka, Lehigh, and Prairie View.

57. W. B. Stinson to Brethren, *GA* 31 (June 5, 1889), 363; RWO, "Indian Territory," *GA* 31 (July 31, 1889), 495; RWO, "Indian Mission," *OR* 32 (June 13, 1889), 2. See also Reports to the Home Board, 1889, 26; 1890, 188; 1891, 5; and 1892, 380, in Reports to the Home Board, 1884–1918: Indian Territory and Oklahoma, box 16, England Papers, Phillips Theological Seminary Library, Tulsa, Okla. (hereinafter England Papers).

58. RWO, "Indian Territory," *GA* 31 (Dec. 18, 1889), 803; RWO, "An Open Letter," *GA* 42 (Dec. 13, 1900), 798; RWO, "Religious," *Indian Citizen*, May 31, 1890, 1.

59. RWO, "An Open Letter," *GA* 42 (Dec. 13, 1900), 798.

60. "Letter from Brother Parker," *GA* 35 (Sept. 7, 1893), 574.

61. *Indian Citizen*, Jan. 11, 1890, 5 and May 3, 1890, 5; C. C. Parker "Reports," *OR* 35 (May 3, 1892), 6; George F. Whitley, "Indian Territory," *GA* 36 (Aug. 30, 1894), 550; C. C. Parker to Bro. Lipscomb, "From Indian Territory," *GA* 36 (Nov. 1, 1894), 693; C. C. Parker, "What Have I Done?," *GA* 40 (Jan. 6, 1898), 16.

62. C. C. Parker, *OR* 34 (Sept. 3, 1891), 3. Parker subsequently reported that, in all, seventy-five had been added to the Wynnewood church during his meeting, a number that would have included individuals who had been baptized elsewhere but wished to then identify with the congregation in Wynnewood. See C. C. Parker, "Correspondence," *OR* 34 (Sept. 10, 1891), 2. See also, RWO, "From Indian Territory," *OR* 34 (Nov. 26, 1891), 2.

63. C. C. Parker, "Indian Territory," *PC* 1 (Jan. 26, 1893), 2.

64. C. C. Parker to Brethren and Sisters, "Correspondence," *OR* 42 (Aug. 22, 1899), 6; C. C. Parker, "Do You Believe or Not?," *PC* 11 (May 5, 1903), 6; C. C. Parker to Bro.

Whitley, "What the Mission Is," *PC* 3 (May 9, 1895), 1. Parker was one of the few white evangelists in Indian Territory or Oklahoma Territory to acknowledge Cassius, but sending him a copy of *The Negro* has the ring of racial prejudice rather than Christian comradery.

65. RWO, "Report of Work Among the Indians," *GA* 30 (Jan. 4, 1888), 8; RWO, "Indian Territory, *GA* 32 (Dec. 10, 1890), 588; RWO, "Indian Territory," *OR* 33 (Dec. 18, 1890), 6; RWO, "Reports," *FF* (Oct. 11, 1892), 6.

66. RWO, "Religious," *Indian Citizen*, Apr. 5, 1890, 1, and July 9, 1890, 1. Ten years later, Officer placed the number of congregations at seventy-two and the number of neighborhood schools at nineteen. See RWO, "An Open Letter," *GA* 42 (Dec. 13, 1900), 798.

67. J. W. Jackson, "Indian Territory, *FF* (Nov. 13, 1890), 5.

68. Daniel Sommer, "Missions," *OR* 30 (Dec. 29, 1887), 8; Editors, "A Request," *GA* 31 (Dec. , 18 1889), 807.

69. RWO, "Indian Territory," *GA* 33 (Sept. 16, 1891), 588.

70. Editors, "RWO writes," *GA* 31 (Aug. 7, 1889), 506.

71. RWO, "An Open Letter," *PC* 2 (Aug. 31, 1893), 3, and "Indian Mission," *PC* 2 (Oct. 4, 1893), 6.

72. John W. Harris, "Oklahoma Jots," *PC* 4 (Apr. 11, 1895), 4.

73. Editors, "Church News," *GA* 31 (Apr. 17, 1889), 243; RWO, "Indian Mission," *OR* 32 (May 23, 1889), 3. Thirty days after the run, Officer estimated that three hundred church members had left Indian Territory for Oklahoma Territory.

74. RWO, "Indian Territory," *GA* 32 (Nov. 5, 1890), 706.

Chapter 3

1. RWO, "Western Texas," *GA* 44 (Jan. 2, 1902), 11.

2. Stan Hoig, "Land Run of 1889," in *Encyclopedia of Oklahoma History and Culture*, https://www.okhistory.org/publications/enc/entry.php?entry=LA014 (accessed July 18, 2017).

3. Angie Debo, *Oklahoma, Foot-Loose and Fancy-Free* (Norman: University of Oklahoma Press, 1987), 37.

4. As an expression of their gratitude, the men of that class presented Chestnutt with an Oxford Teacher's Bible with their names inscribed inside. Sixty years later, she was buried with that Bible in her hands.

5. Mrs. J. A. Sager, "History of Christian Church in Grady County for 40 years," *Chickasha Daily Express* [1929].

6. Sager, "History of Christian Church in Grady County"; Meta Chestnut to Eva Heiliger, Sept. 3, 1944, folder 2, Eva Heiliger Materials, Meta Chestnutt Sager Collection, Special Collections, Oklahoma History Center, Oklahoma City, Okla. (hereinafter Chestnutt Sager Collection).

7. Sager, "History of Christian Church in Grady County."

8. Ibid.; Eva Heiliger, "A True Story," dated Jan. 13, 1940, folder 2, Chestnutt Sager Collection.

9. Sager, "History of Christian Church in Grady County" [1929].

10. Ibid.; "Report from Minco, IT," *American Home Missionary* 1 (Mar. 1895), in box 16, England Papers.

11. "Minco Remembers El Meta," *Daily Oklahoman* (hereinafter *DO*), Aug. 27, 1939, D1.

12. S. E. Kennedy, "A College in the Indian Territory," *CE* 31 (Oct. 4, 1894), 636; Kennedy to Sir, Sept. 18, 1894, *Minco Minstrel*, Sept. 24, 1894; and [Meta Chestnutt Sager] to [Eva Heiliger], Nov. 18, 1946, folder 2, Chestnutt Sager Collection.

13. "Work on the New Foundation Christian College is progressing," *Minco Minstrel*, Aug. 24, 1894, 3.

14. "Minco Remembers El Meta," *DO*, Aug. 27, 1939, D1.

15. "The Celebration," *Minco Minstrel*, Oct. 5, 1894, 3.

16. D. T. Broadus, "Kansas Notes," *GA* 40 (May 22, 1902), 335; Nelle Holshouser, "Only Memory of Christian College Is Left," *DO*, Sept. 9, 1928.

17. "Mr. Larimore . . . Is Here," *Minco Minstrel*, May 25, 1895, 4.

18. "A Big Camp Meeting," *Minco Minstrel*, Aug. 2, 1895, 4.

19. "An Awakening in Minco Churches," *Minco Minstrel*, Nov. 13, 1908, 3.

20. Meta Chestnutt Sager to Eva, Dec. 14, 1945, folder 2, Chestnutt Sager Collection.

21. "In the Matter of the Estate of Meta Chestnutt Sager, Deceased, Executor's First and Final Account," Jan. 26, 1948, Clerk of the Court, Grady County, Chickasha, Okla.

22. F. D. Srygley, "Biographical Sketch of R. Wallace Officer," in *Biographies and Sermons: A Collection of Original Sermons by Different Men, with a Biographical Sketch of Each Man Accompanying His Sermon*, ed. F. D. Srygley (Nashville: Gospel Advocate, 1898), 318.

23. R. W. Officer to C. E. Adams, Kiowa Indian Agency, Anadarko, I.T., Nov. 1, 1890, Churches, Kiowa Agency Records, Indian Archives Division, Oklahoma History Center, Oklahoma City (Microcopy KA 50) (hereinafter Kiowa Agency Records).

24. W. L. Swinney, Florence, Texas, "Bro. Officer's Enemies," *FF* (Mar. 2, 1891), 6.

25. Acting Commissioner of Indian Affairs to Charles E. Adams, Kiowa Indian Agent, Anadarko, I.T., May 19, 1891, Churches, Kiowa Agency Records (Microcopy KA 50); George Day, Kiowa Agency, to Commissioner of Indian Affairs, Anadarko, Feb. 23, 1892, Letterpress Book, vol. 38, Kiowa Agency Records; George Chandler, Acting Sec. of Interior, to Commissioner of Indian Affairs, Washington, D.C., March 9, 1892, Churches, Kiowa Agency Records (Microcopy KA 50).

26. RWO, "Indian Mission," *GA* 32 (Apr. 28, 1892), 272; RWO, "Among the Wild Tribes," *OR* 35 (June 28, 1892), 6.

27. RWO, "Indian Territory," *OR* 35 (May 31, 1892), 6; RWO, "Among the Wild Tribes," *OR* 35 (June 28, 1892), 6.

28. RWO, "Indian Territory," *GA* 38 (Apr. 9, 1896), 237.

29. RWO, "Good News from Bro. Erwin," *GA* 37 (July 4, 1895), 428; RWO, "From the Field," *GA* 40 (July 28, 1898), 479; RWO, "An Appeal from Brother Officer," *GA* 40 (Oct. 13, 1898), 658.

30. RWO, "Indian Territory," *GA* 34 (Dec. 15, 1892), 791.

31. RWO, "Indian Territory," *OR* 34 (Aug. 27, 1891), 6, and "Breshear and Officer Debate," *OR* 34 (Sept. 17, 1891), 3.

32. RWO, "Indian Territory," *GA* 34 (Dec. 15, 1892), 791.

33. RWO, "Indian Territory," *OR* 36 (Aug. 8, 1893), 3. See also *The Officer-Smith Debate: A Religious Discussion on the Design of Baptism and the Influence of the Holy Spirit, Held at Leader, Ind. Ter., Commencing July 13, 1893* (Garland, Tex.: M. A. Smith, 1896).

34. J. W. Atkisson, "The Officer-Frost Debate," *GA* 41 (Sept. 21, 1899), 60.

35. Mrs. G. Stewart, "Growth of the Word," *GA* 37 (Sept. 5, 1895), 572; RWO, ed., "Religious," *Indian Citizen*, Mar. 16, 1889, 5, and June 1, 1889, 6; RWO, "Indian Territory," *GA* 34 (Jan. 28, 1892), 64; RWO, "Notes," *GA* 33 (Mar. 11, 1891), 154. So far as is known, *The Sower* was never published.

36. RWO, "The 'Write Up' of the B[eyond] I[ndian] T[erritory]," *FF* (Jan. 28, 1894), 7, 8; RWO, "Indian Territory," *PC* 2 (Jan. 11, 1894), 8; RWO, "Indian Territory," *GA* 36 (Feb. 22, 1894), 124.

37. RWO, "Indian Territory," *GA* 39 (Dec. 23, 1897), 813; RWO, "Indian Territory," *GA* 40 (Jan. 13, 1898), 30; RWO, "From the Field," *GA* 40 (Sept. 15, 1898), 591; RWO, "Indian Territory," *OR* 40 (Dec. 28, 1897), 8.

38. RWO, "Indian Territory," *GA* 35 (July 13, 1893), 441; RWO, "Indian Territory," *GA* 35 (Sept. 28, 1893), 624; M. S. Conwell, "Correspondence," *GA* 40 (Aug. 25, 1898), 537; RWO, "Indian Mission," *PC* 2 (Oct. 4, 1893), 6; RWO, "Reports from Indian Territory," *OR* 36 (Oct. 10, 1893), 6.

39. RWO, "Indian Mission Notes," *OR* 32 (Nov. 7, 1889), 2; RWO, "Letter from West Texas," *GA* (Nov. 30, 1905), 763.

40. RWO, "Indian Territory," *OR* 36 (Mar. 23, 1893), 3.

41. RWO, "To the Saints Scattered Abroad," *OR* 37 (Oct. 30, 1894), 3; RWO, "Indian Mission," *GA* 36 (Mar. 1, 1894), 131.

42. RWO, "Indian Territory," *GA* 32 (Dec. 10, 1890), 588; RWO, "Indian Territory," *GA* 33 (Sept. 16, 1891), 583; C. C. Parker, "From Indian Territory," *GA* (Nov. 1, 1894), 693; RWO, "An Explanation," *GA* 36 (Nov. 22, 1894), 744; RWO, "Indian Territory," *GA* 38 (Jan. 2, 1896), 11; RWO, "Indian Territory, *GA* 39 (July 22, 1897), 462; RWO, "Acknowledgment," *OR* 37 (Feb. 16, 1894), 3.

43. RWO, "Indian Territory," *GA* 35 (Dec. 7, 1893), 773; B. L. Lunser et al., "An Open Letter," *GA* 39 (Mar. 4, 1897), 140; RWO, "An Open Letter," *GA* 42 (Dec. 13, 1900), 798; John A. Stevens, "About R. W. Officer," *OR* 40 (June 29, 1897), 3.

44. W. H. Horn, "Missions and Missionaries," *PC* 12 (Aug. 16, 1904), 3.

45. W. H. Horn to RWO, "An Open Letter," *PC* 2 (Aug. 3, 1893), 6; RWO, "In Regard to Organizing," *OR* 37 (Nov. 27, 1894), 2; and W. H. Horn, "Poor Indian, Poorer Whiteman," *PC* 3 (July 2, 1895), 5.

46. RWO, "An Open Letter," *PC* 2 (Aug. 31, 1893), 3.

47. W. H. Horn, "An Open Letter, II," *PC* 2 (Oct. 4, 1893), 3.

48. RWO, "Indian Territory," *PC* 2 (Nov. 16, 1893), 6.

49. W. H. Horn, "An Open Letter," *PC* 2 (Nov. 30, 1893), 4.

50. RWO, "Religious," *Indian Citizen*, Nov. 9, 1889, 6; RWO, "Indian Territory," *GA* 37 (May 9, 1895), 304; RWO, "The Organ Out of Worship," *GA* 41 (Mar. 2, 1899), 140; RWO, "Indian Territory," *OR* 38 (July 16, 1895), 3.

51. RWO, "The Temptation," *GA* 36 (Feb. 22, 1894), 127.

52. RWO, "Miscellaneous," *FF* (Apr. 16, 1895), 7; RWO, "Officer's Explanation," *FF* (May 7, 1895), 5; RWO, "From the Field," *GA* 40 (Sept. 8, 1898), 568; RWO, "Information Wanted," *GA* 42 (Nov. 20, 1900), 762.

53. T. B. Larimore's position was not dissimilar.

54. T. R. Burnett, "Burnett's Budget," *OR* 42 (Aug. 8, 1899), 2; Henry E. Warlick, "From Oklahoma," *FF* (Apr. 3, 1894), 6, 7, and "Receiving the Sects by 'The Right Hand of Fellowship,'" *FF* (Jan. 15, 1895), 6; D. B. Cargile, "Indian Territory," *PC* 3 (Aug. 23, 1894), 4. "Materialism" is described in J. C. Glover to Brethren, "Miscellaneous," *FF* (Nov. 27, 1894), 6. G. A. T[rott] to T. A. Holland, "Queries," *FF* 22 (Sept. 11, 1906), 5; RWO to Bro. Trott, "Queries," *FF* 22 (Nov. 13, 1906), 5.

55. RWO, "Unmerited Praise and Unnecessary Abuse," *OR* 39 (May. 19, 1896), 6. Officer claimed to be surprised that his name was used so casually by his progressive brothers.

56. Elders of the Church of God, Trinity, Texas, to Editors *Firm Foundation*, "Indian Mission," *FF* (Nov. 10, 1891), 7; RWO, "Information Wanted," *GA* 42 (Nov. 29, 1900), 762.

57. RWO, "I Have Not 'Gone to the Progressives,'" *GA* 42 (Nov. 20, 1900), 763; RWO, "Indian Territory," *GA* 39 (Feb. 4, 1897), 80. See also "Crumley-Taylor Debate," *FF* 25 (Dec. 21, 1909), 5.

58. RWO, "An Open Letter," *OR* 46 (Mar. 3, 1903), 3.

59. RWO, "Indian Territory," *GA* 41 (Jan. 26, 1899), 55; RWO, "Indian Territory," *GA* 40 (July 14, 1898), 451.

60. Editors, "Correspondence," *GA* 39 (Oct. 21, 1897), 664; Mrs. M. B. Wallace to Bro. McQuiddy, "Sister R. W. Officer," *GA* 36 (Apr. 19, 1894), 247.

61. RWO, "An Open Letter," *OR* 46 (Mar. 3, 1903), 3; emphasis added. F. G. Roberts, the Corresponding Secretary of the Home Board, reported to the ACMS thirty-six full-time Indian Territory Stone-Campbell preachers in 1898. He counted 3,272 Disciples and forty-seven churches. See England, *Oklahoma Christians*, 61.

62. T. B. Larimore, "The Indian Mission," *GA* 34 (Sept. 1, 1892), 551.

63. D. T. Broadus, "Kansas Notes," *GA* 38 (Apr. 16, 1896), 256.

64. C. C. Parker, "Brother R. W. Officer," *GA* 40 (June 9, 1898), 371.

65. Jennie Tryon, P.E.I., "Indian Territory," *OR* 36 (Sept. 26, 1893), 3.

66. RWO, "Indian Mission," *Christian Leader and Way* (hereinafter *CL*), Aug. 25, 1898, 13.

67. "Rev. R. W. Officer Dead," *Nashville News*, Aug. 29, 1930, 2. In its notice, the *News* also perpetuated the long-standing myth about Officer's wealth and his service as leader of a Confederate scout detachment, presumably Quantrill's Raiders.

68. C. R. Nichol, "C. H. Kennedy," in *Gospel Preachers Who Blazed the Trail*, comp. Harriett Helm Nichol and C. R. Nichol (Austin, Tex.: Firm Foundation, 1950), n.p. See his reports in *PC* 4 (Apr. 23, 1901), 4 and 9 (Dec. 4, 1900), 4.

69. Nichol, "D. B. Cargile" in *Gospel Preachers Who Blazed the Trail*; D. B. Cargile, "Indian Territory," *PC* 3 (Aug. 23, 1894), 4.

70. John W. Harris, "Notes from the Nation," *PC* 2 (July 5, 1894), 4; John W. Harris, "Oklahoma Jots," *PC* 3 (Nov. 1, 1894), 1; John W. Harris, "Oklahoma Jots," *PC* 4 (Apr. 11, 1895), 4.

71. G. F. Whitley to Friends in Christ, "Serious Facts," *PC* 2 (Mar. 22, 1894), 6; D. W. Nay, "A Letter to Brother G.F. Whitley, *PC* 3 (Sept. 9, 1894), 4.

72. Nichol, "W. D. Ingram," in *Gospel Preachers Who Blazed the Trail*; W. D. Ingram [to Bro. Moore], *PC* 8 (Oct. 10, 1899), 4.

Chapter 4

1. J. H. G[arrison], "The Oklahoma and Indian Territorial Convention," *CE* 32 (May 17, 1894), 308; England, *Oklahoma Christians*, 78–79.

2. John C. Howard to Bro. Moore, *PC* 13 (Jan. 12, 1905), 7; W. M. Davis, "Oklahoma Items," *PC* 15 (Feb. 21, 1907), 6.

3. C. M. Sharpe, "What Home Missions are to Oklahoma," *CE* 32 (Apr. 26, 1894), 265; *Disciples of Christ Year Book, 1945* (Indianapolis: Year Book Publication Committee, 1945), ii.

4. Such congregations were located at Chickasha, Duncan, Ardmore, Purcell, Henryetta, and South McAlester.

5. U. G. Wilkinson, "Indian Territory Notes," *PC* 14 (Feb. 1, 1906), 6.

6. J. H. Lawson, "Oklahoma Findings," *PC* 16 (June 18, 1908), 3.

7. Visual evidence of this settlement pattern is apparent in Edwin Scott Gaustad and Philip L. Barlow, *New Historical Atlas of Religion in America* (New York: Oxford University Press, ca. 2000), figs. 2.104 and 2.105.

8. England, *Oklahoma Christians*, 28–29; Melva L. Martin to brother and friend, *PC* 17 (July 30, 1909), 6.

9. The church, named "Bethel Church of Christ," and cemetery is located seven miles north and three miles east of Chandler.

10. J. C. Estes, "Mission Work in Western Oklahoma Territory," *GA* 51 (Mar. 23, 1909), 187.

11. J. H. Lawson, "Oklahoma Gleanings," *PC* 11 (Apr. 21, 1903), 7.

12. J. B. Nelson, "Notes from Oklahoma Territory," *GA* 45 (Aug. 27, 1903), 554.

13. U. G. Wilkinson, "Indian Territory Notes," *PC* 14 (Feb. 1, 1906), 6.

14. William Barker, "The Church at Auburn, Okla.," *PC* 9 (July 6, 1901), 6.

15. Angie Debo, *Prairie City: The Story of an American Community* (New York: Alfred A. Knopf, 1944), 32.

16. Laura C. Gordon, "Cheyenne Items," *PC* 3 (Nov. 1, 1894), 8.

17. Hicklin Albert Harrel Jr., *The Harrel Family* (Oak Ridge, Tenn.: Privately printed, ca. 1997), 106–11; D. B. Cargile, "Indian Territory," *PC* 3 (Aug. 23, 1894), 4.

18. Quoted in Hughes, *Reviving the Ancient Faith*, 25.

19. J. H. Lawson, "Three Good Debates," *GA* 52 (Jan. 13, 1910), 53.

20. RWO, "Indian Territory," *PC* 2 (May 31, 1894), 4.

21. J. B. Nelson, "Oklahoma Gleanings," *GA* 44 (Dec. 25, 1902), 823.

22. Joseph E. Cain, "Zephyrs," *PC* 11 (May 26, 1903), 2.

23. "David T. Broadus," *Christian Worker* 70 (Apr. 1984), 1.

24. Fanning Yater Tant, *J. D. Tant—Texas Preacher: A Biography* (Erlanger, Ky.: Faith and Facts Press, 1958), 187–210.

25. J. H. Lawson, "Oklahoma Territory," *GA* 44 (Apr. 10, 1902), 237; "Field Gleanings," *GA* 44 (Apr. 24, 1902), 267; "Field Gleanings," *GA* 44 (Oct. 16, 1902), 669.

26. J. H. Lawson, "Report on Mission Work," *GA* 45 (Jan. 8, 1903), 30; "Field Gleanings," *GA* 46 (Jan. 14, 1904), 29.

27. "John H. Lawson," in Boyd E. Morgan, *Arkansas Angels* (Paragould: College Book Store and Press, 1967), 43–44.

28. Nichol, "J. H. Lawson," in *Gospel Preachers Who Blazed the Trail*, n.p.; C. J. Dull, "Fundamentalism," in Foster et al., *Encyclopedia of the Stone-Campbell Movement*, 346.

29. J. H. Lawson, "Army Service, *CL* (May 7, 1918), 16; J. H. Lawson, "Camp Bowie Notes," *CL* (July 23, 1918), 8.

30. Nichol, "W. F. Ledlow," in *Gospel Preachers Who Blazed the Trail*, n.p.

31. "U. G. Wilkinson," in Loyd L. Smith, *Gospel Preachers of Yesteryear*, 426–29.

32. In this discussion of S. R. Cassius, I have drawn upon the work of Edward J. Robinson, specifically *To Save My Race from Abuse: The Life of Samuel Robert Cassius* (Tuscaloosa: University of Alabama Press, 2007), and "Heaven to Hell: Samuel Robert Cassius and Black Life in Oklahoma, 1891–1923," *Chronicles of Oklahoma*, 84 (Spring 2006): 78–99. The quoted material is from page 79 of the latter.

33. That Allen and Cassius were acquaintances during the time of the Twin Territories is deduced from the fact that Cassius visited Allen in Oakland, California, where Allen was minister of the Church of Christ, in 1924.

34. Robinson, *To Save My Race from Abuse*, 157. Today, no African American Church of Christ in Oklahoma traces its roots to Cassius, just as no white church traces its roots to R. W. Officer.

35. "Dynamite Under a Church," *Kansas City Star*, Apr. 16, 1901; and I. J. Honaker et al., and Frank Pickerill to Brethren of the P.C., Ingalls, Okla., *PC* 9 (May 14, 1901), 8.

36. Theresa Gable, ed., *Davis, Oklahoma* (Oklahoma City: Arbuckle Historical Society, 1981), 168.

37. Sherman Kelly, "Oklahoma," *GA* 53 (Nov. 16, 1911), 1332. This congregation must have been short-lived in that the two current Church of Christ congregations in Davis date their origins to the late 1930s and early 1940s.

38. H. L. Taylor, "Personal," *GA* 48 (June 7, 1906), 357. The current congregation in Holdenville dates its origin to this event. In the same year, Taylor also organized a conservative church at Wewoka. See "Work in Indian Territory," *GA* 48 (Feb. 3, 1906), 93.

39. H. L. Taylor, "Personal," *GA* 48 (May 24, 1906), 325.

40. At the invitation of two women in 1903, J. H. Lawson conducted a meeting in Henryetta, which he described as a "mining town" where "wickedness abounds." Some five or more were baptized and agreed to meet regularly for worship. This effort apparently had no long-range consequence, for no Stone-Campbell congregation existed three years later. See J. H. Lawson, "Field Gleanings," *GA* 45 (Nov. 12, 1903), 731.

41. H. L. Taylor, "The Church at Henryetta, I.T.," *GA* 49 (July 25, 1907), 427. Today, the Henryetta Church of Christ dates its origin to 1900, probably the date of the establishment of the first Stone-Campbell congregation.

42. RWO, "Indian Territory," *OR* 34 (Sept. 10, 1891), 2.

43. From the history of the First Christian Church in Muskogee, quoted in England, *Oklahoma Christians*, 58.

44. Ibid.

45. RWO, "Indian Territory," *OR* 34 (Aug. 27, 1891), 6; England, *Oklahoma Christians*, 59.

46. England, *Oklahoma Christians*, 58. In 1904, a second structure was erected in brick on the same site. It served the congregation until 1926, when the leadership sold the building to the Church of Christ, and constructed a new edifice across the street at Sixth and Kansas.

47. "Notes from Oklahoma Territory," *GA* 44 (Aug. 28, 1902), 222. In fact, Putman would report from time to time in the *Gospel Advocate*, a newspaper that strongly opposed innovations. See J. H. Putman, "Handmaidens," *GA* 45 (Aug. 13, 1903), 525. See also England, *Oklahoma Christians*, 88.

48. D. B. Killebrew, et al., "The Church at Poteau, Okla.," *GA* 50 (July 16, 1908), 461.

49. J. W. Chism, "Meeting at Henryetta, Okla.," *GA* 50 (June 4, 1908), 366. The effort to "drown out" opposing revivalists by scheduling simultaneous meeting was a common technique. See C. C. Parker, "Indian Territory," *OR* 34 (Sept. 24, 1891), 6.

50. W. M. Davis, "Oklahoma Items," *PC* 15 (Feb. 21, 1907), 6.

51. [J. C. Howell], "Our Preachers," *Pioneer Christian* 1 (Aug. 15, 1901), 1, 12, in box 17, England Papers.

52. Ibid.

53. L. B. Grogan, "A Historical Sketch of the Missionary Work of the Christian Church in Indian Territory from its beginning to September 1906" [1906], box 17, England Papers.

54. Ibid.

55. [J. C. Howell], "Our Preachers," *Pioneer Christian* 1 (Aug. 15, 1901), 1, 12, in box 17, England Papers.

56. Jimmie Lewis Franklin, *Born Sober: Prohibition in Oklahoma, 1907–1959* (Norman: University of Oklahoma Press, 1971), 12. Franklin takes this information from U.S. Bureau of the Census, *Thirteenth Census of the United States, 1910: Abstract, with Supplement for Oklahoma*, (Washington, D.C.: GPO, 1913), 590–91; and U.S. Bureau of the Census, *Special Reports: Religious Bodies, 1906*, pt. 1, *Summary and General Tables* (Washington, D.C.: GPO, 1910), 252.

57. "Cuts Out the Campbellites," *Oklahoman*, May 13, 1908, 7.

58. Harriett Helm Nichol, comp., *Gospel Preachers in Texas and Oklahoma* (Clifton, Tex.: Nichol, 1911).

59. U.S. Bureau of the Census, *Religious Bodies, 1916*, pt. 2, *Separate Denominations, History, Description, and Statistics* (Washington, D.C.: GPO, 1919), 208, 247; U.S. Bureau of the Census, *Religious Bodies: 1926*, vol. 1, *Summary and Detailed Tables* (Washington, D.C.: GPO, 1930), 394.

60. The Oakland congregation, just northwest of Madill, was established in 1888 and is mentioned frequently in the literature, while Allen and Gilmore are not. The 2000

edition of the Church of Christ directory, however, shows Allen as having organized the earlier of the two.

Chapter 5

1. *Fourteenth Census of the United States, 1920: Abstract, with Supplement for Oklahoma*(Washington, D.C: GPO, 1923), 80–83.
2. B. F. Rhodes, "Oklahoma Notes," *PC* 17 (July 1, 1909), 14; Loyd L. Smith, *Gospel Preachers of Yesteryear*, 18–20, 100–07; "A. Leroy Elkins," Indian-Pioneer Papers, vol. 27, 327–41, Western History Collection, University of Oklahoma Library, Norman.
3. Smith, *Gospel Preachers of Yesteryear*, 149–51, 426–29; Nichol, *Gospel Preachers in Texas and Oklahoma*, n.p.
4. L. C. Sears, *For Freedom: The Biography of John Nelson Armstrong* (Austin, Tex.: Sweet, 1969), chaps. 8–10; A. W. Luce, "Cordell Christian College Notes," *PC* 16 (Nov. 19, 1908), 5.
5. Dee Bills, "Echoes from the Comanche Meeting," *Gospel Herald* (hereinafter *GH*) 2 (Jan. 15, 1914), 1.
6. J. N. Armstrong, "Echoes from the Comanche Meeting," *GH* 2 (Jan. 8, 1914), 1; A. Leroy Elkins, "Echoes from the Comanche Meeting," *GH* 2 (Jan. 15, 1914), 1.
7. U. G. Wilkinson, "Echoes from the Comanche Meeting," *GH* 2 (Feb. 19, 1914), 1.
8. Andy T. Ritchie, "Reports from the Field," *GA* 52 (Sept. 15, 1910), 1045.
9. J. L. Wood, "Oklahoma," *GA* 49 (Nov. 14, 1907), 736.
10. A. LeRoy Elkins, "Cheerful Messages," *GA* 52 (Aug. 4, 1910), 901.
11. D. S. Ligon, "Cheerful Messages," *GA* 56 (Oct. 29, 1914), 1132.
12. D. L. Haily, "Call for a Meeting at McAlester, Okla," *GA* 51 (Apr. 29, 1909), 543; Mrs. W. M. Anderson, "The Church at Ardmore, Okla.," *GA* 52 (June 30, 1910), 768.
13. "Directory for 1935–1936, Tenth and Francis Church of Christ, Oklahoma City, Oklahoma," in Oklahoma Churches, Vertical File, Center for Restoration Studies, Brown Library, Abilene Christian University (hereinafter CRS); "Church Notices," in *Oklahoman*, Dec. 24, 1905, 10; Apr. 13, 1913, 36; and Nov. 10, 1918, 34; J. F. Smith, "Among the Churches," *GH* 1 (Feb. 7, 1913), 3, and 2 (Apr. 22,1915), 5; E. A. Bedichek, *Word and Work* (1914).
14. S. H. Brown to Robert L. Cowell, [1917], Church History Archives, Beam Library, Oklahoma Christian University, Oklahoma City; "Directory for 1935–1936, Tenth and Francis Church of Christ"; "Church of Christ Springs from Small Numbers," *Oklahoman*, Feb. 5, 1922, 5; "Church of Christ Has Recorded Many Achievements in Spite of Discouragements at Its Start," *Oklahoman*, May 29, 1922, 3. On the new building, A. W. Lee, C. H. Wright, and Frank Winters constituted the finance committee, while L. E. Diamond, D. L. Strong, and J. D. Fine composed the architectural committee. The building cost $20,000.
15. Among the leaders were Ira Blackwell (a barber), W. T. Schrimpshire (a cotton mill laborer), L. E. Diamond (a carpenter), Frank Winters (a salesman), A. W. Lee (Champlain oil and gas dealer), T. P. Prickett (a school janitor), C. R. Todd (an accountant), and J. D. Fine (candy factory manager). Preachers through 1940 included John Allen Hudson,

Foy E. Wallace Jr., K. C. Moser, Christopher A. Norred, A. O. Calley, H. C. Sweet, and c. e. McGaughey. See "Directory for 1927, Tenth and Francis Church of Christ," and "Directory for 1935–1936, Tenth and Francis Church of Christ," both in CRS.

16. Noble Patterson and Terry J. Gardner, eds., *Foy E. Wallace, Jr.: Soldier of the Cross* (Ft. Worth, Tex.: Wallace Memorial Fund, 1999), 130, 214. Brown account ledger, 1939–58, Historical Records, Tenth and Francis Church Archives, Seminole Pointe Church of Christ, Oklahoma City, Okla. (hereinafter Tenth and Francis Archives).

17. "Church History," in the *Membership Directory: Tenth and Rockford Church of Christ* (Tulsa: privately printed, 1970). See also *Polk's City Directory, Tulsa, Oklahoma* (Dallas: R. L. Polk, 1917–18), entries under "church."

18. *The Tulsa Lectures Delivered at The Church of Christ, Tenth and Rockford, Tulsa, Oklahoma, January 9–16, 1938*, ed. L. R. Wilson (Nashville, Tenn.: Gospel Advocate, ca. 1938). When compared to the Tulsa city directories, church sources vary significantly on terms of service of the ministers, especially Hudson and Wilson.

19. Carl H. Royster, comp., *Churches of Christ in the United States* (Nashville: 21st Century Christian, 2006), 442–62. I have followed Royster on dates of beginning, although other sources—WPA records, county histories, and the survey of the author conducted in August 2008—may give ones that are slightly different.

20. Lawton Church of Christ, Sixth and Arlington, Church Inventory Forms, Church of Christ, folder 1–17, MS 21–4–1, WPA Historical Records Survey, Church Records, State Archives Oklahoma State Library, Oklahoma City (hereinafter WPA Historical Records).

21. [Cleon Lyles], Attachment to inventory of the Muskogee Church of Christ, Church Inventory Forms, Church of Christ, folder 1–17, MS 21–4–1, WPA Historical Records. A congregation had been organized in June 1907 and met temporarily in a building at E and Dayton Streets, but it disbanded sometime before 1913. See "Church of Christ Organized," *Muskogee Times Democrat*, June 11, 1907, 5.

22. J. H. Lawson, "Field Gleanings," *GA* 49 (Mar. 21, 1907), 190; D. L. Maile, "A Call for a Meeting at McAlester, Okla.," *GA* 51 (Apr. 29, 1909), 543; "Church of Christ One of City's Oldest," *Kiamichi Magazine*, Oct. 13, 1968.

23. RWO, "Indian Territory," *PC* 2 (Oct. 26, 1893), 4; Mrs. W. M. Anderson, "The Church at Ardmore, Okla.," *GA* 55 (June 30, 1910), 768–69.

24. "Central Church of Christ," *Daily Ardmoreite*, Apr. 19, 1987, 9.

25. Sometimes the instructor taught the school with no reference to the church. See "Normal School of Music," *Haskell News*, Aug. 2, 1917, 1, in Slater file, Banowsky Papers, University Archives and Special Collections, University Libraries, Pepperdine University, Malibu, Calif.

26. "Will Slater," in Smith, *Gospel Preachers of Yesteryear*, 315–18. Slater was the grandfather of William S. Banowsky, who would serve as president of the University of Oklahoma in the 1970s and 1980s.

27. Lindell Mitchell, "Albert Edward Brumley," History of the Restoration Movement (2002), http://www.therestorationmovement.com/_states/tennessee/brumley.htm (accessed June 10, 2009).

28. "The Lord Has Been Mindful of Me: An Autobiography of L. O. Sanderson," *GA* 146 (Sept. 2004), 26–28, at History of the Restoration Movement, http://www .therestoration movement .com/_states/tennessee/sanderson.htm (accessed June 10, 2008); Patterson and Gardner, *Foy E. Wallace, Jr.*, 149.

29. "J. H. Lawson," in Nichol, *Gospel Preachers in Texas and Oklahoma*.

30. "Ira Y. Rice, Sr.," in Smith, *Gospel Preachers of Yesteryear*, 286–89.

31. Patterson and Gardner, *Foy E. Wallace, Jr.*, 146.

32. "Mrs. J. N. Armstrong, of Cordell, Okla., Says—," *GA* 57 (Oct. 28, 1915), 1079–1080.

33. J. F. Smith, "Notes and Comments," *GH* 1 (Jan. 9, 1913), 4; Matthew C. Morrison, *Like a Lion, Daniel Sommer's Seventy Years of Preaching* (Murfreesboro, Tenn.: Dehoff Publications, 1975), chap. 6.

34. U. G. Wilkinson, "Notes from Oklahoma," *PC* 16 (June 18, 1908), 6.

35. Robert E. Hooper, *Crying in the Wilderness: A Biography of David Lipscomb* (Nashville: David Lipscomb College, 1979), 211–13.

36. R. L. Whiteside, "Comments on Current Topics," *GH* 1 (June 26, 1913), 6; J. N. Armstrong, "God A Living Power in the Affairs of Men," *GH* 2 (May 21, 1914), 1. See also Hicks and Valentine, *Kingdom Come*, 45–46.

37. J. A. Harding, "Are We Conscious After Death? An Advent Article Considered," *GH* 3 (Mar. 4, 1914), 3; Tice Elkins, "Materialism Dissected," *GH* 3 (Oct. 7, 1915), 6; Herbert Duncan, "The Infidelity of Russellism," *GH* 4 (Mar. 23, 1916), 3. See T. B. Wilkinson, "Life History and Background of the Country Preacher," typescript copy prepared by J. C. Wilkinson, Sept. 1969, private collection of Roy Young, Apache, Okla.

38. Hughes, *Reviving the Ancient Faith*, xii–xiii; B. F. Rhodes, "The Coming of Christ, No. 2," *GH* 3 (Nov. 26, 1914), 2; B. F. Rhodes, "The Second-Coming of Christ, No. 3," *GH* 3 (Jan. 7, 1915), 1.

39. Royce L. Money, "Church-State Relations in the Churches of Christ since 1945: A Study in Religion and Politics" (PhD diss., Baylor University, 1975), 199.

40. J. E. Dunn, "The Christian's Relation to War, Politics, and Human Governments," *GA* reprinted in *GH* 3 (Jan. 28, 1915), 3, 6. This was Armstrong's view as well: "Civil Government," *GH* 2 (Oct. 29, 1914), 1. See also E. C. Fuqua, "Why We Do Not Vote or Otherwise Participate in the Civil Government," *Word of Truth*, in *GH* 3 (Dec. 3, 1914), 1.

41. B. F. Rhodes, "Christian Soldiers," *GH* 2 (Oct. 29, 1914), 3–6.

42. J. H. Lawson, "Reports from the Field," *CL* (May 7, 1918) and (July 23, 1918).

Chapter 6

1. Elizabeth C. Parsons, ed., *The Greatest Work in the World, Education as a Mission of Early Twentieth-Century Churches of Christ: Letters of Lloyd Cline Sears and Pattie Hathaway Armstrong* (Eugene, Ore.: Wipf and Stock, 2015), 52.

2. Norman L. Parks, *Cordell's Christian College: A History* (Cordell, Okla.: Fourth and College Church of Christ, 1994), 2; Loyd L. Smith, *Gospel Preachers of Yesteryear*, 166–69. Cordell was one of thirty-six congregations Harrel set in order either in Washita County or along its borders. He was still planting churches in 1922, when he

and Everette Baird established the congregation in Edmond, Oklahoma. See Harrel *Harrel Family*, 106.

3. Parks, *Cordell's Christian College*, 2. Timber for the three-room frame building, located just north of the courthouse square on College Street, had come from El Reno, Minco, and North Texas. The academy enrolled as many as 150 students and had a religious atmosphere. Jim Harrel was president; brother John Harrel was business manager.

4. The property was deeded to the Church of Christ in 1905, with a restrictive covenant regarding the use of instrumental music in worship. The covenant was removed in 1946. See Harrel, *Harrel Family*, 104.

5. Park, *Cordell's Christian College*, 3; Smith, *Gospel Preachers of Yesteryear*, 224–28, 326–36.

6. "Cordell Bids For Another College," *DO*, May 22, 1906, 9. This article notes that a Dutch Reformed–related school had located in Cordell. It also confuses Churches of Christ with the Christian Church, in that it reports a membership of 23,117, church property valued at $814,000, 196 church buildings, 376 church organizations, 237 Sunday schools with a membership of 21,300, and 72 "Endeavor Societies."

7. Robert E. Hooper, *A Distinct People, A History of the Churches of Christ in the 20th Century* (West Monroe, La.: Howard, 1993), 73–74.

8. Other board members included E. F. Grogan, T. L. Cook, H. E. Warlick, A. E. Freeman, T. F. Brown, and J. W. Ballard.

9. Parks, *Cordell's Christian College*, 3–4; J. W. Harrel, "Oklahoma Items," *PC* 16 (Feb. 6, 1907), 6.

10. The board first offered the presidency to John E. Dunn, a Tennessee evangelist who had spent considerable time in Oklahoma Territory. Dunn declined the position because the board would not make daily lessons from the Bible mandatory. See John E. Dunn, "Miscellany," *GA* 49 (May 23, 1907), 325. See also Parks, *Cordell's Christian College*, 4. Because the board saw a special need to educate preachers and teachers for the churches, it determined to build the boy's dormitory first. Girls would board in private homes in town, with their campus housing needs met later.

11. Parks, *Cordell's Christian College*, 5; Sears, *For Freedom*, 104; J. H. Lawson, "Miscellany," *GA* 49 (Dec. 26, 1907), 821; West, *Search for the Ancient Order*, 3:279–80. See also Morgan, *Arkansas Angels*, 43–44.

12. Parks, *Cordell's Christian College*, 7; Sears, *For Freedom*, 18–98. See also "Church College has Good Year," *DO*, May 10, 1908, 15.

13. Sears, *For Freedom*, 104–9.

14. Ibid.; Park, *Cordell's Christian College*, 5. Park is far more sympathetic to Harrel and Fleming than Sears. See also "Peace and Harmony Reigns at Cordell, Okla.," *GA* 52 (Aug. 25, 1910), 975.

15. Sears, *For Freedom*, 143; J. N. Armstrong, "Cordell Christian College, Cordell, Okla.," *GA* 57 (July 29, 1915), 748.

16. Parks, *Cordell's Christian College*, 9. "The Women of the Faculty of Cordell Christian College," *GH* 1 (July 24, 1913), 8. For the response of Lloyd Cline Sears to this suggestion, see Parsons, *Greatest Work in the World*.

17. See West, *Search for the Ancient Order*, 3:292–93. West estimated Thorp Springs enrollment as "almost" three hundred in 1917.

18. *Mid-Year Bulletin of the Cordell Christian College, 1909–1910*, Cordell Christian College, Christian Colleges, Miscellaneous, Vertical File, CRS.

19. Ibid.; Parks, *Cordell's Christian College*, 8.

20. *Mid-Year Bulletin of the Cordell Christian College, 1909–1910*, 3.

21. Parks, *Cordell's Christian College*, 8. According to Parks, students were advised not to date just one person. Handholding was limited to engaged couples; kissing presumed that you were married.

22. Ibid., 11. P. W. Adams commented that the Cordell Church was the "largest and most liberal congregation in Oklahoma that I have met." He noted that 60 adults showed up for prayer meeting and 150 for worship even when it rained. P. W. Adams, "Correspondence," *PC* 18 (Dec. 23, 1909), 11.

23. West, *Search for the Ancient Order*, 3:281.

24. See *GH* 1 (Oct. 31, 1912). The *Herald* published between 1912 and 1922. Only the first four years seemed to have survived, however. Those issues are available on microfilm at Pepperdine University, Abilene Christian University, and Harding University.

25. L. C. Sears, *What Is Your Life?* (Dallas: Temple, 1979), 79.

26. For an extensive exposition of the pacifist tradition within the Churches of Christ, see Harrell, *Social Sources of Division in the Disciples of Christ*. See also West, *Search for the Ancient Order*, vol. 3, chap. 13.

27. Parks, *Cordell's Christian College*, 19; see John E. Dunn, "The Christian's Relation to War, Politics, and Human Government," *GH* 3 (Jan. 28, 1915), 3.

28. James H. Fowler II, "Tar and Feather Patriotism: The Suppression of Dissent in Oklahoma during World War I," *Chronicles of Oklahoma*, 56 (Winter 1979): 409–30.

29. Sears, *What Is Your Life?*, 80–81.

30. Ibid., 79.

31. Michael W. Casey, "The Closing of Cordell Christian College: A Microcosm of American Intolerance during World War I," *Chronicles of Oklahoma* 76 (Spring 1998): 25. Since 1915, in fact, the *GH* had published frequent articles on the duty of Christians to government during wartime. See, for example, E. C. Fuqua, "Why We Do Not Vote or Otherwise Participate in the Civil Government," *GH* 4 (Dec. 3, 1914), 1.

32. Michael W. Casey, "From Pacifism to Patriotism: The Emergence of Civil Religion in the Churches of Christ during World War I," *Mennonite Quarterly Review* 66 (July 1992): 389–90. See also J. H. Lawson to Editors, Apr. 27, [1918], *CL* 32 (May 7, 1918), 16, and "Camp Bowie Notes," *CL* 32 (July 23, 1918), 8.

33. Ibid., 27.

34. Casey, "Closing of Cordell Christian College," 28–29.

35. Quoted in Sears, *What Is Your Life?*, 84. See also "Defense Council Closes College, Disloyalty Alleged," *DO*, Aug. 18, 1918, 17.

36. Casey, "Closing of Cordell Christian College," 30–31.

37. Ibid.

38. Ibid., 31–32.

39. Ibid., 33; Sears, *What Is Your Life?*, 84.

40. Sears, *For Freedom*, 158.

41. A partial list of alumni who were ministers included John G. Bills, Roy Cogdill, Vaughn Crumley, J. Harvey Dykes, Byron Fullerton, Wilburn C. Hill, W. Don Hockaday, John Allen Hudson, W. L. Oliphant, and Loyd Smith. See "Ministers," [Cordell, Okla., Church of Christ] *Christian Chronicle*, Special Edition (1941), 9.

42. Hooper, *Distinct People*, 112.

43. U. G. Wilkinson, "Shall We Go to War?," *FF* (May 27, 1917), 3.

44. Michael W. Casey, "From Religious Outsiders to Insiders: The Rise and Fall of Pacifism in the Churches of Christ," *Journal of Church and State*, 44 (Summer 2002): 462–63; John C. Stevens, *No Ordinary University: The History of a City Set on a Hill* (Abilene: Abilene Christian University Press, 1998), 55–56.

Chapter 7

1. Jim Bissett, *Agrarian Socialism in America: Marx, Jefferson, and Jesus in the Oklahoma Countryside, 1904–1920* (Norman: University of Oklahoma Press, 1999), 3–7.

2. Oscar Ameringer, *If You Don't Weaken: The Autobiography of Oscar Ameringer*, with an introduction by James Green (Norman: University of Oklahoma Press, 1983), 232.

3. J. W. Chism, "Meeting at Francis, Okla.," *GA* 50 (June 25, 1908), 411.

4. See Joe Klein, *Woody Guthrie: A Life* (New York: Alfred A. Knopf, 1980), 56–60; and Ron Briley, "The Christian Left's Vision (Remember Woody Guthrie?)," History News Network (Aug. 8, 2005), http://hnn.us/articles/13445.html (accessed Apr. 4, 2008).

5. The bulk of the material on Enfield that follows hereafter is taken from a six-page "Memoirs" document and a multiple-page "Letters to Roy" piece, both written by Enfield after ca. 1950 and now filed in box 1, Biography and Family History, Orville E. Enfield Collection, Special Collections, Oklahoma History Center (hereinafter Enfield Collection). Unless part of my narrative is drawn verbatim from the "Memoirs," I will not refer to it again. Material from other sources will be cited traditionally.

6. Letters to Roy, [post 1948], 119, Enfield Collection.

7. Vera Tefertiller, "Enfield, Orville E., Packsaddle," *Our Ellis County Heritage, 1885–1979* (Gage, Okla.: Ellis County Historical Society, 1979), 150.

8. D. T. Broadus, "Texas Notes," *Christian Companion* (Mar. 27, 1910), 13.

9. J. F. Smith, "Enfield-Wadsworth Debate," *GH* 2 (Jan. 1, 1914), 5.

10. O. E. Enfield, "Our Tin Wedding," *GH* 1 (Sept. 18, 1913), 5; "The 'Come' and 'Go' of the Bible, Number One," *GH* 1 (Sept. 18, 1913), 2; "The 'Come' and 'Go' of the Bible, Number Two," *GH* 1 (Sept. 18, 1913), 1; "The 'Come' and "Go" of the Bible, Number Three," *GH* 1 (Sept. 25, 1913), 1, 2; O. C. [*sic*] E[nfield] to Brethren, "Baptist Preacher Wanted My Picture," *GH* 1 (Nov. 30, 1913), 1, 5; "The Come and Go of the Bible, Number Four," *GH* 1 (Oct. 30, 1913), 1, 2; J. F. Smith, "Enfield-Wadsworth," *GH* 1 (Jan. 1, 1914), 2, 5; O. E. Enfield, "Induction into the School of Agnosticism," *GH* 1 (Jan. 1, 1914), 2, 3; "Think of This," *GH* 1 (Mar. 12, 1914), 2, 5; "The Dying Wife," *GH* 1 (June 3, 1915), 3, 6.

11. Letters to Roy, [post 1948], 120–22, Enfield Collection.

12. Letters to Roy, [post 1948], 127–28, Enfield Collection. In Garin Burbank, *When Farmers Voted Red: The Gospel of Socialism in the Oklahoma Countryside, 1910–1924* (Westport, Conn.: Greenwood Press, 1977), 28, the author sees Enfield as "outwardly socialist but inwardly and powerfully millenarian." The reality of the kingdom of God on earth, of course, was fundamental to the theology of Barton Stone, David Lipscomb, and J. A. Harding, in which Enfield had been well trained.

13. The list of known advocates of socialism within Churches of Christ in Oklahoma is very short. In addition to Enfield, also on the list is Robert L. Allen, who defended the cause in a debate at Minco in 1914 and Thomas H. McLemore. See "Notes," *FF* 31 (Feb. 24, 1914), 4; and Bissett, *Agrarian Socialism in America*, 95.

14. Henry Warlick, "Appeal for Help," *FF* (Jan. 15, 1915), 7.

15. U. G. Wilkinson, *Why I Am Not a Socialist* (Comanche, Okla.: American Print, 1915), 4. Another forceful and controversial analysis was W. F. Lemmons, *The Devil and Socialism* (Cincinnati: F. L. Rowe, 1914). Lemmons, a Texan, was particularly exercised over the socialist interest in social equality, taking offense at the "Great Coon Dinner" held in New York ca. 1908. Neither Wilkinson nor Lemmons critiqued socialism as it actually manifested itself in Oklahoma. The same was true of A. Leroy Elkins, a physician, an Indian Territory evangelist after 1894, and one of the founders of the Tipton Home for orphan children, whose musings often appeared in the *Firm Foundation*. See, for instance, "Notes," *FF* 31 (Feb. 24, 1914), 7; and "A. Leroy Elkins," Indian-Pioneer Papers, vol. 27, 327–41. See also "A Challenge Accepted," *FF* 31 (Mar. 17, 1914), 2, where the editor of the periodical, G. H. P. Showalter, gives his take on socialism in specific and politics in general.

16. James R. Green, *Grass-Roots Socialism, Radical Movements in the Southwest, 1895–1943* (Baton Rouge: Louisiana State University Press, 1978), 377–78; *Directory of Oklahoma, 1981* (Oklahoma City: State Election Board, 1981), 689.

17. Hughes, *Reviving the Ancient Faith*, 147.

18. O. E. Enfield, "Memoirs," n.d., 3, Enfield Collection. Contemporary reports in the *Daily Oklahoman* place the arrest in Shattuck, while Enfield's memoirs clearly associate it with Seiling. See "Enfield, Socialist Federal Prisoner," *DO*, Aug. 17, 1917, 24.

19. "Enfield, Socialist Federal Prisoner," *DO*, Aug. 17, 1917, 24.

20. Bissett, *Agrarian Socialism in America*, chap. 7.

21. Ibid., 150–51.

22. Ibid., 151–52.

23. I deduce the relationship from "Witnesses Tell of Rioting in Prospect in Western County . . . ," Enid, Okla., *DO*, Sept. 21, 1918, 1, where the reporter makes a direct connection.

24. "Draft Rebellion Planned in the West," *DO*, June 2, 1918, 6; "Hicks Drawn into Enfield Trial Here," *DO*, June 4, 1918, 9; "Arguments Begin in Enfield Case Today," *DO*, June 5, 1918, 4; and "Witnesses Tell of Rioting in Prospect in Western Country . . . ," *DO*, Sept. 21, 1918, 1. See also *U.S. vs. O. E. Enfield*, case 75882–3, Old German files, Records of the FBI, National Archives, Washington, D.C. (RG 65, microfilm roll 443).

25. "Enfield Jury, Out 10 Hours, Rests," *DO*, June 6, 1918, 10.

26. O. E. Enfield, "Memoirs," 3, Enfield Collection. See also Dr. J. E. Enfield, *The Man from Packsaddle* (Hollywood: House-Warven Publishers, 1951), 90–92. Although authorship is attributed to his brother, O. E. Enfield wrote *The Man From Packsaddle*. In what appears to be references to his June 1918 trial, he includes a soliloquy critical of the judge and witnesses. The judge was "swayed, not by the sublime principles of law and justice, but rather by passion and prejudice." As for the witnesses, "it must be said that they absolutely disregarded their oaths, and knowingly and emphatically falsified their testimony."

27. *Clinton Chronicle*, in *Cordell Herald-Sentinel*, Aug. 12, 1918, 4, Gateway to Oklahoma History, Oklahoma Historical Society.

28. Enfield, *The Man from Packsaddle*, 168–69.

29. "Enfield Wins Office Fight," *DO*, Jan. 1, 1937, 4.

30. Letters to Roy, 105–6, Enfield Collection; O. E. Enfield, Elk City, to Frank Winters, Oklahoma City, May 12, 1935, and O. E. Enfield, Arnett, to Franklin D. Roosevelt, Washington, D.C., Feb. 24, 1944, both in box 1, Miscellaneous Correspondence, Enfield Collection.

31. Enfield to Winters, May 12, 1935, Miscellaneous Correspondence, Enfield Collection. See also poem entitled "My God," and O. E. Enfield to Elder Rhodes, Reyden, Okla., May 9, 1954, box 5, and Letters to Roy, 103, box 1, Enfield Collection.

Chapter 8

1. Dan T. Boyd, "Oklahoma Oil: Past, Present, and Future," *Oklahoma Geology Notes*, 62 (Fall 2002): 98.

2. *Directory of Oklahoma, 1981*, 638; Charles Robert Goins and Danney Goble, *Historical Atlas of Oklahoma*, 4th ed. (Norman: University of Oklahoma Press, 2006), map 86.

3. Franklin, *Born Sober*, 72.

4. Ameringer, *If You Don't Weaken*, 365–90.

5. Danney Goble, comp., *Final Report of the Oklahoma Commission to Study The Tulsa Race Riot of 1921* (Oklahoma City: Oklahoma Commission to Study the Tulsa Race Riot of 1921, 2001); Jimmie Lewis Franklin, *Journey toward Hope: A History of Blacks in Oklahoma* (Norman: University of Oklahoma, 1982); Scott Ellsworth, *Death in a Promised Land: The Tulsa Race Riot of 1921* (Baton Rouge: Louisiana State University, 1982).

6. Mark A. Noll, *A History of Christianity in the United States and Canada* (Grand Rapids, Mich.: William B. Eerdmans, 1992), 373; Robert C. Cottrell, *The Social Gospel of E. Nicholas Comfort: Founder of the Oklahoma School of Religion* (Norman: University of Oklahoma Press, 1997), 65–68.

7. Arrell Morgan Gibson, *Oklahoma: A History of Five Centuries*, 2nd ed. (Norman: University of Oklahoma Press, 1965), 232.

8. Maxie B. Boren, "John Darrell Boren," History of the Restoration Movement (2004), http://www.therestorationmovement.com/_states/texas/boren,jd.htm (accessed Jan. 25, 2016). Boren was born in Wynnewood, Indian Territory, in 1898. He began preaching in Texas; he achieved the rank of lieutenant colonel in the U.S. Army as a chaplain;

and he preached for the North Pennsylvania congregation in Oklahoma City for a decade after leaving active duty. He was the uncle of Governor David Boren.

9. Forty-thousand is an estimate based upon the trend lines of the U.S. Census Bureau, which counted 21,700 members in 1916 and 34,645 in 1926. That increase of 37 percent was nearly double the increase in the state's general population between 1920 and 1930, from just over 2 million to just under 2.4 million. It is true, however, that the U.S. religious census for 1936 counted only 25,996 as members of the Oklahoma Churches of Christ. U.S. Bureau of the Census, *Census of Religious Bodies, 1936*, pt. 1, *Summary and Detailed Tables* (Washington, D.C.: GPO, 1940), table 32, 804.

10. See Church Inventory Forms, Church of Christ, file 1–17, MS 21–4–1, WPA Historical Records.

11. See Walter C. Pray, Inventory sheet of Lamont, or Wynn's Chapel Church of Christ, March 13, 1939; Inventory Sheet on Gotebo Church of Christ, n.d.; and W. E. Meek, Inventory on Stillwater Church of Christ, Mar. 8, 1938, Church Inventory Forms, Church of Christ, file 1–17, MS 21–4–1, WPA Historical Records.

12. Inventory sheet of Tishomingo Church of Christ, n.d., Church Inventory Forms, Church of Christ, file 1–17, MS 21–4–1, WPA Historical Records.

13. J. Doyle Farrell, Inventory sheet of Berlin Church of Christ, n.d., Church Inventory Forms, Church of Christ, file 1–17, MS 21–4–1, WPA Historical Records.

14. Ibid.; Orpha Ewert, Inventory sheet of the Springdale Church of Christ, Sept. 17, 1938, Church Inventory Forms, Church of Christ, file 1–17, MS 21–4–1, WPA Historical Records.

15. Ina C. Womack, Inventory sheet of the Woodward Church of Christ, Dec. 4, 1937, and J. Doyle Farrell, Inventory Sheet of the Berlin Church of Christ, n.d., Church Inventory Forms, Church of Christ, file 1–17, MS 21–4–1, WPA Historical Records.

16. The figures do not quite match up, because the church growth statistics come from the religious censuses of 1916 and 1926.

17. Royster, *Churches of Christ in the United States*, 440–62, lists them as Stillwater (1920); Blackwell (1920); Burns Flat (1920); Moore (1920); Tahlequah (1920); Seminole (1920); Locust Grove (1920); Soper (1920); Sulphur (1920); Wayne (1920); Woodward (1920); Waynoka (1921); Bartlesville (1922); Broken Arrow (1922); Edmond (1922); Sayre (1922); Ponca City (1923); Lindsay (1923); Newalla (1923); Hydro (1923); Foster (1923); Stonewall (1925); Tahlequah (1927); Okemah (1928); Tyrone (1928); Pernell (1929); and Terral (1929).

18. Ibid. identifies them as Grove (1930); Guymon (1930); Lone Wolf (1930); Boise City (1930); Kiowa (1930); Wilson (1930); Wynnewood (1930); Muskogee (1931); Crowder (1931); Perry (1932); Wetumka (1933); Claremore (1933); Morris (1934); Okmulgee (1934); Collinsville (1935); Prague (1935); Pryor (1935); Wagoner (1936); Fort Cobb (1937); Mannford (1937); Sallisaw (1937); El Reno (1938); Hinton (1938); Purcell (1938); Davis (1939); Eufaula (1939); Choctaw (1939); and Newkirk (1939).

19. Ibid. lists them as Coweta (1940); Alex (1940 and 1942); Colbert (1940); Dill City (1940); Marietta (1940); McLoud (1940); Porter (1940); Roland (1940); Stigler (1940); Stillwell (1940); Tulsa, Cincinnati St. (1940); Vinita (1940); Cyril (1941); Oklahoma City, Britton

Rd. (1941); Yale (1941); Atoka, Fourth Ward (1942); Davis, Third St. (1942); Walters (1942); Midwest City, Ridgecrest (1943); Muskogee, Westside (1944); Keota (1945); Duncan, Elk St. (1946); Jay (1946); Lawton, Eighth and Lee (1946); Talihina (1946); Oklahoma City, Barnes (1947); Wellston (1947); Chickasha, First and George (1948); Minco (1948); Ada, Southwest (1948) Bethany (1949); Duncan (1949); and Oklahoma City, Grand Blvd. (1949).

20. Tenth and Francis, Capitol Hill (South Harvey), Southwest (South Agnew), Twelfth and Drexel, South Byars, Culbertson Heights (Northeast Thirteenth), Northeast (Northeast Seventh), Northside (Northwest Forty-Ninth), Northwest Thirteenth, Northwest Thirty-First and Blackwelder, Britton, Midwest City, and Putnam City. See *Polk's Directory for Oklahoma City*, 1945 (Dallas: R. L. Polk, 1945), and *Membership Directory: Culbertson Heights Church of Christ* (Oklahoma City: privately printed, 1945), [3].

21. Tenth and Rockford, Carbondale (South Thirty-Second West), Home Garden (Forty-Third West), Eastside (Admiral Place), Admiral and Phoenix, West Forty-First, East King, and North Main. See *Polk's City Directory, Tulsa*, 1944 and 1946 (Dallas: R. L. Polk, 1944 and 1946).

22. U.S. Bureau of the Census, *U.S. Census of Religious Bodies, 1936*, vol. 2, *Separate Denominations*, pt. 1, *Denominations A–J.* (Washington, D.C.: GPO, 1940), 462.

23. Historian Robert Hooper concludes that the period between 1926 and 1936 was a growth period for Churches of Christ nationwide, despite census returns. He notes, for example, that the *Firm Foundation*, which circulated west of the Mississippi River, reported an average of 13,804 baptisms in 1931, 1932, and 1933. The *Gospel Advocate* carried similar reports. Data in those journals suggested significant growth in Oklahoma as well. See Hooper, *Distinct People*, 133.

24. Patterson and Gardner, *Foy E. Wallace, Jr.*, 130; Foy E. Wallace Jr. to Wilbur E. Brown, Aug. 15, 1936, and Wallace to Brother Showalter, July 28, 1936, both in Foy Wallace Jr. file, box 1, Ruel Lemmons Papers, CRS (hereinafter Lemmons Papers); William E. Wallace, interview by author, October 1, 2008, Talihina, Okla.

25. In 1930, Tenth and Francis in Oklahoma City planned to construct a new building that would have a self-contained radio studio, plans that did not materialize until 1939. See "Church Plans New Building," *DO*, May 14, 1930, 9; Jim Taggart, "L. R. Wilson Broadcasts Regular WOAI Radio Program," *Christian Chronicle* (hereinafter *CC*) 1 (July 21, 1943), 6.

26. "Church Heads to End Meet," *DO*, Jan. 20, 1922, 10.

27. "Church of Christ in Session at Norman," *DO*, July 20, 1929, 11; "Church of Christ Will Hold Parley," *DO*, Jan. 9, 1932, 7.

28. *Tulsa Lectures, Delivered at the Church of Christ, Tenth and Rockford*. Sixty preachers registered for this lectureship, which featured twelve speakers from six states including George Benson, only recently returned from China. Foy E. Wallace Jr., was scheduled to lecture but had to withdraw at the last minute; L. O. Sanderson took his place.

29. "Two Churches Conducting Lectureships," *CC* 1 (Nov. 24, 1943), 4; "Gospel Lectureship in Oklahoma City," *CC* 1 (Mar. 29, 1944), 1.

30. George S. Benson, *Missionary Experiences*, ed. Phil Watson (Delight, Ark.: Gospel Light, ca. 1987); John C. Stevens, *Before Any Were Willing: The Story of George S. Benson* (Searcy, Ark.: Harding University Press, 1991), chaps. 9 and 10.

31. Parks, *Cordell's Christian College*, 25.

32. M. Norvel Young, *A History of Colleges Established and Controlled by Members of the Churches of Christ* (Kansas City: Old Paths Book Club, 1949), 126–27.

33. Batsell Barrett Baxter and M. Norvel Young, eds., *Preachers of Today: A Book of Brief Biographical Sketches and Pictures of Living Gospel Preachers* (Nashville: Christian Press, 1952), 1:375.

34. Parks, *Cordell's Christian College*, 27–32.

35. Ibid.

36. Ibid.

37. Ibid.

38. Ibid., 33–38.

39. Ibid., 33–38, 52.

40. Ibid., 43–53.

41. Ibid., 55–56.

42. Ibid., 56–58; Young, *History of Colleges*, 128–29.

43. Parkes, *Cordell's Christian College*, 56–58.

44. Ronald B. Flowers, "Bible Chair Movement," in Foster et al., *Encyclopedia of the Stone-Campbell Movement*, 91–92. See also Rick Rowland, *Campus Ministries: A Historical Study of Churches of Christ Campus Ministries and Selected College Ministries from 1706 to 1990* (Ft. Worth, Tex.: Star Bible Publications, 1991), 28–29.

45. "Hill Begins Eighth Year's Work in Stillwater, Oklahoma," *CC* 1 (Sept. 15, 1943), 1.

46. Cottrell, *Social Gospel of E. Nicholas Comfort*, chap. 4.

47. Tom Olbricht, "A. R. Holton: A Biography" (unpublished PowerPoint presentation, 2003).

48. John P. Lewis to Dr. William S. Banowsky, Oct. 16, 1980, Vertical File, John P. Lewis Papers, CRS (hereinafter Lewis Papers).

49. John P. Lewis, "The Oklahoma School of Religion," *Bible Banner* (hereinafter *BB*) 2 (Oct. 1939), 22; "The University of Oklahoma Bible Chair," *BB* 3 (Apr. 1941), 10. Lewis did not seem to be quite so fastidious about names or distinctives. He was using "Bible Chair" to describe the Church's ministry to University students by 1941.

50. "The Oklahoma School of Religion," *Oklahoma Journal of Religion* 1 (Dec. 1944): 17.

51. "Program for the Meeting of Church Leaders (June 27–29, 1938)," Handwritten Notes file, Sermons and Misc. Docs. box, Lewis Papers.

52. Otis Durant Duncan, "A Churchman's View of the Church," *Oklahoma Journal of Religion* 2 (Mar. 1945): 3–4, 16.

53. *Oklahoma Journal of Religion* 1 (Aug. 1944): title page; "Oklahoma School of Religion," 17.

54. Cottrell, *Social Gospel of E. Nicholas Comfort*, chap. 9.

55. Hughes, *Reviving the Ancient Faith*, 206.

56. "Lubricating Firm Holds Parley Here," *DO*, Feb. 15, 1933, 4.

57. Brown account ledger, 1939–58, Tenth and Francis Archives.

58. A. W. Lee and C. R. Todd to L. L. Estes, Jan. 5, 1952, Elders Business Meetings file, and Feb. 9, 1952, file L, box 3, Tenth and Francis Archives. The issue at hand was the appointment of additional elders and deacons, which Lee and Todd opposed, but underlying was Estes's limited view of the role and function of the local congregation.

59. "Brother T. E. Burch Dies," [Wewoka, Okla. Church of Christ] *Gospel Herald*, June 20, 1974, 2–3.

60. Ibid.; [Wewoka, Okla., Church of Christ] *Congregational Crusader*, Jan. 2, 1955, and Jan. 16, 1955; Tip Burch, telephone interview by author, July 24, 2009, Wewoka, Okla.; and Patsy Burch Cannon, telephone interview by author, July 29, 2009, Searcy, Ark.

61. "In Memory," *Christian Worker* 70 (Apr. 1984), 3; Stafford North, *Soaring on Wings like Eagles: A History of Oklahoma Christian University* (Oklahoma City: Oklahoma Christian University, 2008), 147–48.

62. Helen Winters Wright, interview by author, September 26, 2008, Oklahoma City, Okla.

63. Ibid.

64. Copies of the lessons and many of the tracts are available at the following: Frank Winters, Leaders, Vertical File, CRS.

65. O. D. Duncan to Edmund de Brunner, Dec. 1, 1956, box 1, Otis Durant Duncan Papers, Archives, Oklahoma State University Library (hereinafter Duncan Papers).

66. O. D. Duncan, "A Churchman's View of the Church," *Oklahoma Journal of Religion* 2 (Mar. 1945): 3–4, 16.

67. Kyle M. Yates Jr., *A History of Religious Programs at Oklahoma State University* (Stillwater: Oklahoma State University, 1991), 68–69.

68. Duncan to de Brunner, Dec. 1, 1956, box 1, Duncan Papers.

69. A handwritten document reciting events beginning March 1936, by [A. C. Grimes], undated, McAlester file, Oklahoma Churches, Vertical File, CRS.

70. Ibid.; *The Church and a Faction* (McAlester, Okla.: B. M. Strother, [1938]).

71. W. E. B[rightwell], "A Shameful Situation," *GA* 76 (May 6, 1934); D. W. Kelley, "Brother Kelley's Letter," *GA* 79 (June 3, 1937), in *Church and a Faction*, 18–23; Wallace, "Editorial," *BB* 1 (Mar. 1939), 3.

72. *Church and a Faction*, 25.

73. *D. B. Killebrew et al. vs. A. C. Grimes et al.*, case 15922, Fifteenth Judicial District of the State of Oklahoma, McAlester, Oklahoma, in Pittsburg County Clerk Records. See "Findings of the Court," Dec. 19, 1936, and "Amendment and Supplement to Motion for New Trial," Nov. 26, 1937.

74. Wallace, "Editorial," *BB* 1 (Mar. 1939), 3.

75. "McAlester, Okla. Church Has Good Progress in '45," *CC* 3 (Dec. 5, 1945), 1.

76. Baxter and Young, *Preachers of Today*, 1:26.

77. J. Porter Wilhite, *The Trail Blazers: Heroes of the Faith* (Houston: J. Porter Wilhite, 1965), 114.

78. "Sessions Open Here Tuesday for Teachers," *DO*, Sept. 23, 1923, 5; "Society," *DO*, Jan. 18, 1924, 6; "Mrs. Mattox Not to Fight Board Ruling," *DO*, June 2, 1924, 14; "Committees Named for P.T.A. Meeting," *DO*, Mar. 8, 1930, 2.

79. "Clothing Need Growing Here," *DO*, Dec. 26, 1930, 12; "Parents, Teachers to Talk . . . ," *DO*, Jan. 9, 1931, 10; "Child Health Will Be Topic . . . ," *DO*, Mar. 20, 1931, 19; Helen Mattox Young, telephone interview by author, August 7, 2007, Malibu, Calif.

80. "Garments Are Collected by Needle Guild," *DO*, Dec. 7, 1930, 54; "Charity Bureau of County Will Move," *DO*, Oct. 8, 1931, 9; "Gardens Set Out by Needy Lost in Flood," *DO*, June 9, 1932, 6; "$38,347 Cut Is Made," *DO*, Oct. 19, 1932, 1.

81. "Three Civic Leaders Are Put Forward," *DO*, Dec. 21, 1931, 1.

82. "Irene Y. Mattox Feted at Dinner by Church Group," *DO*, May 7, 1963, 5.

83. "County Cites $500 Cut in Charity Cost," *DO*, Dec. 15, 1932, 15.

84. *History of Oklahoma State Federation of Women's Clubs, 1898–1969* (Oklahoma City: State Federation of Women's Clubs, ca. 1969), 241–42.

85. "Irene Young Mattox, 'Outstanding Woman of the Century,' Is Dead at 88," *CC* 27 (July 6, 1970), 1; Steven Lemley, "K. C. Moser: Memories and Assessment" (unpublished paper, Pepperdine Bible Lectures, May 4, 2000); Mary Eleanor Williams, "A Tribute to a Great Lady," [1970], in Correspondence. Aug.–Oct. 1970 file, box 3, Howard A. White Papers, Special Collections and University Archives, University Libraries, Pepperdine University, Malibu, Calif. (hereinafter White Papers).

86. Stephen Lemley, interview by author, July 12, 2016, Malibu, Calif.

Chapter 9

1. "'Melody' Given Two Meanings," *DO*, May 10, 1924, 5.

2. "Another Christian Church Takes Stand as Simple Church of Christ, Chandler, Oklahoma," *GA* 77 (May 2, 1935), 428.

3. Inventory by John H. Stockton on the Rush Springs Church of Christ, Nov. 12, 1938, Church Inventory Forms, Church of Christ, file 1–17, MS 21–4–1, WPA Historical Records.

4. Black account ledger, 1957–60, Tenth and Francis Archives.

5. *A Debate on the Sunday School Questions: Is It Scriptural to Have a Sunday School between Joe S. Warlick and George W. Phillips?* (Dallas, Tex.: n.p., 1924).

6. Larry Hart, "Brief History of a Minor Restorationist Group (The Non–Sunday-School Churches of Christ," *Restoration Quarterly* 22 (1979): 212–32; Ronnie F. Wade, *The Sun Will Shine Again, Someday: A History of the Non-Class, One Cup Churches of Christ* (Springfield, Mo.: Yesterday's Treasurers, 1986); Royster, *Churches of Christ in the United States.*

7. For definitions of the eschatological terms used here, see Hughes, *Reviving the Ancient Faith*, xii–xiii. See also Hooper, *Distinct People*, 56.

8. Hans Rollmann, "Boll, Robert Henry," in Foster et al., *Encyclopedia of the Stone-Campbell Movement*, 96–97.

9. Patterson and Gardner, *Foy E. Wallace, Jr.*, 130.

10. Editor, "The Churches of Christ in Oklahoma City," *BB* 1 (Sept. 1938), 10; "Why the Bible Banner Moved," *BB* 1 (Nov. 1938), 12.

11. Terry J. Gardner, "Young Foy, The Early Years, 1896–1938," in Patterson and Gardner, *Foy E. Wallace, Jr.*, 1–19; Hughes, *Reviving the Ancient Faith*, chap. 7.

12. Patterson and Gardner, *Foy E. Wallace, Jr.*, 214.

13. Ibid., 215.

14. Fifteen issues of the *Good Way* have survived and are preserved in the Special Collections of University Libraries, Pepperdine University. The quotation comes from a brief essay titled "All Things Concern the Kingdom," *Good Way* 1 (May 1946) 6.

15. Foy E. Wallace Jr. to Brother Showalter, Nov. 23, 1936, Foy Wallace Jr. file, box 1, Lemmons Papers.

16. Premillennialism was still a divisive topic in the 1950s. The doctrine caused tension between the two congregations in Shawnee, a fuss that was resolved after the elders of the churches "adjusted all differences" between them. Robert E. Seikel, *A Centennial History of Central Church of Christ, Shawnee, Oklahoma, 1907-2007* (Shawnee: Central Church of Christ, 2007), 56–57.

17. John Mark Hicks, "Moser, Kenneth Carl (1893–1976)," in Foster et al., *Encyclopedia of the Stone-Campbell Movement*, 546–47.

18. Hughes, *Reviving the Ancient Faith*, 173–74.

19. C. Leonard Allen, *Distant Voices: Discovering a Forgotten Past for a Changing Church* (Abilene, Tex.: Abilene Christian University Press, 1993), 162–70. Hicks, "Moser, Kenneth Carl," 546–47; "K. C. Moser and Churches of Christ: A Historical Perspective," *Restoration Quarterly* 37, no. 3 (1995): 1–24; and "K. C. Moser and Churches of Christ: A Theological Perspective," *Restoration Quarterly* 37, no. 4 (1995): 193–211.

20. William Wallace interview.

21. "Pastor Also Is Architect and Worker," *DO*, Oct. 25, 1936, 18; Helen Mattox Young, telephone interview with author, August 6, 2009, Malibu, Calif.

22. Helen Mattox Young, telephone interview with author, August 7, 2009.

23. Michael Wilson Casey, "The Interpretation of Genesis One in the Churches of Christ: The Origins of Fundamentalist reactions to Evolution and Biblical Criticism in the 1920s" (master's thesis, Abilene Christian College, 1989), 6.

24. U. G. Wilkinson, "Is the Story of Creation, Fall and Redemption of Man a Legend or Myth?," *FF* (June 19, 1917), 48.

25. Casey, "Interpretation of Genesis One," 30, 26, 49, 42.

26. D. S. Ligon, "Good News," *Christian Worker* (Apr. 10, 1924): 5, in Casey, "Interpretation of Genesis One," 93.

27. A. Leroy Elkins, "Letter from Bro. Elkins," *Christian Worker* (May 20, 1926): 5–6, in Casey, "Interpretation of Genesis One," 93ff.

28. J. L. Barnes, "Monkeyism in Oklahoma," *Christian Worker* (Mar. 3, 1927): 3, in Casey, "Interpretation of Genesis One," 93ff.

29. C. J. Dull, "Fundamentalism," in Foster et al., *Encyclopedia of the Stone-Campbell Movement*, 346; see also Elbert L. Watson, "Oklahoma and the Anti-Evolution Movement of the 1920s," *Chronicles of Oklahoma*, 42 (Winter 1964–65): 396ff.; and J. H. Lawson, "From the Field," *Christian Worker* (May 13, 1926): 6, in Casey, "Interpretation of Genesis One," 110.

30. D. T. Broadus, "Notable Example No. 4," *Christian Worker* (Mar. 1923): 1, in Casey, "Interpretation of Genesis One," 92.

31. U. G. Wilkinson, "Modern Infidelity," *CL* (May 29, 1923): 1, in Casey, "Interpretation of Genesis One," 92.

32. Elkins, "Thought and Action," *FF* (Mar. 27, 1923), 1.

33. Boren, "John Darrell Boren." J. D. Boren was the brother of Congressman Lyle H. Boren and first cousin of Senator David L. Boren and composer/singer Hoyt Axton.

34. *A Debate between W. L. Oliphant and Charles Smith . . . Held in the Church of Christ, Shawnee, Oklahoma, August 15 and 16, 1929* (1929; repr., Nashville, Tenn.: Gospel Advocate, ca. 1952).

35. Casey, "Interpretation of Genesis One," 31–32, chap. 2.

36. Michael Casey, "Bible, Authority and Inspiration of," in Foster et al., *Encyclopedia of the Stone-Campbell Movement,* 77–78.

37. Ibid.; Sears, *For Freedom,* 126–27.

38. E. M. Borden, "Satan Is Wise," *FF* (Aug. 4, 1925), 8, in Casey, "Interpretation of Genesis One," 103.

39. Price Billingsley, "The Bible Inerrant," *GA* 67 (Aug. 13, 1925), 795, in Casey, "Interpretation of Genesis One," 104.

40. Casey, "Interpretation of Genesis One," 119.

41. Hooper, *Distinct People,* 117–18. K. C. Moser, then minister at Wewoka, was an example of Oklahoma churchmen who honored the pacifist roots of Churches of Christ.

42. Ibid., 126–28.

43. L. R. Wilson, "Brother Green Fires a Cannon of War," *FF* (Dec. 24, 1935), 4, in Casey, "From Religious Outsiders to Insiders," 468.

44. Capitol Hill Church of Christ mailing list, [1944], Oklahoma City-Capitol Hill, and Membership Directory, June 1942, Oklahoma City—Twelfth and Drexel, Oklahoma Churches, Vertical File, CRS. See also Seikel, *Centennial History of Central Church of Christ, Shawnee,* 48.

45. Hooper, *Distinct People,* 123.

46. Hugo McCord, "Shall a Young Man—?," *BB* 3 (Apr. 1940), 11.

47. "Conscientious Objectors' Fund Grows Rapidly; Committee asks Cooperation to Liquidate Debt," *CC* 1 (July 21, 1943), 3.

48. Ibid.; The author's cousin by marriage was one of those who suffered the affront of being denied communion.

49. U.S. Bureau of the Census, *Fourteenth Census of the United States, 1920: Abstract, with Supplement for Oklahoma,* 101.

50. Franklin, *Born Sober* 86–87; Larry O'Dell, "Anti-Evolution Movement," https://www.okhistory.org/publications/enc/entry.php?entry=AN011; and "Ku Klux Klan," https://www.okhistory.org/publications/enc/entry.php?entry=KU001, both in *Encyclopedia of Oklahoma History and Culture* (accessed Jan. 17, 2018).

51. Patterson and Gardner, *Foy E. Wallace, Jr.,* 131.

52. Hughes, *Reviving the Ancient Faith,* 282.

53. Wallace, "Negro Meetings for White People," *BB* 3 (Mar. 1941), 7; Edward J. Robinson, *The Fight Is On in Texas: A History of African American Churches of Christ in the Lone Star State, 1865–2000* (Abilene, Tex.: Abilene Christian University Press, 2008), 127.

54. Some congregations did not allow African American converts to be baptized in the church house baptistery, holding the rite in farm ponds instead. Patsy Burch Cannon, telephone interview by author, July 29, 2009, Searcy, Ark.

55. J. E. Choate, *Roll Jordan Roll: A Biography of Marshall Keeble* (Nashville: Gospel Advocate, 1974), 67; J. S. Winston, interview by R. Vernon Boyd, [1968], in West Texas Digital Archives, Boyd Collection of Oral Libraries, Abilene Christian University Library, Abilene, Tex. (hereinafter West Texas Archives).

56. Choate, *Roll Jordan Roll*, 70.

57. *Dedication, North Eastern Avenue Church of Christ, March 30, 1969* (Oklahoma City: n.p., 1969); C. E. Steward, "The Outlook," *Christian Echo* 35 (Jan. 5, 1940), 7.

58. Choate, *Roll Jordan Roll*, 118. Winrow is now the minister of the Reseda, California, Church of Christ. Another one of Keeble's boys was Fred Gray, who was Rosa Parks's and Martin Luther King Jr.'s attorney.

59. Robinson, *The Fight Is On in Texas*, 70; C. E. Steward, "The Outlook," *Christian Echo* 39 (May 20, 1944), 4.

60. R. N. Hogan, interview by R. Vernon Boyd, 1968/1969, Chicago, Ill., in West Texas Archives; "In Memory of G. P. Bowser's Movement, Fort Smith, Ark., 1933–1946," Miscellaneous, Race, Vertical File, CRS. In 1945, three Oklahomans were among the students at Bowser Christian Institute in Fort Smith: F. A. Geeter of Okmulgee, later a preacher in Georgia; Isaac Venson of Atoka, later a preacher in Tulsa; O. B. Butler Jr. of Oklahoma City, later a preacher in Kansas City.

61. Calvin H. Bowers, "A Rhetorical Analysis of the Preaching of R. N. Hogan," (master's thesis, Pepperdine University, 1972), 20–21. See also R. N. Hogan, Wichita, Kans., to James L. Lovell, Sept. 2, 1937, James L. Lovell Papers, box 1, CRS; and Edward J. Robinson, *Show Us How You Do It: Marshall Keeble and the Rise of Black Churches of Christ in the United States, 1914–1968* (Tuscaloosa: University of Alabama Press, 2008), 130. "A Working Group in Oklahoma City," *Christian Echo* 35 (Aug. 5, 1940), 7; Weathers (1938–43) was followed by G. E. Steward (1943–49), G. P. Holt (1949–57), Vanderbilt Lewis (1957–59), Eugene Lawton (1959–61), N. L. Evans, L. L. Randle, W. B. Barkus, and Thomas O. Jackson (1966–).

62. K. K. Mitchell, *History of Black Evangelism in America* (N.p.: n.p., n.d.), Miscellaneous, Race, Vertical File, CRS; Royster, "Oklahoma," *Churches of Christ in the United States, 2006* (Nashville, Tenn.: 21st Century Christian, 2006).

63. Bowers, "Rhetorical Analysis of the Preaching of R. N. Hogan," 23.

64. [G.] E. Steward, "Our Pulpit," *Christian Echo* 40 (May 20, 1945): 1–2; Clyde Muse, ed., *After Pentecost, 50th Annual National Lectureship, March 20–24, 1994, Oklahoma City, Oklahoma* (Oklahoma City: Unique Printing, ca. 1994).

65. J. S. Winston, "History of Annual National Lectureship," in Muse, *After Pentecost*, 16.

66. Robinson, *The Fight Is On in Texas*, 106. Local history has Winston as ministering to the East Main Church of Christ in Ardmore in the early 1930s.

67. Goble, *Final Report of the Oklahoma Commission to Study The Tulsa Race Riot*; Franklin, *Journey toward Hope*.

68. "Working Group in Oklahoma City," 7.

69. Patsy Burch Cannon interview.

70. Hughes, *Reviving the Ancient Faith*, 204–9.

71. L. E. Fooks, *The Tipton Home Story* (Austin, Tex.: Firm Foundation, 1958).

72. Ibid., 31–41.

73. Ibid., chaps. 4–5.

74. Ibid., 260, chaps. 12 and 13.

75. Ibid., chap. 14. For a photographic glimpse of Tipton as of 1952, see Erma DeYoung, "The Tipton Home, a Children's Haven, *Frederick Leader,* Aug. 18, 1952, A7ff.

76. See the Tipton Children's Home homepage at https://www.tiptonchildrenshome .com/ (accessed July 14, 2009).

77. James Burton Coffman, *Tales of Coffman: An Autobiography* (Abilene, Tex.: Abilene Christian University Press, 1992), 53.

Chapter 10

1. Hooper, *Distinct People*, 184–85.

2. Seikel, *Centennial History of Central Church of Christ, Shawnee*, 56.

3. North, *Soaring on Wings like Eagles*. For this section on Oklahoma Christian University, I have relied greatly on Stafford North's history of the university. When I have supplemented his text, I cited the source.

4. Ibid., 81, 90.

5. Ibid., 307.

6. Ruth Murray Brown, *For a "Christian America": A History of the Religious Right.* (Amherst, N.Y.: Prometheus Books, 2002), 36.

7. North, *Soaring on Wings like Eagles*, 307–8.

8. Ibid., 227–28.

9. Ibid., 106; Erik Tryggestad, "After 50 Years, an Apology," *CC* 76 (Apr. 2019), 17–19.

10. North, *Soaring on Wings like Eagles*, 106–7; "18 OCC Students Arrested; Protests Lodged," *CC* 26 (Mar. 17, 1969), 1; W. David Baird, *Quest for Distinction: Pepperdine University in the 20th Century* (Malibu, Calif.: Pepperdine University, 2016), 167; Tryggestad, "After 50 Years," 19.

11. North, *Soaring on Wings like Eagles*, 357.

12. Ibid., 108.

13. Thomas Olbricht, email letter to author, Feb. 24, 2018.

14. North, *Soaring on Wings like Eagles*, 118.

15. Ibid., 128–32.

16. "Stillwater Church in 30th Year of Work with Oklahoma State," *CC* 17 (Aug. 19, 1960), 10. In the possession of Sylvia Duncan at Stillwater, there is a picture of Joe Watson teaching a class in a university building, with text implying that classes began in 1931. Other documents support the 1929 date.

17. Mike Casey, "Campus Ministry/Churches of Christ," in Foster et al., *Encyclopedia of the Stone-Campbell Movement*, 150.

18. "Directory of Church of Christ Bible Chairs," *Bible Chair Journal* (Fall 1960): 8.

19. "Living Word Falters Again . . . ," *CC* 42 (Sept. 1985), 6; "LWA to close. . . ." *CC* 44 (Apr. 1987), 15; "Our History," Oklahoma Christian Academy (2006), http://www .ocacademy.org/about/our-history.aspx (accessed July 8, 2008).

20. Jeff Brown, interview by author, September 18, 2008, Tulsa, Okla.

21. "Preaching School: Study Opportunities," *CC* 38 (Sept. 1981), 6, 7.

22. "Faculty," Winter 2007, Oklahoma City School of Biblical Studies; Barnes Church of Christ, http://okcsbs.com/school-info/faculty/ (accessed Mar. 15, 2018).

23. "A Statement of Conviction," Brown Trail School of Preaching, https://www.brown trailschoolofpreaching.com/ourconviction.html (accessed Mar. 15, 2018).

24. Ardmore, Atoka, Chickasha, Guthrie, Langston, Lawton, Madill, Mangum, Muskogee, Oklahoma City, Ponca City, Shawnee, Tulsa, and Wewoka.

25. Circulating among Churches of Christ at the time was a small book by James Marvin Powell and M. Norvel Young entitled *The Church Is Building* (Nashville, Tenn.: Gospel Advocate, 1956), which spoke to most aspects of constructing a church building, from selecting an architect, to the amount of money to spend, to the size of the church lawn.

26. [Mayfair Church of Christ] *Bulletin*, Jan. 5, 1969, in Congregational Files, Disciples of Christ Historical Society, Nashville, Tenn.

27. Gray Carter to Mr. and Mrs. A. E. Perry, May 7, 1940, and Preston Cotham to Mr. and Mrs. A. E. Perry, Dec. 14, 1944, Blanche Perry Collection, box 2, folder 13 (Lawton, Okla.), CRS; "Baptistry Portraits From Coast to Coast," *CC* 5 (Jan. 28, 1948), 1. The thirteen paintings were at Adams, Boise City, Bristow (1950), Hooker (1950), Chickasha (1949), Durant (1944), Forgan (1950), Frederick (1943), Lawton (Sixth and Arlington) (1940), Marietta (1951), Pauls Valley, Prague (1949), and Rush Springs (1949).

28. "Herald of Truth Budget Set as $1.9 million," *CC* 20 (Nov. 29, 1963), 1; "The Herald of Truth," *CC* 21 (June 5, 1964), 14; Hooper, *Distinct People*, 187–88.

29. C. C. McGaughey to L. W. McFee, Feb. 17, 1948, McGaughey Papers, Special Collections, Beam Library, Oklahoma Christian University, Okla. City; "New Church Building in D.C.," *CC* 8 (Feb. 12, 1950), 1.

30. "National Drive Set for Manhattan," *CC* 14 (Mar. 5, 1957), 1; "Manhattan Goal: March 30," *CC* 15 (Mar. 18, 1958), 1.

31. "World's Fair Plans Unfolding," *CC* 20 (Nov. 22, 1963), 1; Walter E. Burch, "Thousands Throng to Fair Exhibit," *CC* 21 (June 5, 1964), 1; Glover Shipp, "Signs Tell the Story: Churches of Christ Growing, Expanding," *CC* 21 (June 5, 1964), 1; "World Fair begins April 21, 1965," *CC* 22 (Mar. 5, 1965).

32. "60 Families May Move . . . ," *CC* 19 (Mar. 2, 1962), 1; "Top Story of 1962," *CC* 20 (Feb. 1, 1962), 1; Don Haymes, "A Response . . . A Revealing," *CC* 21 (June 5, 1964), 11. See also "The Campbellites Are Coming," *Time Magazine*, Feb. 15, 1963; and "Exodus/ Bay Shore: A Thirty-five Year Retrospective," *CC* 55 (Aug. 1998), 20.

33. [Mayfair Church of Christ] *Bulletin*, Sept. 20, 1964, in Congregational Files, Disciples of Christ Historical Society, Nashville; Kent Allen, et al., *The History of a Church: The Forty-Year History of Memorial Road Church of Christ* (Oklahoma City: Memorial Road Church of Christ, 2003), 9.

34. "25th and Geraldine," *CC* 21 (July 3, 1964), 2; "Oklahoma Church Plans Campaigns Through '72," *CC* 24 (Oct. 20, 1967), 7; "The Art of Campaigning," *CC* 25 (Nov. 11, 1968), 1.

35. "Oklahoma Churches Schedule Summer Canadian Campaign," *CC* 18 (May 5, 1961), 1; "Oklahoma Group to Renew Canada Effort," *CC* 20 (June 7, 1963), 6; "18 Baptized in Edmonton Campaign," *CC* 21 (Sept. 25, 1964), 1; Ivan Stewart, interview by author, September 18, 2008, Oklahoma City.

36. "The Art of Campaigning," *CC* 25 (Nov. 11, 1968), 1; James O. Baird, "Are Campaigns Worth the Cost?," in program for *"17th Annual Oklahoma Christian Spring Dinner,"* April 1990.

37. "Oklahoma City Churches to Hold Lectures," *CC* 5 (Jan. 14, 1948), 1; "Marshall Keeble Visits Oklahoma," *CC* 19 (Mar. 23, 1962), 3; "Thousands Expected . . . ," *CC* 21 (Apr. 10, 1964), 1; "Tulsa Meeting . . . ," *CC* 21 (May 8, 1964), 3.

38. "Second Singing Normal Set . . . ," *CC* 18 (July 21, 1961), 1.

39. Eldred Stevens and Eric Beevers, *Stevens-Beevers Debate on the New Testament and Roman Catholicism: A Public Discussion* (Ft. Worth, Tex.: Eldred Stevens, 1953). See also "Stillwater Preacher Accepts Challenge to Debate Catholic," *CC* 9 (Jan. 16, 1952), 1; "Stevens' Debate with Catholic in Stillwater, Okla.," *CC* 9 (Apr. 30, 1952), 1; "5,000 Hear 4-Night Debate on Catholicism," *CC* 9 (May 21, 1952), 1; Royal H. Bowers, "Accomplishments in Several Fields Seen in Stillwater," *CC* 12 (Feb. 2, 1955), 1.

40. Don Williams, interview by author, September 5, 2008, Cyril, Okla.

41. "A New Thrust Rousing the Sleeping Giant," *CC* 26 (Nov. 17, 1969), 2. One of the standard guides for the ministry was Carl W. Wade, *Joy Bus Evangelism* (1974).

42. "Cordell, Oklahoma Church . . . ," *CC* 4 (July 11, 1947), 1; "Oklahoma Camps," *CC* 15 (June 3, 1958), 3; "Camp Rock Creek Originated in 1956," *CC* 22 (May 7, 1965), 1; "Burnt Cabin Camp," *CC* 18 (Apr. 18, 1961), 5; Paula Johnson, "A History of the Sixth and Arlington Church of Christ, Lawton, Okla." (unpublished paper prepared for the author, 2008).

43. "Missionaries in 34 Foreign Areas," *CC* 16 (Feb. 17, 1959), 2B.

44. Ibid.

45. "H. E. Pierces to Be Sponsored by Frederick, Okla.," *CC* 7 (Oct. 5, 1949), 1.

46. "Edward Brown Returns after 5 Years in Japan," *CC* 12 (Oct. 6, 1954), 7.

47. "Thomas Ward, Jr. Dies of Polio on African Mission," *CC* 8 (July 26, 1950), 1.

48. "Join Robert James," *CC* 20 (July 20, 1963), 7.

49. "Bob Douglas to Leave," *CC* 18 (Nov. 25, 1960), 1; "Libya May Oust Bob Douglas," *CC* 18 (Dec. 8, 1961), 1; "1,000 Egyptians Now Enrolled," *CC* 20 (Aug. 2, 1963), 7; "Bob Douglas Ends Mission among Arabs," *CC* 24 (May 26, 1967), 1.

50. "Okla. Church Launches New Mission," *CC* 29 (Mar. 13, 1972), 1; Allen et al., *History of a Church*, 16.

51. "Joe and Polly Watson Are Going to South Africa," *CC* 23 (Jan. 7, 1966), 2.

52. David Roper, *Voices Crying in the Wilderness: A History of the Lord's Church with Special Emphasis on Australia* (Salisbury, South Australia: Restoration Publications, 1979), 399, 443.

53. "Italian Government Closes Churches . . . ," *CC* 10 (Sept. 17, 1952), 1; "Italy Shuts Up All Church of Christ Programs," *CC* 10 (Sept. 16, 1952), 12; "Italian Government Lifts Ban . . . ," *CC* 10 (Oct. 8, 1952), 1; "Documentary Evidence Requested by Howard," *CC* 12 (June 22, 1955), 1; Ad, "What Is Church of Christ Teaching in Italy?," *Daily Ardmoreite*, Jan. 20, 1950, 7, History Scrapbook, Church Office, McLish Street Church of Christ, Ardmore.

54. Ralph Burcham and Gladys Burcham, *Vietnam, Triumphs and Tragedies: Our Mission Story* (N.p.: Xulon Press, 2007); Allen, et al., *History of a Church*, 19.

55. "Caged Uruguay Captive Prays for Enemies," *CC* 28 (Oct. 25, 1971), 1; Barbara Fleming, "Dr. Fly, Hostage of Revolutionary Movement Tupamaro," *Coloradoan*, Apr. 16, 2017, https://www.coloradoan.com/story/news/2017/04/16/fleming-dr-fly-hostage-revolutionary-movement-tupamaro/100553144/ (accessed Feb. 27, 2018).

56. Draft Notes for a Chronological History of Turley Children's Home, 1997–2000, directors office, Hope Harbor Children's Home and Academy, Claremore, Okla.; "Turley Home Has Face-Lifting . . . ," *CC* 18 (Dec. 2, 1960), 15; "Cal Tinney Visits Tulsa Home for Children," *CC* 8 (Dec. 20, 1950), 4.

57. Draft Notes for a Chronological History of Turley Children's Home.

58. Ibid.; "70th Anniversary Edition," *Christian Worker* 70 (Apr. 1984), 1–3.

59. "Turley Children's Home to Move," *CC* 52 (May 1995), 4.

60. "Southwest Boys' Home Gets Property at Hollis," *CC* 15 (Sept. 17, 1957), 1.

61. Ron Bruner, "A Multi-Frame Perspective of the Hollis Church of Christ: A Paper Presented to Dr. Charles Siburt," (Abilene Christian University, 2007), 24; Bruner, "History and Purpose," Westview Boys' Home, https://westviewboyshome.com/transitions/history-and-purpose/ (accessed Feb. 14, 2018).

62. Bruner, "History and Purpose."

63. "$400,000 Aged Home Opening in Cordell," *CC* 19 (Feb. 2, 1962), 1; "Cordell Home Is Serving the Elderly," *CC* 23 (Nov. 5, 1965), 2; "History," Cordell Christian Home, http://www.cordellchristianhome.org/history.html (accessed Feb. 15, 2018).

64. "Notes," *CC* 47 (Mar. 1990), 4.

65. Tealridge Retirement Community (website), https://www.tealridge.com/ (accessed Apr. 8, 2019).

66. List of retirement homes, *CC* 40 (Mar. 1982), 12; Jeff Brown interview, September 15 2008.

Chapter 11

1. The pink sheet, paragraph 3, in Brown, *For a "Christian America,"* 40.

2. Ibid.

3. Hooper, *Distinct People*, 286.

4. Money, "Church-State Relations in the Churches of Christ since 1945," 93–97.

5. [East Okmulgee Street Church of Christ] *Reflector*, May 15, 1960. The same bulletin for April 17, 1960, printed other articles opposing a vote for Kennedy. The bulletin of the Hollis Church of Christ, for April 12, 1959, defended an earlier charge that Catholics

were free to lie by quoting the *Catholic Encyclopedia* and the *Manual of Moral Theology*. See also [Wewoka Church of Christ] *Congregational Crusader*, May 15, 1960.

6. Money, "Church-State Relations in the Churches of Christ since 1945," 93–97.

7. Ibid., 116–34.

8. Ibid., 250.

9. Brown, *For a "Christian America,"* 29–45, 69. Joann North attended an anti-ERA meeting of Church of Christ women at the Twenty-Fifth and Geraldine congregation. Stafford North, email to author, Oct. 24, 2018.

10. Brown, *For a "Christian America,"* 16, 76, 99.

11. Hugo McCord, "A Sorry Viewpoint," *GA* 111 (Mar. 20, 1969), 190–91, as cited in Hughes, *Reviving the Ancient Faith*, 305–6.

12. "New Preacher for East Side Church," *CC* 21 (Sept. 4, 1964), n.p.; "Race Relations Workshop Set," *CC* 25 (Dec. 2, 1968), 3.

13. "Things of the Spirit," [Culbertson Heights Church of Christ] *Bulletin*, May 20, 1954, Oklahoma City, Okla., in Roy Young Collection, Apache, Okla.

14. "Thirty Reasons Why Christians Should Not Dance," [East Okmulgee Street Church] *Reflector*, Nov. 20, 1960, Muskogee, Okla.

15. Jack Meyer, "Comments," [Tenth and Francis Streets Church of Christ] *Gospel Visitor* 1 (Oct. 6, 1949), 4.

16. Budget for 1951, Budget file, box 3, Tenth and Francis Archives.

17. Garth Black remembered that Lee never led public prayers or taught Bible classes. Garth Black, telephone interviews by author, February 17, 2010, and February 4, 2016.

18. Contributing to the tension was Jack Meyer's sermon on the qualification of elders, which had negative connotations for Lee. Garth Black remembers that Lee took the pulpit immediately after Meyer had finished and said, "That man would never preach again in this building." Estes followed Lee and said that other elders were in disagreement and that Meyer would preach again. Garth Black interviews, February 17, 2010, and February 4, 2016; email from Garth Black to David Baird, Feb. 16, 2010. See also A. W. Lee and C. R. Todd to L. L. Estes, Feb. 9, 1952, file L, box 3, Tenth and Francis Archives.

19. A. W. Lee and C. R. Todd to L. L. Estes, Jan. 5, 1952; L. L. Estes et al. to Lee and Todd, Jan. 7, 1952; Lee and Todd to Estes, Feb. 9, 1952; and Estes to the Regular Business Meeting, May 5, 1952, Minutes of the Business Meeting, 1952–1957, all in box 2, Tenth and Francis Archives. See also Elder's report on Business Meeting, in *Gospel Visitor* 4 (July 31, 1952), 3.

20. J[ames] W. A[dams], "Meet L. L. Estes," *Gospel Visitor* 15 (Nov. 27, 1963), 2–3. Estes died in early 1968 in a tragic car accident.

21. Born in New York, Jack Meyer Sr. took degrees from David Lipscomb College and Abilene Christian. He had preached at congregations in Alabama and Texas before coming to Tenth and Francis in Oklahoma City. Meyer was the author of the much-read *The Preacher and His Work* (1955 and 1959) and associate editor of *Truth in Love*. See Baxter and Young, *Preachers of Today* 2:290.

22. Adams was a native of California, an alumnus of Freed Hardeman College, and held at least six preaching posts in Texas before coming to Oklahoma City in 1956. He was known for his evangelistic meetings, moderating debates, and journalistic work. See Baxter and Young, *Preachers of Today* 2.

23. Spears was an alumnus of David Lipscomb College and Harding College, who had preached in Arkansas before coming to the Tenth and Francis congregation. Dudley Spears, email to author, Feb. 4, 2016.

24. C. A. Ward et al. to the members at Tenth and Francis, n.d., in *Gospel Visitor* 10 (Sept. 18, 1958), 1–4.

25. Ibid.

26. Ibid.

27. L. E. Diamond et al. to Whom it May Concern, Oct. 31, 1948, file C, box 3, Tenth and Francis Archives.

28. Ibid.

29. "Note from the elders," *Gospel Visitor* 10 (Sept. 18, 1958), 3. Annual contributions to Tipton totaled $2,400 in 1954. See brown account ledger, 1939–58, Tenth and Francis Archives.

30. Howard E. Miller file, box 2, and Monthly Business Meeting Minutes, Apr. 10, 1967, Tenth and Francis Archives.

31. Monthly Business Meeting Minutes, Jan. 4, 1965, and Aug. 2, 1965, Tenth and Francis Archives.

32. L. E. Diamond et al. to Whom it May Concern, Oct. 31, 1948; and [Elders] to John Banister, Apr. 17, 1945, file B, box 3, both in Tenth and Francis Archives.

33. A. W. Lee et al. to Robert Alexander, Aug. 11, 1946, file A, box 3, Tenth and Francis Archives; Jack Meyer, "Comments," *Gospel Visitor* 1 (Oct. 6, 1949), 4, and 1 (Oct. 20, 1949), 2.

34. Dudley R. Spears to Ted, Nov. 17, 1966, Institutions file, box 2, Tenth and Francis Archives; "D[udley] R. S[pears], "Bible Chairs Are Denominational," *Gospel Visitor* 22 (Sept. 11, 1970), 2.

35. Minutes of June 4, 1956, Minutes of Business Meeting, 1952–1958, box 3, Tenth and Francis Archives; Garth Black interview, February 4, 2016.

36. Dudley R. Spears, "The Downtown Church of Christ," *Gospel Visitor* 21 (Apr. 11, 1969), 2ff.; Peter Christy to Harley K. Bromley, Sept. 27, 1975, Misc. Incoming Letters file, box 2, Tenth and Francis Archives.

37. Minutes of June 2, 1959, and Sept. 16, 1959, Minutes of Elders and Deacons Business Meeting, 1958–1963, box 2, Tenth and Francis Archives. The leadership sold the removed pews to the Atoka Church of Christ for $650.

38. *Directory of Churches of Christ, 2003-2004* (Bowling Green, Ky.: Guardian of Truth Foundation, 2004), 59–60.

39. Douglas A. Foster, "Rice, Ira Young Jr.," in Foster et al., *Encyclopedia of the Stone-Campbell Movement*, 649.

40. Hooper, *Distinct People*, 297–301; Hughes, *Reviving the Ancient Faith*, 327–33.

41. "History of the Eastside Church of Christ, 1957–2000" (unpublished paper prepared for the Eastside Church in Midwest City, Okla., 2000).

42. Terry J. Gardner, "Wallace, Foy Esco," in Foster et al., *Encyclopedia of the Stone-Campbell Movement*, 767–68; William Wallace interview.

43. Hughes, *Reviving the Ancient Faith*, 367.

44. Lewis Hale, interview by author, September 16, 2008, Oklahoma City.

45. Johnson, "History of the Sixth and Arlington Church of Christ, Lawton."

46. Robert M. Randolph, "Mission," in Foster et al., *Encyclopedia of the Stone-Campbell Movement*, 533.

47. William Wallace interview.

Chapter 12

1. Hooper, *Distinct People*, 286; "Growth and Decline," *CC* 65 (Jan. 2008), 20–21; Lee Keele, "An Action Plan for the Church of Christ in Seminole, Okla., 1994–2000" (unpublished paper prepared for the elders of the Seminole Church of Christ, 1994). Records enumerating membership and numbers of congregations in Oklahoma give widely varying numbers; the directory of congregations published periodically by the Firm Foundation Publishing House, *Where the Saints Meet*, counted 601 in 1969, 585 in 1977, and 632 in 1987.

2. Flavil R. Yeakley Jr., "Survey of the Churches of Christ in Oklahoma" [1980], Garnett Road Church of Christ Historical Records, file 1, drawer 2, Journey Church, Tulsa, Okla.

3. Rowland, *Campus Ministries*, 26–29.

4. *Stubbs et ux., Appellants, v. North Pennsylvania Avenue Church of Christ et al., Appellees*, 44 OBJ 556–61 (OKC TCIV APP 1973).

5. Ibid.

6. Ibid.

7. Ibid. What followed the decision of the Supreme Court is unknown. The public records are barely sufficient, and memories of the case are vague.

8. James M. McGoldrick Jr., *Marian Guinn vs. the Collinsville, Oklahoma Church of Christ* [Dec. 1984], James McGoldrick file, box 39, White Papers. In my presentation of the facts of the Collinsville case, I have leaned heavily on the McGoldrick brief. Also helpful was "Brotherhood Generally Sympathetic with Collinsville Elders Re: Trial," *Contending for the Faith* 15 (May 1984), in Collinsville, Oklahoma Churches, Vertical File, CRS.

9. Trial Transcript, *Marian Guinn vs. The Church of Christ Collinsville, Oklahoma*, vol. 1–3 (Mar. 12–15, 1984): 50–54, 555–58.

10. Judy Fessett, "$390,000 Awarded in Church Lawsuit," *DO*, Mar. 16, 1984, 109; "Elders Invaded Privacy, Woman Tells Tulsa Jury," *DO*, Mar. 14, 1984, 99. See also Richard L. Cupp Jr., 19 UC Davis L. Rev. 949 (1986).

11. *Time Magazine*, Mar. 26, 1984, 70; Emerson L. Flannery, "The Separation of Church and State," *Guardian of Truth* 28 (Aug. 2, 1984): 470.

12. Associated Press, "Woman Sues Church Elders on Punishment," *New York Times*, Mar. 11, 1984, 1001025.

13. McGoldrick, *Marian Guinn vs. the Collinsville, Oklahoma Church of Christ*.

14. "Church of Christ United in Opposition to Court Judgment," *DO*, Mar. 23, 1984, 107; Lindy Adams, "A Conversation with Truman Rucker," *CC* 31 (Feb. 1, 2004).

15. Adams, "Conversation with Truman Rucker"; Bill Braun, "Church, Woman Settle Lawsuit," *Tulsa World*, Aug. 12, 1989.

16. Jimmie C. Smith, "Those Church Lawsuits," Church of Christ (Mar. 1, 1986), https://www.newtestamentchurch.org/OPA/Articles/1986/03/those_church_lawsuits.htm; Adams, "Conversation with Truman Rucker." For additional evaluation of the significance of the case, see Charles Colson, *Kingdoms in Conflict* (New York: Harper, 1987); Robert E. Cochran Jr. and Robert M. Ackerman, *Law and Community: The Case of Torts* (Lanham, Md.: Rowman and Littlefield, 2004), 98–101; and Richard Cupp Jr., 19 UC Davis L. Rev. 949 (1986), 949–85.

17. "A Letter to the Editor," *GA* 126 (July 5, 1984), 388.

18. "Mack Lyon: Televangelist Reaches the World," *CC* 54 (Aug. 1997), 4; "History," In Search of the Lord's Way, http://www.searchtv.org/history.html (accessed Feb. 20, 2018).

19. "Heavenward Bound," *Christian Worker* (Mar. 1979); "Tulsa: Thousands at Workshop," *CC* 39 (Mar. 30, 1982), 1; Chellie Ison and Erik Tryggestad, "Tulsa Workshop Canceled," *CC* 74 (Feb. 2017), 1, 8.

20. [Ada Central Church of Christ] *Central Proclaimer*, Dec. 27, 1970.

21. Johnson, "History of the Sixth and Arlington Church of Christ, Lawton."

22. "Campaigns Augment Soviet Churches," *CC* 48 (Aug. 1991), 1; "Let's Start Talking's Impact Continues to Grow," *CC* 49 (Nov. 1992), 1; "Signs of 'Coming of Age,'" *CC* 53 (Jan. 1996), 1.

23. "Oklahoma," *CC* 56 (Jan. 1, 1996), 1.

24. Lyssa Sperrazza, "A Shining Light," *DO*, July 15, 2017, A12. The Light House ministry operates as a 501c(3) agency with a special interest in hepatitis-three clients.

25. "Missions from 3rd World Come Home," *CC* 61 (Jan. 2004), 17; "Compassion Outreach Center," Compassionate Outreach, Central Church of Christ Ada, http://www.compassionada.org/ (accessed July 20, 2008).

26. "The Kids' Place," Edmond Church of Christ, http://edmondchurchofchrist.com/ministries/the-kids-place (accessed Apr. 2, 2017); "Oklahoma," *CC* 55 (Mar. 1998), 4.

27. Jennifer Taylor, "Serving Them Right," *CS* (May 25, 2000), 398.

28. "Oklahoma," *CC* 57 (Nov. 2000), 5.

29. "Oklahoma," *CC* 55 (Mar. 1998), 4.

30. "New Housing Project," *CC* 61 (Mar. 2004), 1; Rosalind Crenshaw, "Federal Stimulus Aids Okla. City Development Company," *Christian Echo* 110 (Sept.–Oct. 2011), 1; "Church to Show Film on Tulsa Race Riots at History Center," *DO*, Sept. 12, 2014, 12A; "Clergy Offer Forum on Youths, Racism, Violence," *DO*, Aug. 8, 2013, 11A.

31. "When the Unthinkable Happens," *CC* 52 (June 1995), 1.

32. "Oklahoma," *CC* 59 (June 2002), 5.

33. The other sixteen are congregations at Alva, Ardmore (Maxwell), Chickasha, Clinton, Comanche, Crescent, Enid, Grove, Kingfisher, Oklahoma City (Airport; Memorial Road; and Wilshire), Owasso, Ponca City, Sayre, and Seminole (Little).

34. Jerry Frazier, *Vital Fundamentals: Simply Discussed* (Owasso: Owasso Church of Christ, 2005).

35. Bailey McBride, "*Chronicle* Affirms Mission of Former Editor," *CC* 38 (Sept. 1981), 8–9; "OCC takes *Christian Chronicle*," *CC* 38 (Sept. 1981), 1; McBride, "An Historical Overview," *CC* 60 (June 2003), 17–19; McBride, "Reflecting on Chronicle's 65-year mission to serve Churches of Christ," *CC* 65 (July 2008), 38.

36. North, *Soaring on Wings like Eagles*, 118–19.

37. Hughes, *Reviving the Ancient Faith*, 365–67.

38. Tom Olbricht, *Hearing God's Voice* (Abilene, Tex.: Abilene Christian University Press, 1995), 289.

39. Leroy Garrett, *A Lover's Quarrel, An Autobiography: My Pilgrimage of Freedom in Churches of Christ* (Abilene: A.C.U. Press, 2003), 13–138.

40. Tom Olbricht, "Hermeneutics in the Churches of Christ," *Restoration Quarterly* 37, no. 1 (1995): 1–24.

41. Thomas H. Olbricht, *Reflections on My Life in the Kingdom and the Academy* (Eugene, Ore.: Wipf and Stock, 2012), 156, 314–15.

42. Ralph Schaefer, "Talking a Way of Life for Howard," *Tulsa World*, Sept. 12, 2013; Jerry Rushford, telephone interview by author, April 10, 2018.

43. Rick Popejoy, "Oklahoma Christian University of Science and Arts' 'Kingdom of Inclusion' Includes Too Much," *Contending for the Faith*, Jan. 2004, 1.

44. "Two Announcements," *Search for the Lord's Way*, Jan. 2004, 1; Mack Lyon interview by author, September 24 2008, Edmond, Okla.

45. Mike O'Neal to Brothers and Sisters, May 11, 2004, College of Biblical Studies files, Oklahoma Christian University.

46. Lynn A. McMillon to Brethren, Mar. 5, 2004, College of Biblical Studies files, Oklahoma Christian University. Hershel Dyer, interview by author, June 4, 2018, Tulsa, Oklahoma.

47. Dale I. Royal, "Let the Bible Speak," *Daily Oklahoman*, Aug. 3, 2008, 8, and Sept. 10, 2008, 9A.

48. Ben Baily, *Liberalism: Are We Drawing Closer to God?* [Ardmore: McLish Street Church of Christ, 2008]. History Scrapbook, Church Office, McLish Street Church of Christ, Ardmore.

49. Roy B Young to Mike O'Neal, Feb. 18, 2004, College of Biblical Studies files, Oklahoma Christian University.

BIBLIOGRAPHY

Archives

Abilene Christian University, Abilene, Tex.
    Center for Restoration Studies, Brown Library
        Vertical Files
        Oklahoma Churches
        Texas Churches
        Leaders
            Banister, John
            Fullerton, Byron
            Miller, Luke
            McDaniel, Lindy
            Tant, Yater
            Winters, Frank
        Miscellaneous
            Bible Chairs
            Blacks—Religion
            Booklets and Tracts
            Christian Colleges
            Race
    Blanche Perry Collection
    Burton K. Coffman Papers
    James L. Lovell Papers
    John P. Lewis Papers
    Reuel Lemmons Papers
    Tom Olbricht Papers, *Mission* Surveys
Disciples of Christ Historical Society, Nashville, Tenn.
    Congregational Files
        Mayfair Church of Christ, Oklahoma City
        Sixth and Arlington Church of Christ, Lawton, Okla.

Biographical Files
James J. Trott
Oklahoma Christian University, Oklahoma City, Okla.
Beam Library, Special Collections
C. E. McGaughey Collection
Tenth and Francis Church Collection
Bulletins of the Wewoka Church of Christ
College of Biblical Studies
Oklahoma History Center, Oklahoma City, Okla.
Chickasaw Nation Records
Miscellaneous-Schools (Microcopy CKN-27)
Choctaw Nation Records
Marriage Register, Atoka County (Microcopy CTN-22)
Deed Records, Atoka County (Microcopy CTN-22
Miscellaneous-Schools (Microcopy CTN-27)
Kiowa Agency Records
Churches (Microcopy KA 50)
Letterpress Book, vol. 38
Miscellaneous-Schools (Microcopy KA 50)
Special Collections
Meta Chestnut Sager Collection
Orville E. Enfield Collection
Encyclopedia of Oklahoma History and Culture
Oklahoma State Library, Oklahoma City, Okla.
State Archives
WPA Historical Records Survey, Church Inventory Forms
Christian Church, Churches of Christ (Conservative), MSS 21–4–1, Folders 2–19
Church of Christ, MSS 21–4–1, Folders 1–36
Church of Christ (Negro), MSS 21–4–1, Folders 1–36
Disciples of Christ, MSS 21–4–1, Folders 1–39 and 1–41
Disciples of Christ (First Christian), MSS 21–4–1, Folders 1–40
Oklahoma State University, Stillwater, Okla.
Oklahoma State University Libraries, Archives
Otis Durant Duncan Papers
Pepperdine University, Malibu, Calif.
Special Collections and University Archives, University Libraries
William S. Banowsky Papers
Howard A. White Papers
Phillips Theological Seminary Library, Tulsa, Okla.
Beasley Archives
England Papers
Individual Church Archives

Elm and Hudson Church of Christ, Altus, Okla.
Historical Records
The Journey Church, Tulsa, Okla.
    Garnett Road Church of Christ Collection
    International Soul Winning Workshop programs
McLish Street Church of Christ, Ardmore, Okla.
    History Scrapbook
Seminole Church of Christ, Seminole, Okla.
    Historical Records
Seminole Pointe Church of Christ, Oklahoma City, Okla.
    Tenth and Francis Church Archives
U. S. National Archives, Washington, D.C.
    Records of the Bureau of Indian Affairs
University of Oklahoma, Norman, Okla.
    Western History Collection
        Indian-Pioneer Papers

Records of County Clerks

Hall County, Memphis, Tex.
Franklin County, Winchester, Tenn.
Limestone County, Athens, Ala.
Grady County, Chickasha, Okla.
Pittsburg County, McAlester, Okla.

Journals and Newspapers

Atoka Independent, 1880s
American Christian Review, 1887
Bible Banner (Oklahoma City), 1938–47
Choctaw Champion (Atoka, I.T.), 1888–90
Christian Chronicle (Oklahoma City), 1943–2019
Christian Companion, 1910
Christian Echo, 1935–49, 1978–80
Christian Worker, 1923-27, 1984
Christian Standard, 1884–87
Firm Foundation (Austin, Tex.), 1890–1909
Gospel Advocate (Nashville, Tenn.), 1878–1915
Gospel Guardian (Oklahoma City), 1935–36
Gospel Herald (Cordell, Okla.), 1912–16
Indian Citizen (Atoka, I.T.), 1889, 1890, 1892
Indian Missionary (Atoka, I.T.), 1886–91
Minco Minstrel, 1894–1920
Muskogee (Oklahoma) Times Democrat, 1907, 1909

Muskogee (Oklahoma*) Dailey Phoenix*, 1909, 1987, 1994
Nashville (Arkansas*) News*, 1921–30
Octographic Review, 1887–1905
Oklahoma Christian (Guthrie, Okla.), 1895–1900
Oklahoma Journal of Religion (Norman)
Primitive Christian, 1893–1909
Star of Hope (Noble, Okla.), 1906
Tulsa World, 1980–89

Books

Adams, James W. *Words Fitly Spoken.* Bowling Green, Ky.: Guardian of Truth Foundation, 1988.

Allen, C. Leonard. *Distant Voices: Discovering a Forgotten Past for a Changing Church.* Abilene, Tex.: Abilene Christian University Press, 1993.

———. *Things Unseen: Churches of Christ in (and after) the Modern Age.* Siloam Springs, Ark.: Leafwood Publishers, 2004.

Allen, C. Leonard, and Richard T. Hughes. *Discovering Our Roots: The Ancestry of Churches of Christ.* Abilene, Tex.: Abilene Christian University Press, 1983.

Allen, Kent, et. al. *The History of a Church: The Forty-Year History of Memorial Road Church of Christ.* Oklahoma City: Memorial Road Church of Christ, 2003.

Ameringer, Oscar. *If You Don't Weaken: The Autobiography of Oscar Ameringer.* With an introduction by James R. Green. Norman: University of Oklahoma Press, 1983.

Atoka County Historical Society. *Tales of Atoka County Heritage.* Atoka, Okla.: Atoka County Historical Society, ca. 1983.

Baird, W. David. *Quest for Distinction: Pepperdine University in the 20th Century.* Malibu, Calif.: Pepperdine University Press, 2016.

Baxter, Batsell Barrett, and M. Norvel Young, eds. *Preachers of Today: A Book of Brief Biographical Sketches and Pictures of Living Gospel Preachers.* 3 vols. Nashville, Tenn.: Christian Press, 1952.

Beeman, William O. *Oklahoma Christian College: The Story of the First Twenty Years, 1950–1970.* Delight, Ark.: Gospel Light, 1970.

Benson, George S. *Missionary Experiences.* Edited by Phil Watson. Delight, Ark.: Gospel Light, ca. 1987.

Bissett, Jim. *Agrarian Socialism in America: Marx, Jefferson, and Jesus in the Oklahoma Countryside, 1904–1920.* Norman: University of Oklahoma Press, 1999.

Bowers, Calvin H. *Realizing the California Dream: The Story of Black Churches of Christ in Los Angeles.* Los Angeles: Calvin H. Bowers, 2001.

Boyd, R. Vernon. *Undying Dedication: The Story of G. P. Bowser.* Nashville, Tenn.: Gospel Advocate, 1985.

Brown, Ruth Murray. *For a "Christian America": A History of the Religious Right.* Amherst, N.Y.: Prometheus Books, 2002.

Burcham, Ralph, and Gladys Burcham. *Vietnam, Triumphs and Tragedies: Our Mission Story.* N.p.: Xulon Press, 2007.

Burbank, Garin. *When Farmers Voted Red: The Gospel of Socialism in the Oklahoma Countryside, 1910–1924.* Westport, Conn.: Greenwood Press, 1977.

Casey, Michael W. *Saddlebags, City Streets, and Cyberspace: A History of Preaching in the Churches of Christ.* Abilene, Tex.: Abilene Christian University Press, 1995.

Casey, Michael, and Doug Foster, eds. *The Stone-Campbell Movement: An International Religious Tradition.* Knoxville: University of Tennessee Press, 2002.

Choate, J. E. *Roll Jordan Roll: A Biography of Marshall Keeble.* Nashville, Tenn.: Gospel Advocate, 1974.

The Church and a Faction. McAlester, Okla.: B. M. Strother Publisher, [1938].

Cochran, Robert E., Jr., and Robert M. Ackerman. *Law and Community: The Case of Torts.* Lanham, Md.: Rowman and Littlefield, 2004.

Coffman, James Burton. *Tales of Coffman: An Autobiography.* Abilene, Tex.: Abilene Christian University Press Press, 1992.

Colson, Charles W. *Kingdoms in Conflict.* New York: Harper, 1987.

Cottrell, Robert C. *The Social Gospel of E. Nicholas Comfort: Founder of the Oklahoma School of Religion.* Norman: University of Oklahoma Press, 1997.

Cupp, Richard L., Jr. 19 UC Davis L. Rev. 949 (1986).

A Debate between W. L. Oliphant and Charles Smith . . . Held in the Church of Christ, Shawnee, Oklahoma, August 15 and 16, 1929. Nashville, Tenn.: Gospel Advocate, ca. 1952. First published 1929 by F. L. Rowe, Cincinnati.

A Debate on the Sunday School Questions: Is It Scriptural to Have a Sunday School between Joe S. Warlick and George W. Phillips? Dallas, Tex.: n.p., 1924.

Debo, Angie. *Oklahoma, Foot-Loose and Fancy-Free.* Norman: University of Oklahoma Press, 1987.

———. *Prairie City: The Story of an American Community.* New York: Alfred A. Knopf, 1944.

Dedication, North Eastern Avenue Church of Christ, March 30, 1969. Oklahoma City: n.p., 1969.

Dewitz, Paul W. H. *Notable Men of Indian Territory at the beginning of the Twentieth Century, 1904–05.* Muskogee, I.T.: Southwestern Historical Co., [1905].

Directory of Churches of Christ, 2003–2004. Bowling Green, Ky.: Guardian of Truth Foundation, 2004.

Directory of Oklahoma, 1981. Oklahoma City: Oklahoma State Election Board, 1981.

Disciples of Christ Year Book, 1945. Indianapolis: Year Book Publication Committee, 1945.

Eckstein, Daniel. *History of the Churches of Christ in Texas, 1824–1950.* Austin, Tex.: Firm Foundation, 1963.

Ellsworth, Scott. *Death in a Promised Land: The Tulsa Race Riot of 1921.* Baton Rouge: Louisiana State University, 1982.

Enfield, Dr. J. E. *The Man from Packsaddle.* Hollywood, Calif.: House-Warven Publishers, 1951.

England, Stephen J. *Oklahoma Christians: A History of Christian Churches and of the Start of the Christian Church (Disciples of Christ) in Oklahoma.* Oklahoma City: Christian Church in Oklahoma, 1975.

Fooks, Leslie Eugene. *The Tipton Home Story*. Austin, Tex.: Firm Foundation, ca. 1958.

Foster, Douglas A., Anthony L. Dunnavant, Paul M. Blowers, and D. Newell Williams. *The Encyclopedia of the Stone-Campbell Movement*. Grand Rapids, Mich.: William B. Eerdmans, 2004.

Franklin, Jimmie Lewis. *Born Sober: Prohibition in Oklahoma, 1907–1959*. Norman: University of Oklahoma Press, 1971.

———. *Journey toward Hope: A History of Blacks in Oklahoma*. Norman: University of Oklahoma, 1982.

Frazier, Jerry. *Vital Fundamentals: Simply Discussed*. Owasso, Okla.: Owasso Church of Christ, 2005.

Gable, Theresa, ed. *Davis, Oklahoma*. Oklahoma City: Arbuckle Historical Society, 1981.

Gaines, Carl E., and John C. Whitley. *Black Preachers of Today: Churches of Christ*. N.p.: n.p., 1974.

Garrett, Leroy. *A Lover's Quarrel, an Autobiography: My Pilgrimage of Freedom in Churches of Christ*. Abilene, Tex.: Abilene Christian University Press, 2003.

Garrison, Winfred Ernest, and Alfred T. DeGroot. *The Disciples of Christ: A History*. Saint Louis: Christian Board of Publication, 1948.

Gaustad, Edwin Scott, and Philip L. Barlow. *New Historical Atlas of Religion in America*. New York: Oxford University Press, 2000.

Gibson, Arrell Morgan. *Oklahoma: A History of Five Centuries*. 2nd ed. Norman: University of Oklahoma Press, 1965.

Gideon, D. C. *Indian Territory: Descriptive, Biographical and Genealogical*. New York: Lewis, 1901.

Goble, Danney, comp. *Final Report of the Oklahoma Commission to Study The Tulsa Race Riot of 1921*. Oklahoma City: Oklahoma Commission to Study the Tulsa Race Riot of 1921, 2001.

Goins, Charles Robert, and Danney Goble. *Historical Atlas of Oklahoma*. 4th ed. Norman: University of Oklahoma Press, 2006.

Green, James R. *Grass-Roots Socialism: Radical Movements in the Southwest, 1895–1943*. Baton Rouge: Louisiana State University Press, 1978.

Harrell, David Edwin, Jr. *The Churches of Christ in the Twentieth Century: Homer Hailey's Personal Journey of Faith*. Tuscaloosa: University of Alabama Press, 2000.

———. *A Social History of the Disciples of Christ*. Vol. 1, *Quest for a Christian America: The Disciples of Christ and American Society to 1866*. Nashville, Tenn.: Disciples of Christ Historical Society, 1966.

———. *A Social History of the Disciples of Christ*. Vol. 2, *The Social Sources of Division in the Disciples of Christ, 1865–1900*. Atlanta: Publishing Systems, 1973.

Harrel, Hicklin Albert, Jr. *The Harrel Family*. Oak Ridge, Tenn.: Privately printed, ca. 1997.

Hatch, Nathan O. *The Democratization of American Christianity*. New Haven: Yale University Press, 1989.

Hicks, Olan. *1946–1947 Yearbook of Churches of Christ*. Abilene, Tex.: Christian Chronicle, 1946.

History of Oklahoma State Federation of Women's Clubs, 1898–1969. Oklahoma City, Okla.: Federation of Women's Clubs, ca. 1969.

Hoig, Stan. *The Oklahoma Land Rush of 1889.* Oklahoma City: Oklahoma Historical Society, 1984.

Holloway, Gary, and Douglas A. Foster. *Renewing God's People: A Concise History of Churches of Christ.* Abilene, Tex.: Abilene Christian University Press Press, 2001.

Hooper, Robert E. *Crying in the Wilderness: A Biography of David Lipscomb.* Nashville, Tenn.: David Lipscomb College, 1979.

———. *A Distinct People: A History of the Churches of Christ in the 20th Century.* West Monroe, La.: Howard, 1993.

Hughes, Richard T. *Reviving the Ancient Faith: The Story of Churches of Christ in America.* Grand Rapids, Mich.: William B. Eerdmans, 1996.

Hughes, Richard T., and R. L. Roberts. *The Churches of Christ.* Westport, Conn.: Greenwood Press, 2001.

Kennedy, Anthony Ward. *They Came from Everywhere and Settled Here.* Vol. 3. Conway, Ark.: Rapid Rabbit, 1995.

Klein, Joe. *Woody Guthrie: A Life.* New York: Alfred A. Knopf, 1980.

Lemmons, W. F. *The Devil and Socialism.* Cincinnati: F. L. Rowe, 1914.

Lewis, Warren, and Hans Rollman, eds. *Restoring the First-Century Church in the Twenty-First Century: Essays on the Stone-Campbell Restoration Movement.* Eugene, Ore.: Wipf and Stock, 2005.

Lynn, Mac, comp. *Churches of Christ in the United States.* Nashville, Tenn.: Gospel Advocate, 1991.

———. *Where the Saints Meet: A Directory of Churches of Christ, 1987–1988.* Pensacola, Fla.: Firm Foundation, ca. 1987.

Marian Guinn vs. Collinsville, Okla. Church of Christ, Trial Manuscript. Vols. 1–3. March 12–15, 1984.

Marshal, Frank H. *Phillips University: First Fifty Years.* 3 vols. Enid, Okla.: Phillips University, 1957.

McCormack, Joe E., ed. *The History of a Church: The Forty-Year History of Memorial Road Church of Christ.* Edmond: Memorial Road Church of Christ. 2004.

McLoughlin, William G. *The Cherokee Ghost Dance: Essays on the Southeastern Indians, 1789–1861.* Macon, Ga.: Mercer University Press, 1984.

Membership Directory: Culbertson Heights Church of Christ. Oklahoma City: privately printed, 1945.

Membership Directory: Tenth and Rockford Church of Christ. Tulsa: privately printed, 1970.

Miller, Luke. *Miller's Sermons.* Austin, Tex.: Firm Foundation, 1940.

Mitchell, K. K. *History of Black Evangelism in America.* Montgomery, Ala.: privately printed, 1980.

Morgan, Boyd E. *Arkansas Angels.* Paragould, Ark.: College Bookstore and Press, 1967.

Morrison, Matthew C. *Like a Lion, Daniel Sommer's Seventy Years of Preaching.* Murfreesboro, Tenn.: Dehoff Publications, 1975.

Murch, James DeForest. *Christians Only.* Cincinnati: Standard, 1962

Muse, Clyde, ed. *After Pentecost: 50th Annual National Lectureship, March 20–24, 1994, Oklahoma City, Oklahoma.* Oklahoma City: Unique Printing, ca. 1994.

Neville, Alexander White (Sandy). *Backward Glances,* Vol. 3, *1932–33.* Edited by Skipper Steely. Paris, Tex.: Wright Press, ca. 1987.

———. *The Red River Valley, Then and Now.* Paris, Tex.: North Texas Publishing, 1948.

Nichol, Harriett Helm, and C. R. Nichol, comps. *Gospel Preachers Who Blazed the Trail.* 1911. Reprint, Austin, Tex.: Firm Foundation, 1950.

Nichol, Harriett Helm. *Gospel Preachers in Texas and Oklahoma.* Clifton, Tex.: Nichol, 1911.

Noll, Mark A. *A History of Christianity in the United States and Canada.* Grand Rapids, Mich.: William B. Eerdmans, 1992.

North, Stafford. *Soaring on Wings like Eagles: A History of Oklahoma Christian University.* Oklahoma City: Oklahoma Christian University, 2008.

The Officer-Smith Debate: A Religious Discussion on the Design of Baptism and the Influence of the Holy Spirit, Held at Leader, Ind. Ter., Commencing July 13, 1893. Garland, Tex.: M. A. Smith, 1896.

O'Beirne, H. F. *Leaders and Leading Men of the Indian Territory, with interesting Biographical Sketches.* Vol. 1, *Choctaws and Chickasaws.* Chicago: American Publishers Association, 1891.

Olbricht, Thomas. *Hearing God's Voice.* Abilene, Tex.: Abilene Christian University Press, 1995.

———. *Reflections on My Life in the Kingdom and the Academy.* Eugene, Ore.: Wipf and Stock, 2012.

Our Ellis County Heritage, 1885–1979. Gage, Okla.: Ellis Co. Historical Society, 1979.

Parks, Norman L. *Cordell's Christian College: A History.* Cordell, Okla.: Fourth and College Church of Christ, 1994.

Parsons, Elizabeth C., ed. *The Greatest Work in the World: Education as a Mission of Early Twentieth-Century Churches of Christ: Letters of Lloyd Cline Sears and Pattie Hathaway Armstrong.* Eugene, Ore.: Wipf and Stock, 2015.

Patterson, Noble, and Terry J. Gardner, eds. *Foy E. Wallace, Jr.: Soldier of the Cross.* Fort Worth, Tex.: Wallace Memorial Fund, 1999.

Phillips, Thomas W. *The Church of Christ.* 15th ed. Cincinnati: Standard, 1915.

Poe, Betty, comp. and ed. *History of Coal County, Oklahoma.* Dallas, Tex.: Curtis Media, 1986.

Polk's City Directory for Oklahoma City, McAlester, Muskogee, Okmulgee, and Tulsa. Dallas, Tex.: R. L. Polk, 1945 and 1946.

Polk's City Directory, Tulsa, Oklahoma. Dallas, Tex.: R. L. Polk, 1917–18.

Polk's City Directory, Tulsa, Oklahoma. Dallas, Tex.: R. L. Polk, 1944–46.

Richardson, Robert. *Memoirs of Alexander Campbell.* 2 vols. 1897 and 1898. Reprint, Germantown, Tenn.: Religious Book Service, n.d.

Robinson, Edward J. *The Fight Is On in Texas: A History of African American Churches of Christ in the Lone Star State, 1865–2000.* Abilene, Tex.: Abilene Christian University Press, 2008.

———. *Show Us How You Do It: Marshall Keeble and the Rise of Black Churches of Christ in the United States, 1914–1968.* Tuscaloosa: University of Alabama Press, 2008.

———. *To Save My Race from Abuse: The Life of Samuel Robert Cassius.* Tuscaloosa: University of Alabama Press, 2007.

Roper, David. *Voices Crying in the Wilderness: A History of the Lord's Church with Special Emphasis on Australia.* Salisbury, South Australia: Restoration Publications, 1979.

Rowland, Rick. *Campus Ministries: A Historical study of Churches of Christ Campus Ministries and Selected College Ministries from 1706 to 1990.* Fort Worth, Tex.: Star Bible Publications, 1991.

Royster, Carl H., comp. *Churches of Christ in the United States: Inclusive of Her Commonwealth and Territories.* Nashville, Tenn.: 21st Century Christian, 2006.

Schug, Howard L., and Jesse P. Sewell, eds. *Harvest Field.* Athens, Ala.: Bible School Bookstore, 1947.

Sears, L. C. *For Freedom: The Biography of John Nelson Armstrong.* Austin, Tex.: Sweet, 1969.

———. *What Is Your Life?* Dallas: Temple, 1979.

Seikel, Robert E. *A Centennial History of Central Church of Christ, Shawnee, Oklahoma, 1907–2007.* Shawnee, Okla.: Central Church of Christ, 2007.

Showalter, G. H. P. *Travel Talks.* Austin, Tex.: Firm Foundation, 1938.

Stubbs et ux., Appellants, v. North Pennsylvania Avenue Church of Christ et al., Appellees. 44 OBJ 556–61. OKC TCIV APP 1973.

Smith, Loyd L. *Gospel Preachers of Yesteryear.* Allen, Tex.: Loyd L. Smith, 1986.

Stevens, Eldred, and Eric Beevers. *Stevens-Beevers Debate on the New Testament and Roman Catholicism: A Public Discussion.* Fort Worth, Tex.: Eldred Stevens, 1953.

Stevens, John C. *Before Any Were Willing: The Story of George S. Benson.* Searcy, Ark: Harding University Press, 1991.

———. *No Ordinary University: The History of a City Set on a Hill.* Abilene, Tex.: Abilene Christian University Press, 1998.

Strickland, Rennard. *The Indians in Oklahoma.* Norman: University of Oklahoma Press, 1980.

Tant, Fanning Yater. *J. D. Tant—Texas Preacher: A Biography.* Erlanger, Ky.: Faith and Facts Press, 1958.

Tucker, William E., and Lester G. McAllister. *Journey in Faith: A History of the Christian Church (Disciples of Christ).* Saint Louis: Bethany Press, 1975.

The Tulsa Lectures Delivered at The Church of Christ, Tenth and Rockford, Tulsa, Oklahoma, January 9–16, 1938. Edited by L. R. Wilson. Nashville, Tenn.: Gospel Advocate, ca. 1938.

Wade, Ronny F. *The Sun Will Shine Again, Someday: A History of the Non-Class, One Cup Churches of Christ.* Springfield, Mo.: Yesterday's Treasures, 1986.

Weather, Eva Jean. *Alexander Campbell: Adventurer in Freedom: A Literary Biography.* 2 vols. Fort Worth: Texas Christian University Press and Disciples of Christ Historical Society, 2005–2007.

West, Dorothy Arnote. *Pushmataha County: The Early Years.* N.p.: n.p., 2002.

West, Earl Irvin. *The Search for the Ancient Order.* Vol. 1, *1849–1865.* Nashville: Gospel Advocate, 1964. Vol. 2, *1866–1906.* Indianapolis: Religious Book Service, 1950. Vol. 3,

1900–1918. Indianapolis: Religious Book Service, 1979. Vol. 4, *1919–1950*. Germantown, Tenn: Religious Book Service, 1987.

West, William Garrett. *Barton Warren Stone: Early American Advocate of Christian Unity*. Nashville, Tenn.: Disciples of Christ Historical Society, 1954.

Wilhite, J. Porter. *The Trail Blazers: Heroes of the Faith*. Houston, Tex.: J. Porter Wilhite, 1965.

Wilkinson, U. G. *Why I Am Not a Socialist*. Comanche, Okla.: American Print, 1915.

U.S. Bureau of the Census. *Census of Religious Bodies, 1936*. Vol. 1, *Summary and Detailed Tables*. Washington, D.C.: Government Printing Office, 1940.

———. *Census of Religious Bodies, 1936*. Vol. 2, *Separate Denominations*. Pt. 1, *Denominations A–J*. Washington, D.C Government Printing Office, 1940.

———. *Fourteenth Census of the United States, 1920: Abstract, with Supplement for Oklahoma*. Washington, D.C.: Government Printing Office, 1923.

———. *Religious Bodies, 1916*. Pt. 2, *Separate Denominations, History, Description, and Statistics*. Washington, D.C.: Government Printing Office, 1919.

———. *Religious Bodies: 1926*. Vol. 1, *Summary and Detailed Tables*. Washington, D.C.: Government Printing Office, 1930.

———. *Special Reports: Religious Bodies, 1906*. Pt. 1, *Summary and General Tables*, Washington, D.C.: Government Printing Office, 1910.

———. *Special Reports: Religious Bodies, 1906*. Pt. 2, *Separate Denominations: History, Description, and Statistics*. Washington, D.C.: Government Printing Office, 1920.

———. *Thirteenth Census of the United States, 1910: Abstract, with Supplement for Oklahoma*. Washington, D.C.: Government Printing Office, 1913.

U.S. Department of Commerce and Labor, Bureau of Census. *Population of Oklahoma and Indian Territory, 1907*. Washington, D.C.: Government Printing Office, 1907.

Where the Saints Meet. Austin, Tex.: Firm Foundation, 1969, 1977, and 1987.

Yates, Kyle M., Jr., comp. *A History of Religious Programs at Oklahoma State University*. Stillwater: Oklahoma State University, 1991.

Young, M. Norvel. *A History of Colleges Established and Controlled by Members of the Churches of Christ*. Kansas City, Mo.: Old Paths Book Club, 1949.

Articles and Chapters

Associated Press. "Woman Sues Church Elders on Punishment." *New York Times*, Mar. 11, 1984. https://www.nytimes.com/1984/03/11/us/woman-sues-church-elders-on-punishment.html.

Baird, James O. "Are Campaigns Worth the Cost?" In *17th Annual Oklahoma Christian Spring Dinner*. April 1990.

Baird, W. David. "R. W. Officer and the Indian Mission: The Foundational Years (1880–1886)." In *And the Word Became Flesh: Studies in History, Communication, and Scripture in Memory of Michael W. Casey*, edited by Thomas H. Olbricht and David Fleer, 3–20. Eugene, Ore.: Pickwick Publications, 2009.

Bennett, Joseph R., II. "The Biography of James Jenkins Trott, 1800–1868." History of the Restoration Movement. http://www.therestorationmovement.com/_states/tennessee/trott.htm (accessed Mar. 20, 2009).

Boren, Maxie B. "John Darrell Boren." History of the Restoration Movement. 2004. http://www.therestorationmovement.com/_states/texas/boren,jd.htm (accessed Jan. 25, 2016).

Boyd, Dan T. "Oklahoma Oil: Past, Present, and Future." *Oklahoma Geology Notes* 62 (Fall 2002): 98–106.

Braun, Bill. "Church, Woman Settle Lawsuit." *Tulsa World*, Aug. 12, 1989.

Briley, Ron. "The Christian Left's Vision (Remember Woody Guthrie?)." History News Network, Aug. 8, 2005. http://hnn.us/articles/13445.html (accessed Apr. 4, 2008).

"Brotherhood Generally Sympathetic with Collinsville Elders Re: Trial." *Contending for the Faith* 15 (May 1984): 50–54, 555–58.

"The Campbellites Are Coming." *Time Magazine*, Feb. 15, 1963.

Casey, Michael W. "The Closing of Cordell Christian College: A Microcosm of American Intolerance during World War I." *Chronicles of Oklahoma* 76 (Spring 1998): 20–37.

———. "From Pacifism to Patriotism: The Emergence of Civil Religion in the Churches of Christ during World War I." *Mennonite Quarterly Review* 66 (July 1992): 389–90.

———. "From Religious Outsiders to Insiders: The Rise and Fall of Pacifism in the Churches of Christ." *Journal of Church and State* 44 (Summer 2002): 455–75.

"Central Church of Christ." *Daily Ardmoreite*, Apr. 19, 1987, 9.

"Church of Christ One of City's Oldest." *Kiamichi Magazine*, Oct. 13, 1968.

Debo, Angie, ed. "The Diary of Charles Hazelrigg." *Chronicle of Oklahoma* 25 (Autumn 1947): 229–70.

"Directory of Church of Christ Bible Chairs." *Bible Chair Journal* (Fall 1960): 8.

Duncan, Otis Durant. "A Churchman's View of the Church." *Oklahoma Journal of Religion* 2 (March 1945): 3–4.

"Dynamite under a Church." *Kansas City Star*, Apr. 16, 1901.

Flannery, Emerson L. "The Separation of Church and State." *Guardian of Truth* 28 (Aug. 2, 1984): 470.

Fowler, James H. II. "Tar and Feather Patriotism: The Suppression of Dissent in Oklahoma during World War I." *Chronicles of Oklahoma* 56 (Winter 1979): 409–30.

Gardner, Terry J. "The Influence of Foy E. Wallace, Jr." In *Restoring the First-Century Church in the Twentieth-First Century: Essays on the Stone-Campbell Restoration Movement*, edited by Warren Lewis and Hans Rollman, 193–204. Eugene, Ore.: Wipf and Stock, 2005.

Hart, Larry. "Brief History of a Minor Restorationist Group (The Non–Sunday-School Churches of Christ)." *Restoration Quarterly* 22 (1979): 212–32.

Hicks, John Mark. "K. C. Moser and Churches of Christ: An Historical Perspective." *Restoration Quarterly* 37 (1995): 1–24.

———. "K. C. Moser and Churches of Christ: A Theological Perspective." *Restoration Quarterly* 37 (1995): 193–211.

Hoig, Stan. "Land Run of 1889." *Encyclopedia of Oklahoma History and Culture*. https://www.okhistory.org/publications/enc/entry.php?entry=LA014 (accessed July 18, 2017).

Kilpatrick, Wayne. "Murrell Askew: The Reluctant Baptist." History of the Restoration Movement. http://www.therestorationmovement.com/_states/oklahoma/askew.htm (accessed Dec. 2, 2008).

Lemley, Steven. "K. C. Moser: Memories and Assessment." Paper delivered at Pepperdine Bible Lectures, May 4, 2000.

[Mattox, Judge]. "All Things Concern the Kingdom." *Good Way* 1 (May 1946): 6.

Mitchell, Lindell. "Albert Edward Brumley." History of the Restoration Movement. 2002. http://www.therestorationmovement.com/_states/tennessee/brumley.htm (accessed June 10, 2009).

Olbricht, Thomas H. "Hermeneutics in the Churches of Christ." *Restoration Quarterly* 37 (1995): 1–24.

"Rev. R. W. Officer Dead." *Nashville [Ark.] News*, Aug. 29, 1930.

Robinson, Edward J. "Heaven to Hell: Samuel Robert Cassius and Black Life in Oklahoma, 1891–1923." *Chronicles of Oklahoma* 84 (Spring 2006): 78–99.

Sager, Mrs. J. A. "History of Christian Church in Grady County for 40 years." *Chickasha Daily Express* [1929].

Scott, Laurence W., ed. *Texas Pulpit by Christian Preachers*. Saint Louis: Christian Publishing, 1888.

Slate, Michael D. "R. W. Officer: An Example of Frontier Individualism." *Restoration Quarterly* 22 (1979): 144–59.

Srygley, F. D. "Biographical Sketch of R. Wallace Officer." In *Biographies and Sermons: A Collection of Original Sermons by Different Men, with a Biographical Sketch of Each Man Accompanying His Sermon*, edited by F. D. Srygley, 309–20. Nashville, Tenn.: Gospel Advocate, 1898.

Trustees. "The Oklahoma School of Religion." *Oklahoma Journal of Religion* 1 (Dec. 1944): 17.

Watson, Elbert L. "Oklahoma and the Anti-Evolution Movement of the 1920s." *Chronicles of Oklahoma* 42 (Winter 1964–65): 396–407.

"What Is Church of Christ Teaching in Italy?" *Daily Ardmoreite*, Jan. 20, 1950.

Unpublished Dissertations, Theses, Papers, and Presentations

Bowers, Calvin H. "A Rhetorical Analysis of the Preaching of R. N. Hogan." Master's thesis, Pepperdine University, 1972.

Bruner, Ron. "A Multi-Frame Perspective of the Hollis Church of Christ: A Paper Presented to Dr. Charles Siburt." Abilene Christian University, 2007.

Casey, Michael Wilson. "The Interpretation of Genesis One in the Churches of Christ: The Origins of Fundamentalists reactions to Evolution and Biblical Criticism in the 1920s." Master's thesis, Abilene Christian College, 1989.

Fenno, Wyatt E. "Living Waters: An Invitation to Contemplative Spirituality for the Quail Springs Church of Christ." Doctor of Ministry thesis, Abilene Christian University, April 2005.

Henderson, Robert Mark. "Leadership and the Life of God: Distribution of Ministerial Gifts and Leadership Practices at the Quail Springs Church of Christ." Doctor of Ministry thesis, Abilene Christian University, March 2004.

"History of the Eastside Church of Christ, 1957–2000." Unpublished paper prepared for the Eastside Church in Midwest City, Okla., 2000

Johnson, Paula. "A History of the Sixth and Arlington Church of Christ, Lawton, Okla."
    Unpublished paper prepared for the author, 2008.
Keele, Lee. "An Action Plan for the Church of Christ in Seminole, Okla., 1994–2000."
    Unpublished paper prepared for the elders of the Seminole Church of Christ, 1994.
Lemley, Steven. "K. C. Moser: Memories and Assessment." Unpublished paper delivered
    at the Pepperdine Bible Lectures, May 4, 2000.
Money, Royce Lynn. "Church-State Relations in the Churches of Christ since 1945: A Study
    in Religion and Politics." PhD diss., Baylor University, 1975.
Olbricht, Thomas H. "A. R. Holton: A Biography." Unpublished PowerPoint presentation,
    2003.
Wilkinson, T. B. "Life History and Background of the Country Preacher." Typescript
    copy prepared by J. C. Wilkinson. September 1969. Private collection of Roy Young,
    Apache, Oklahoma.

Church Bulletins

(Ada) *Central [Church of Christ] Proclaimer,* 1960–2008.
(Altus) [Elm and Hudson Church of Christ] *Bulletin* and *The Messenger,* 1950–65.
(Lawton) [Sixth and Arlington Church of Christ] *Bulletin.*
(Muskogee) [East Okmulgee Street Church of Christ] *Reflector,* 1958–60.
(Oklahoma City) [Culbertson Heights Church of Christ] *Things of the Spirit* newsletter,
    1953–54.
(Oklahoma City) [Mayfair Church of Christ] *Bulletin,* 1957.
(Oklahoma City) [Tenth and Francis Streets Church of Christ] *Gospel Visitor,* 1949–74.
(Seminole) *Church Messenger,* 1946–49, and *Family News,* 1970–86.
(Wewoka) [Church of Christ] *Congregational Crusader,* 1955.
(Wewoka) [Church of Christ] *Gospel Herald,* 1969–74.

Personal Interviews

Black, Garth, email interview, Feb. 16, 2010, and telephone interviews, Feb. 17, 2010, and
    Feb. 4, 2016
Blakney, Warren G., Sr., Tulsa, July 14, 2008
Brown, Jeff, Tulsa, Sept. 18, 2008
Burch, Tip, telephone interview, Wewoka, Okla., July 24, 2009
Cannon, Patsy Burch, telephone interview, Searcy, Ark., July 29, 2009
Crenshaw, Arnelious, Oklahoma City, Sept. 15, 2008
Deffenbaugh, David, Tahlequah, Okla., Sept. 29, 2008
Dyer, Hershel, Tulsa, July 15, 2008, and June 4, 2018
Elliott, Scott, Wilburton, Okla., Sept. 30, 2008
Fletcher, Harold, Oklahoma City, Sept. 13, 2008
Hale, Lewis, Oklahoma City, Sept. 16, 2008
Hunter, Ralph, Owasso, Okla., Sept. 23, 2008
King, Eric, Edmond, Okla., Sept. 15, 2008
Lemley, Stephen, Malibu, Calif., July 12, 2016

Lyon, Mack, Edmond, Okla., Sept. 24, 2008

Mattox Young, Helen, telephone interview, Malibu, Calif., Aug. 7, 2007, and Aug. 6, 2009

McMillian, Lynn, Oklahoma City, June 4, 2018

McPherson, Gene, Oklahoma City, Sept. 16, 2008

Olbricht, Thomas, email interview, Feb. 24, 2018

Phillips, Marvin, Tulsa., Sept. 25, 2008

Ross, Bud, Ada, Okla., Sept. 8, 2008

Rush, Terry, Tulsa, July 15, 2008

Rushford, Jerry, telephone interview, Apr. 10, 2018

Stewart, Ivan, Oklahoma City, Okla., Sept. 18, 2008

Stinnett, Chris, Seminole, Okla., Sept. 9, 2008

Williams, Don, Cyril, Okla., Sept. 5, 2008

Winters Wright, Helen, Oklahoma City, Sept. 26, 2008

Wallace, William E., Talihina, Okla., October 1, 2008

Young, Roy, Apache, Okla., Sept. 5, 2008

INDEX

Page numbers in *italics* refer to illustrations.

CPSIA information can be obtained
at www.ICGtesting.com
Printed in the USA
LVHW042344130120
643462LV00003B/383/P

9 780806 164625